In Performance

EDITED BY
CAROL MARTIN

In Performance is a book series devoted to national and global theater of the twenty-first century. Scholarly essays providing the theatrical, cultural, and political contexts for the plays and performance texts introduce each volume. The texts are written both by established and emerging writers, translated by accomplished translators and aimed at people who want to put new works on stage, read diverse dramatic and performance literature and study diverse theatre practices, contexts, and histories in light of globalization.

In Performance has been supported by translation and editing grants from the following organizations:

The Book Institute, Krakow
TEDA Project, Istanbul
The Memorial Fund for Jewish Culture, New York
Polish Cultural Institute, New York
Zbigniew Raszewski Theatrical Institute, Warsaw

THOUSAND YEARS WAITING

WAITING

AND OTHER PLAYS

Chiori Miyagawa

Seagull
BOOKS

LONDON NEW YORK CALCUTTA

Seagull Books, 2012

Thousand Years Waiting © Chiori Miyagawa, 2006
Comet Hunter © Chiori Miyagawa, 2003
Leaving Eden © Chiori Miyagawa, 2005
Awakening © Chiori Miyagawa, 2000
FireDance © Chiori Miyagawa, 2010
Broken Morning © Chiori Miyagawa, 1997
Red Again © Chiori Miyagawa, 2004
Songs in *Awakening* © Mark Campbell, 2000
Songs in *Broken Morning* © Mark Campbell, 2003

Photographs © Individual photographers

ISBN-13 978 0 8574 2 020 6

British Library Cataloging-in-Publication Data
A catalog record for this book is available from the British Library

Printed and bound by Hyam Enterprises, Calcutta, India

CONTENTS

ACKNOWLEDGEMENTS

This book is in memory of Paul Walker (1952–93).

I would like to thank Carol Martin, Naveen Kishore, Lori Fromo-witz, Elaine Devlin, Sonoko Kawahara, Mark Campbell, Sophia Skiles, Morgan Jenness, Greg Leaming, Caridad Svich, Daniella Topol and all the actors, directors, designers, composers, stage managers, producers, funders, and everyone else who contributed to making these plays come to life. I could not have written *Leaving Eden* without the SMU Commission and Lark Play Development Center; could not have written *Comet Hunter* without the EST/Alfred P. Sloan Commission and New Dramatists; could not have written *Broken Morning* without the Theater Communication Group Extended Collaboration Grant and Dallas Theater Center; could not have written *Awakening* without the New York Theater Workshop's summer retreat program; could not have written *FireDance* without the McKnight Playwriting Fellowship from Playwrights Center and New Georges; could not have put this book together without the Radcliffe Advanced Studies Fellowship at Harvard University and a research fund from Bard College. I feel very fortunate for all the support I have received for my work. Thank you. I am grateful to Lyn Austin (1922–2000) of Music-Theatre Group for getting me started on this fantastic journey. And to Hap Tivey, for absolutely everything.

A BODY OF REMEMBRANCE:
CHIORI MIYAGAWA'S THEATRE

Caridad Svich

The characters in Chiori Miyagawa's plays are haunted by fragmented historical and cultural memories.[1] From her theatrical
re-imagining of Kate Chopin's 1899 novel *The Awakening* to her
inquiry into Chekhov's life and short stories in *Leaving Eden* to her
portrayal of Murasaki Shikibu's influential *The Tale of Genji* in her
play *Thousand Years Waiting*, Miyagawa's dramatic attention is on
the intricate cultural affiliations and continuity of identities in nonlinear narratives. Informed by both Eastern and Western aesthetics, Miyagawa's discontinuous shifts in time and place signal both
the fragility of human existence and the elasticity of memory.
Characters can find themselves in Japan in the year 1000 in one
moment and in New York City in the year 2000 the next and are
bound to a spiritual world beyond their comprehension—a world
that can claim them or heal them. Their fragmented cultural memories convey "a feeling that we can all recall from somewhere in
our lives, from sometime in our pasts."[2]

---

1 For additional resources, see *I Have Been to Hiroshima mon Amour*, in
TheatreForum 37 (Fall) (2010); *Red Again*, in *Antigone Project* (South Gate, CA:
NoPassport Press, 2009); *America Dreaming*, in *Global Foreigners* (London, New
York, Calcutta: Seagull Books, 2006); *Antigone's Red*, in *TAKE TEN II* (New York:
Vintage, 2003); *Nothing Forever*, in *Positive/Negative Women* (San Francisco:
Aunt Lute Books, 2002); *Woman Killer*, in *Plays & Playwrights 2002* (New York:
New York Theatre Experience, 2002) and as single edition playtext (South Gate,
CA: NoPassport Press, 2010); *Jamaica Avenue*, in *Tokens?: The NYC Asian
American Experience on Stage* (New York: Asian American Writers Workshop,
1999); and, *Yesterday's Window*, in *TAKE TEN* (New York: Vintage, 1997).

2 Chiori Miyagawa, "Do Poets Keep Secrets?" Available at www.drunkenboat.-
com/db9/poetics_essays/-miyagawa/poetics_miya.html (last accessed on
January 20, 2012).

Born in Nagano, Japan, Miyagawa came to the US shortly after her sixteenth birthday to take part in a high-school exchange program, never going back to live in Japan again.[3] Deeply engaged in shifting boundaries of cultural affiliation, Miyagawa writes about her adaptation of Chopin's *Awakening*:

> All of my theatrical characters are outsiders in different ways, because I am one. I don't think I have a choice in the matter. I was not born in the United States, and I did not learn to speak English until I was sixteen. [. . .] Part of me is intentionally attached to being an outsider. It allows me to metamorphose into characters that temporarily reside in bardo, the realm after death and before rebirth, and to think mystically about the next reincarnation. I suspect that my feet are always consciously or unconsciously touching the ancient soil of Japan, and I conjure ghosts of all kinds from my ancestral past. Edna is one.[4]

Karma shapes the past, present, and future experiences of Miyagawa's characters as they gain knowledge in a limitless afterlife where they have the opportunity to change collective and personal memory.[5] In *Awakening*, Edna walks into the ocean at the same time that Chopin finishes her novel; in *FireDance* (a radical reworking of Shakespeare's *Hamlet* from Ophelia's perspective), Ghost jumps off a bridge while Alice escapes her literary fate; and in *Thousand Years Waiting*, Woman A, in modern-day New York City, enters *The Tale of Genji* in Kyoto in the year 1000 where she

---

3 Although she has visited Japan several times since.

4 Chiori Miyagawa, "A Mythical Place Called Grand Isle—Adapting Kate Chopin's Awakening," in Sharon Friedman (ed.), *Feminist Revisions of Classic Works* (Jefferson, NC: McFarland & Co, 2009), p. 203.

5 In Buddhism, karma is directly linked to the motives behind an action. Motivation usually makes the difference between good and bad actions, but included in the motivation is also the aspect of ignorance: a well-intended action from an ignorant mind can subsequently be interpreted as a bad action for it may create unpleasant results.

acquires her feminist sensibility.[6] All her characters engage in acts of defiance and liberation.

THOUSAND YEARS WAITING (2006)

In *Thousand Years Waiting*, Miyagawa illustrates the compelling grasp that selective memories can have on women as she re-imagines eleventh-century Japan through a contemporary American character, Woman A, reading the memoir of Lady Sarashina in which Lady Sarashina is reading the famous novel *The Tale of Genji*.[7] Woman A steps into in the old Kyoto depicted by Lady Sarashina (Woman B) who in the play is an elderly woman looking back at the young girl she once was.

> B *(Lady Sarashina as an adult)*. They disappeared into the mountains. It snowed the next day. We arrived in Kyoto on December second.

> A *(Contemporary Woman)*. On December second, I'm already here. I've been in New York City since November when we all left home. My trip was faster. I've been waiting for you to arrive for a thousand years.

---

6 Miyagawa grew up reading and rereading *shojyo manga* stories (graphic novels for girls), in particular *The Poe Clan* and *The Rose of Versailles* (Miyagawa's translation). *The Poe Clan* follows a gang of teenage orphan vampires from nineteenth-century England to 1959 Germany. *The Rose of Versailles*, spanning from 1755 to 1793, centers on a transsexual protagonist who befriends Marie Antoinette and then betrays her to join the Revolution and storm the Bastille.

7 *Thousand Years Waiting* was first performed at Performance Space 122 in New York City on February 23, 2006, as a co-production between Crossing Jamaica Avenue and Performance Space 122. For the world premiere of the play, Miyagawa's longtime collaborator, director Sonoko Kawahara, encouraged her to wed the staging intentions of the play with *otome* (female) *bunraku*, the early twentieth-century Japanese puppetry form that was created because women were not allowed to perform traditional puppetry. Miyagawa did so, and *Thousand Years Waiting* marked the first time an *otome bunraku* artist performed in an American play.

B (*Lady Sarashina as a girl*). In Kyoto, women play many musical instruments. My sister and I write poetry and make paintings. My stepmother gives me incense I have never smelled before. It smells like plum blossoms.

A (*Contemporary Woman*). Time passes in discoveries of new things. I find your diary again in a dusty used bookstore downtown.

B (*Lady Sarashina*). In Kyoto, I find books. I read them all day long. I enter the stories and do not come out except to have tea. I'm fourteen. I read *The Tale of Genji*.

[. . .]

B (Lady Sarashina) becomes a character from the book.

Miyagawa challenges conventional dramatic notions of time and space as the narrative is layered with shifts in time and memory through which the women find themselves and one another. "The woman in *Thousand Years Waiting* is able to acquire this knowledge because of many, many years of storytelling by those who came before her," says Miyagawa. "The future is possible because of memory. Women are good at remembering. We have always resisted forgetting, however sad, however difficult the particulars. In *Thousand Years Waiting*, the woman in the present realizes that life is not an individual trajectory that begins and ends, but rather a cycle that continues and is shared by the whole of humanity."[8] For Miyagawa, as for many artists working across cultures, finding and re-inscribing lost or forgotten stories is an important dramatic device. As scholar Sharon Friedman explains, "Miyagawa's characters hold fast to their fragile memories and mystical thinking to ward off loss and achieve a kind of immortality."[9]

---

8 Caridad Svich, "Resisting Forgetting with Chiori Miyagawa," *The Brooklyn Rail* (February 2006). Available at http://www.brooklynrail.org/2006/02/theater/in-dialouge.

9 Sharon Friedman, "A Soul Raging and Homeless" in Chiori Miyagawa, *Woman Killer* (South Gate, CA: NoPassport Press, 2010), p. 12.

Comit Hunter traces Caroline Herschel's journey through life in the company of the stars that she discovers through which she searches for spiritual meaning. The play begins with Herschel, the first recognized female astronomer in the world, discovering her first comet in 1786 in Slough, England.[10] "There was motion since last night! It *is* a comet! *I* have discovered a comet!" The play returns to this moment throughout the telling of Herschel's life story.[11] Caroline is guided by Time, her personal companion whom only she can see and a prophet of humanity who presents historically accurate scientific knowledge throughout the play. As a theatrical device, Time enables Miyagawa to both portray the astronomical worldview during Herchel's life and linguistically merge Caroline's poetic and professional lives. Time is also Caroline's confessor: she confides her feelings, her doubts, and her frustrations with the limits forced on her professional life because of her gender.

Early in her life, Herschel moves from Germany to England to join her beloved brother, William, the discoverer of the planet Uranus, with whom she remained until his death. Despite her brilliant scientific contributions, Herschel is marginalized by society because she is physically deformed, unmarried, and a woman working in the world of science, a world of men. Her love for her brother is her only solace. With his guidance Caroline becomes an astronomer in her own right, paving the way for the future women comet hunters.

---

10 Caroline Herschel (1750–1848) discovered eight comets and several astronomical objects during her lifetime, including the second companion to the Andromeda galaxy. Yet she was not inducted as an honorary member into the Royal Historical Society of Astronomy until 1835, and was, even then, only one of two women inducted.

11 *Comet Hunter* was commissioned and developed by Ensemble Studio Theater in New York City and the Alfred P. Sloane Science and Technology Foundation.

Stars come up around them. Time rewinds. 1789.
William is fifty-one, Caroline is thirty-nine. He gets up on
his 40-foot telescope. Caroline is at the foot of the telescope.

TIME. Rewind time to 1789. William erects a 40-foot telescope which took the Herschels four years to build. August 28. The world's largest telescope's first light.

CAROLINE. William! Say something!

WILLIAM. Such brilliance! We have been near blind until now. Oh, Lina, the greatness of the heavens is unmistakable.

CAROLINE. And you!

WILLIAM. How strange is fate? Was I always meant to find this brightness? I was just an ordinary boy once.

CAROLINE. You were never ordinary. There was always greatness to come.

WILLIAM. Lina, I am looking at Saturn.

CAROLINE. Yes, I know. You have been wanting to see it closer.

WILLIAM. My suspicion was right. The sixth moon of Saturn exists.

CAROLINE. Are you certain that the sixth is not a star?

WILLIAM. Its ranging is exact as the other four moons and with the ring.

CAROLINE. The retrograde motion should amount to nearly four and half minutes per day. So in about two hours you should be able to ascertain if it is in fact a moon.

WILLIAM. Will you stay up with me until then?

CAROLINE. Of course, William. I will always stay with you.

Caroline shares with William a special love of the stars, a love that serves as an antidote to her physical deformity and society's response to it. This love animates the play and its visions of the heavens. Generations later, her comet is known to reappear periodically, linking her discovery to a kind of immortality.

LEAVING EDEN (2005)

In *Leaving Eden,* Miyagawa interweaves five separate short stories by Anton Chekhov in which characters appear and reappear.[12] Each protagonist is a combination of several Chekhov characters. The play follows the lives of 22 people (played by seven actors) over a span of 25 years(1880–1905), concluding in the present. At the beginning of the play, in a dingy room in Moscow we meet Anyuta, a young working-class woman, suffering from unbearable cold, sharing her room with her lover Stepan, a medical student. When their friend, the artist Nikolai, shows up, he raises questions about happiness that make them face the limitations of their lives.

But, by the beginning of the 1900s, the privilege of acquiring an education begins to have significance for women's lives. It is at this moment that Nadya and her fading bourgeois way of life appears. In the face of new possibilities, her adopted brother Sasha tries to talk her out of entering into a conventional marriage.

NADYA. I don't know. I just want to cry. Since I was sixteen, I dreamed of marriage. I was very glad that a wedding was arranged for me at last. But suddenly, I'm not happy.

SASHA. It's because you live a meaningless life. You do nothing. Your mother does nothing. Your fiancé does nothing. Other people have to work so you can be idle. Don't you think it's immoral? You're devouring other lives so you can have leisure.

NADYA. My mother is a sensitive and unique woman.

SASHA. Is she?

NADYA. The other morning, she came to me in tears because she had started reading a novel and got to a place where she could not help but cry.

---

12 *Leaving Eden* was written on commission from the Meadows School of the Arts of Southern Methodist University, Texas, where it premiered in 2005, directed by Greg Leaming.

SASHA. Nadya, she's a kind woman. She is very kind to me. But look at how her maids live. Four of them sleep on the floor in the kitchen, no beds, just bedbugs. Your mother speaks French, for God's sake.

NADYA. I wish you would say something new sometime. Every summer it's the same.

SASHA. Because nothing changes.

The last scene is a wedding reception in present-day New York City where Chekhov shows up as the unexpected guest, expounding on class and social responsibility and observing the ways in which humanity is not yet free of suffering. Sophia is the other unexpected guest in the last scene. She is a descendant of Nadya: Chekhov reminisces with Sophia about Nadya as an actual person from his own life rather than a fictional character he created. Thus, through Sophia, Miyagawa blurs fiction and perceived reality in the world. In this contemporary scene, serious political debates about health care in the context of class issues are woven with jokes about the food served at weddings, the weather, and other social niceties. The festive atmosphere of the scene puts the entire play in relief while exposing how Miyagawa uses Chekhov's life and writing as a prism. The combination of humor and tragedy in *Leaving Eden* leads to one of the most redemptive endings in Miyagawa's work. In a tableau of hope, all the characters have their glasses raised, ready to toast the unseen bride and groom as Chekhov looks on.

AWAKENING (2000)

Awakening[13] is Miyagawa's radical adaptation of Chopin's novel *The Awakening*. Using the events in Chopin's novel, Miyagawa creates two stories that inhabit the stage simultaneously: one, the

---

13 *Awakening* was originally written in 1998 and produced in 2000 by Crossing Jamaica Avenue, Performance Space 122 and Dance Theater Workshop in New York City, directed by Sonoko Kawahara, with lyrics by Mark Campbell.

story of Chopin, and the other, the story of Edna, the protagonist in Chopin's novel. Chopin watches the play as she writes Edna's story and, at the same time, she reminisces about writing *The Awakening*. Miyagawa uses this layering of experience to show us both the completed work and the process of becoming complete.

In Chopin's novel, Edna Pontellier struggles with the established social attitudes of turn-of-the-century South. Vacationing on the Grand Isle resort in the Gulf of Mexico with her husband Leonce and two sons, she meets Robert Lebrun. As the attraction between Edna and Robert grows, Edna begins to dream about an independent life away from her husband and sons. She returns to New Orleans with her family but can't forget the awakening of desire she experienced with Robert. When her husband goes on a trip and sends the children to stay with his mother, Edna has another affair with a charming, irresponsible cad, Alcee Arobin. The affair is fleeting and does not end well but further ignites Edna's hunger for a life other than the conventional one expected of her. Months later, when Robert is in New Orleans, Edna meets him again. Robert admits that as much as he loves her he cannot stay with her. Edna is devastated and goes back to Grand Isle where she walks into the sea and drowns herself.

For Miyagawa, suicide is the only way Edna can find release from the social constraints that bind her. At the end of the play Edna says, "I am a melange of things lost / things that cannot be obtained— / but with this act, I will return to the present, / to who I am now, / and release the memory of everything / all that I suffered / all that I am yet to suffer. / I walk into the ocean. / I am awake." In this final moment, Chopin, who has both created and witnessed Edna's life, reflects upon her own life and on how critics harshly attacked her novel. Chopin declares her love for her subject and her art-making, mirroring Miyagawa's admiration for Chopin's novel. *Awakening* is ultimately about the act of writing itself.

CARIDAD SVICH

FireDance is a drastic revision of Shakespeare's *Hamlet* that begins with a woman hanging herself.[14] Matt (the Hamlet character) is haunted by female ghosts reciting the history of women's suffering. Alice (the Ophelia character) is a waitress looking for a thread to connect her to her mother and, through her, to the history of female experience. Her brother Peter (the Laertes character) has chosen the life of a homeless man singing on the streets of the city. Swirling in their midst is Alice's haunting memory of her missing mother. A ghost glimpses portions of devastating events such as the massacre at Wounded Knee and the imprisonment of Japanese Americans during the Second World War.

By using fragments of history that get repeated and then forgotten, Miyagawa revises Ophelia's fate. Alice desires not only her beloved but also history and truth. When she learns of her father's death, she attempts to kill herself but is saved by the ghost who, in her place, leaps from a bridge in a parallel universe. At that moment Alice decides to live with the loss of her mother and abandon the insanity that justifies her self-destruction: "We dance the last tango to take us back to the beginning of time, to forget our names, to kill the fire in my eyes. Hold my hand, Matt. I'll read your future. There is a curse on your life. On the nights you are afraid of death, you will miss me." In the face of the endless history of violence, Matt is left behind to continue suffering his own story.

BROKEN MORNING: STORIES FROM THE DEATH ROW FACTORY (2003)

Broken Morning is based on a collage of interviews Miyagawa conducted in Texas with 12 men on death row at the Huntsville

---

14 *FireDance* was written in 1996 and produced in 1998 by Voice & Vision at the Connelly Theater in New York City, directed by Marya Mazer. The play published in this volume is a newly revised version from a production at Bard College in 2010, directed by Daniella Topol.

Prison, a woman on death row in Gatesville Prison, the death row guards, a captain, a chaplain, a warden, and family members of the victims.[15] Stories of grief, loss, and collective trauma resulting from inexplicable acts of violence are tied together by a character named Sheila who attempts to order her shattered world after her child is kidnapped and murdered. The Writer, a stand-in for Miyagawa, introduces us to each character by describing their physical attributes and revealing their crimes.

WRITER (*reads from the fact sheet*). Edward Cruz was convicted of capital murder of a nineteen-year-old woman on June 13, 1986. Police said the woman was raped and beaten to death with a motorcycle chain under an overpass in East Austin. An autopsy showed that the Hispanic female was hit sixteen times on the head and eight times on the face with the chrome-plated chain.

Woman remains frozen. Edward walks back to the prison area.

EDWARD. Eight years later, I got an execution date— August 4 or 5, I think. Back in '94. They gave me the date on Good Friday, so my mom had to give up Easter. Can you believe that? They couldn't wait until it was over? It bothered Mom a lot she had to miss Easter, but she brought my daughter and my son to see me. Mallie started crying. She was seven then. I've never even touched her once. She was born when I was going to court for this case, and I've been here since. I got a stay four months later. Mallie was real

---

15 Originally commissioned by Dallas Theater Center through a Theater Communications Group Extended Collaboration Grant in 1996, and presented in the Big D Festival of the Unexpected at Dallas Theater Center, directed by Richard Hamburger in 1997. *Broken Morning*, with lyrics by Mark Campbell, had its premiere in February 2003 as a co-production of Crossing Jamaica Avenue and HERE Arts Center, directed by Sonoko Kawahara.

happy. She says she's gonna become rich so she can
get me outta here. She is my angel girl.

*As Edward and the woman fade, lights come up on Sheila
again.*

SHEILA. Why didn't I hear it? The window breaking in my
angel girl's room during the night.

The stories in *Broken Morning* are as varied as the men and the
woman Miyagawa interviewed. With their vernacular speech, the
characters are ethnically diverse and have great differences in class,
education, and ambitions. The accumulation of fragmented stories
about broken lives produces moments of shared humanity between
the individuals consigned to death and the people on the "outside." Miyagawa does not exonerate the prisoners for their crimes
but excoriates the capital-punishment industry by showing the
poor, uneducated, and abused backgrounds of the accused and the
sorrows of surviving family members.

RED AGAIN (2004)

Red Again begins where Sophocles' *Antigone* ends.[16] Ensconced in
the underworld with her fiancé Harold, Antigone is in a bardo
state of psychic remembrance, complicity, guilt, and collective
mourning.[17] Irene, Antigone's sister, is left in the world of the
living where all the human atrocities in history converge.

IRENE. I'm reporting a double suicide. My sister Antigone
hanged herself, and her boyfriend Harold found her

---

16 *Red Again* was originally written in 2003 and produced in 2004 as part of the
full-length *Antigone Project* as a co-production of Crossing Jamaica Avenue and
the Women's Project in New York City, directed by Barbara Rubin.

17 The Tibetan word *bardo* signifies the liminal state between life and death.
There are six levels of liminality in Tibetan Buddhism: (1) between birth and life
(2) dream state (3) meditation (4) the moment of death (5) luminosity after
death (6) transmigration.

body and then stabbed himself. My name is Irene. I
live in Manhattan. Please hurry. We are being evacuated. All people of Japanese descent received notice
to relocate in forty-eight hours. I'm packing my life
into two suitcases that I can carry. I can't carry two
dead bodies. I can't carry my sister. I can't carry her. I
have to carry linen and silver and our family curse.
Antigone is dead. Forever. I can't carry anymore.
I'm being sent far far away from home. Somewhere
called Treblinka. Do you know where it is? I think it's
in Bosnia. Or Cambodia. Please. I need help. I'm
reporting a broken heart, broken bodies, broken
humanity.

As Irene becomes more and more distressed at the loss of her
sister and her future brother-in-law, Antigone and Harold discover incomplete books corresponding to every life.

ANTIGONE. Irene, Irene. Can you hear me? I want to tell
you about the books I found in the underworld. Each
person has a book, and as one lives her life, her story
gets recorded in the book. I looked in your book. You
have many blank pages still. Your story continues.

IRENE. You were right. The damage done to human decency, democracy, and rational thinking is too great.
There is no turning back. We live in lies and racial
profiling and threats disguised as freedom speeches,
and no one will help me bury your paleness and
Harold's bloody red. The city is under high security
alert, the color Red.

Even in bardo, Antigone and Harold realize that they have
work to do for the living. Marianne McDonald writes, "Each has
different approaches to the world: Harold thinks the world can be
changed through meditation, whereas Antigone opts for defiance

and revolution."[18] In the mode of a sublime shared dream, the play ends with the task of learning book by book, story by story, written and unwritten, how each of us can change the world. Antigone and Harold carry out this task as they are about to enter the last level of bardo—transmigration.

Red Again was conceived as part of five one-act revisions of the Antigone story entitled *Antigone Project*. Taken together, the five one-act plays resituate Antigone from the polis to "women in the third world and other sites, and address mechanism of history, the future, civil rights, individual freedom, and national security."[19] Miyagawa's play was written specifically in response to the war in Iraq and the Patriot Act's erosion of civil rights: "In *Red Again*, Miyagawa flattens the temporal depth of history into an eternally recurring present making it seem like we are being swallowed by the violent and unjust repetitions of history."[20] The playwright Lisa Schlesinger notes, "As *Red Again* comes to a close, Irene reminds us of the very specific Greek way of seeing tragedy and its endless cycles of familial violence. Irene reminds us that Antigone will always be here to remind us." [21]

Miyagawa's plays invoke liquid spaces where memories, dreams, and imagined lives from different times float effortlessly in individual consciousness. Sometimes her words seem to be altogether made strange. Familiar narratives become "foreign" through linguistic, spatial, and temporal displacements. Love in Miyagawa's plays is a catastrophe coupled with failure and hurt and with

---

18 Marianne McDonald, "Antigone Across Time" in *Antigone Project* (South Gate, CA: NoPassport Press, 2009), p. 22.

19 Carol Martin, "The Political is Personal" in *Feminist Revisions of Classic Works*, p. 81.

20 Ibid., p. 86

21 Lisa Schlesinger, Lisa. "O Antigone" in *Antigone Project* (South Gate, CA: NoPassport Press, 2009), p. 9.

the miraculous nature of human perseverance. Seeing the world from this vantage point makes us sorely aware that we live in a wounded place—a place that demands patience, humor, distance, and the immediacy of intimacy. Recurring collapses of time and space and multiple interpolations of alternate realities written in poetic language make Miyagawa a major writer of nonlinear drama.

THOUSAND YEARS
WAITING

Part of the story is based on the events from *The Sarashina Diary* (c.1000 CE), written in the Sarashina region in Japan by a woman as a memoir at the end of her life. As her name is not known, I call her Lady Sarashina in my play. The sections on *The Tale of Genji* are based on characters from the world's first novel, written by Lady Murasaki in the early eleventh century AD. In both cases, the language is entirely mine.

The play exists in three layers of reality—a contemporary woman reads *The Sarashina Diary* and, in the diary, its author, Lady Sarashina, reads *The Tale of Genji*. The past and the present coexist throughout the play.

Lady Sarashina is the narrator of the past—she narrates events as they happen in her world and also as an older woman looking back.

I suggest that the text not be treated preciously. There are comic moments as well as dark ones. Personally, I imagine Prince Genji as a buffoon. A woman waiting for a phantom lover can be poetic, funny, and tragic, all at once.

These pages constitute roughly an hour and a half of performance time. In this version there are three extensive *otome bunraku* dance sections (Japanese traditional puppetry performed by a woman). These sections were originally written for dancers, but the director Sonoko Kawahara chose to collaborate with an *otome bunraku* artist from Japan. Each director is welcome to imagine how to interpret these sections. The passing of time should also be choreographed.

The story covers over 45 years of Lady Sarashina's life. In the New York City production, the piece was layered with original music by Bruce Odland. The music should be used creatively by the director. There are no set cues in the script.

THOUSAND YEARS WAITING

Present. Somewhere in America. A woman stands, holding a book.

A (*Contemporary Woman*). This diary was written a thousand years ago in Kyoto by a woman. Her name is lost but her diary has been translated from old Japanese to modern Japanese to English. I found it first in a local library. I was looking for something unusual. Something that was missing. Something unfamiliar. The librarian said that I was the first person ever to check out the book. *The Sarashina Diary.* It is said that all her diary entries were made toward the end of her life. She wrote it from memory.

The past. Japan. Lady Sarashina is fourteen years old.

B (*Lady Sarashina as a young girl*). I spend my days reading *The Tale of Genji.* I am fourteen. Someone just like Prince Genji will come into my life someday. I wait. I wait for my prince.

Time rushes forward.

(*As an old woman*). I was born in a remote country. Women in my house passed the time telling stories. By the time I was ten I knew there were books called *The Tale of Genji.* I wanted to read it.

One day, during the tea ceremony, I asked my stepmother to get me *The Tale of Genji.* She smiled and said, "Be patient, my dear. Perhaps something will surprise you."

When I was twelve . . .

Lady Sarashina is twelve. Her older sister enters with great excitement.

C (*Sister*). Our father has been appointed at court! We will live in the capital! He has worked hard for this opportunity all his life. It is a great honor for the family.

B (*Lady Sarashina*). Lady Murasaki is at court!

C (*Sister*). Who is Lady Murasaki? Is she our stepmother's friend?

IMAGE 1.2 **Lady Sarashina reads** *The Tale of Genji*. **The contemporary woman reads Lady Sarashina's diary.**

Margi Sharp (left), Sophia Skiles (right).

Photograph by David Altman.

B (*Lady Sarashina*). She wrote books called *The Tale of Genji*. Father will be able to get her books for me at court!

C (*Sister*). It is November. We will begin our journey right away. We are moving to Kyoto/

B (*Lady Sarashina*). Destiny/

A (*Contemporary Woman*). New York City.

I was eighteen when I left home, a small country town of gossip and barbeques. I was older than this girl who dreamed of the capital with the most romantic longing. All I wanted was to leave. I was missing something.

B (*Lady Sarashina*). The servants packed up the house in three days. When the caravan of our belongings lined up to begin the journey, I ran back into the old house one last time. It was empty and lonely.

C (*Sister*). We must go now.

B (*Lady Sarashina*). In that corner, I had built an altar. Do you remember?

C (*Sister*). Of course I remember. It was there until three days ago.

B (*Lady Sarashina*). I prayed to Amida Buddha every day at the altar. I prayed that I would go to the capital and be able to read books there.

C (*Sister*). Why are you so sad then?

Time flows. On the journey.

B (*Lady Sarashina*). After a long day of traveling, we reached a border at the end of the white dunes. The stars were out. The servants built small lodges for the night. I placed my Buddha in the corner.

C (*Sister*). Nanny just had a baby.

Lady Sarashina lets out a joyful little cry.

C (*Sister*). Sh . . . She doesn't have a husband.

B (*Lady Sarashina*). I know. What happened to her husband?

C (*Sister*). He left. It happens to women of her class sometimes.

B (*Lady Sarashina*). Why?

C (*Sister*). Those men can only have one wife. People like our father don't have to leave any women behind because they can have many wives.

B (*Lady Sarashina*). I want to see Nanny.

C (*Sister*). She is ill.

B (*Lady Sarashina*). I want to see her.

A (*Contemporary Woman, reading from the book*). "My sister took my hand and led me to my nanny's hut. Her face was white. Moonlight seeping through the hut, falling on her and her baby. Her body covered in crimson cloth."

A (*As Nanny*). I haven't seen you in so long.

B (*Lady Sarashina*). Only since we left Fujisawa. That was yesterday. Only a day.

A (*Nanny*). How pretty you look!

B (*Lady Sarashina*). Don't cry.

C (*Sister*). We must go now.

B (*Lady Sarashina*). No, let me stay.

A (*Nanny*). Don't cry.

B (*Lady Sarashina*). The next day we left without Nanny. She was too weak to travel.

A (*Nanny*). Don't worry. I'll catch up.

B (*Lady Sarashina as an old woman*). I never see her again.

C (*Sister*). We must go now.

B (*Lady Sarashina as a girl*). No, let me stay.

> C (*Sister*) leads B (*Lady Sarashina*) by the hand away from A (*Nanny*). A (*Contemporary Woman*) reads.

A (*Contemporary Woman reading from the book*). "We followed white sand for three days. On the fourth night we came to a mountain."

B (*Lady Sarashina*). I'm tired and cold. I want to wait here for Nanny to catch up.

C (*Sister*). We'll see Nanny later. Don't think about her.

B (*Lady Sarashina*). Why?

C (*Sister*). Just don't think about her.

A (*Contemporary Woman, reading from the book*) "The sky was sliding into murkiness, and the veil was coming down on another day lived and vanished, when we heard a clear note ringing through the air."

C (*Sister*). Look! Traveling performers. How did they find us?

B (*Lady Sarashina*). Please Father, let them come sing for us.

The traveling performers enter. Music. The "singing" is expressed in movement. Toward the end of the performance, the other three women join the performers.

Blackout in the middle of the movement.

IMAGE 1.3 **On Lady Sarashina and her sister's journey to Kyoto, they encounter a traveling performer. (In this production, the performer was played by an** *otome bunraku* **puppet, performed by Masaya Kiritake.)**

Anna Wilson, the puppet, Margi Sharp, Sophia Skiles (from left tpo right).

Photograph by Theresa Squire.

IMAGE 1.4 **Prince Genji makes a night visit to one of his lovers. Contemporary Woman in New York City imagines old Japan.**

Sophia Skiles, Anna Wilson, Margi Sharp (from left to right).

Photograph by David Altman.

When the lights come up, the performers are gone.

B (*Lady Sarashina as an adult*). They disappeared into the mountains. It snowed the next day. We arrived in Kyoto on December second.

A (*Contemporary Woman*). On December second, I'm already here. I've been in New York City since November when we all left home. My trip was faster. I've been waiting for you to arrive for a thousand years.

B (*Lady Sarashina as a girl*). In Kyoto, women play many musical instruments.My sister and I write poetry and make paintings. My stepmother gives me incense I have never smelled before. It smells like plum blossoms.

A (*Contemporary Woman*). Time passes in discoveries of new things. I find your diary again in a dusty used bookstore downtown.

B (*Lady Sarashina*). In Kyoto, I find books. I read them all day long. I enter the stories and do not come out except to have tea. I'm fourteen. I read *The Tale of Genji.*

The Tale of Genji *Episode*

B (*Lady Sarashina*) *becomes a character from the book.*

B (*As Lady Wisteria*). Who is there?

C (*As Prince Genji*). It is Genji. I came to see you, Lady Wisteria.

B (*Lady Wisteria*). Prince Genji, how did you get in here?

C (*Prince Genji*). Your lady-in-waiting kindly helped me. You must know my heart.

B (*Lady Wisteria*). Prince, you're my son.

C (*Prince Genji*). Only a stepson.

B (*Lady Wisteria*). I have been your stepmother since you were twelve.

C (*Prince Genji*). But you're only five years older than me. And now that I am eighteen, I can be a confident lover.

B (*Lady Wisteria*). I'm married to the Emperor. I'm married to your father.

C (*Prince Genji*). Lady Wisteria, you know I have loved you ever since you came to the palace. I have loved you for six years.

B (*Lady Wisteria*). I came to your father when I was your age. I always thought that you were a beautiful young man.

C (*Prince Genji*). You were brought to him because my father was grieving over my mother's death. She was only an imperial concubine, but he loved her very much.

B (*Lady Wisteria*). I was frightened by the older women at court.

C (*Prince Genji*). I missed my mother for many years.

B (*Lady Wisteria*). Our union is forbidden.

C (*Prince Genji*). I must have you.

> *He has her.*

B (*Lady Wisteria*). I was eighteen when I became the Emperor's wife. He seemed old. I always thought you were a beautiful young man.

C (*Prince Genji*). Lady Wisteria, you have my eternal devotion.

> *End of* The Tale of Genji *episode.*

Back to Lady Sarashina's life. Time flows.

B (*Lady Sarashina*). My stepmother gives me books. As fast as she reads them, I follow. But when I am fifteen, my stepmother informs me that she is leaving.

C (*Stepmother*). I shall never forget you.

B (*Lady Sarashina*). Why are you leaving? Don't you love my father anymore?

C (*Stepmother*). He has other wives. I'm tired of wanting and waiting. If you don't leave, all you do is make more painful memories. It is better to stop the history, so at some time in the future you are able to visit it in your mind without grief.

B (*Lady Sarashina*). I don't know what you mean.

C (*Stepmother*). You will someday.

B (*Lady Sarashina*). Do you know what happened to my nanny?

C (*Stepmother*). She died after giving birth to a girl.

A (*Contemporary Woman*). My mother died.

B (*Lady Sarashina*). Shouldn't I have been at her side?

C (*Stepmother*). She was too far away.

A (*Contemporary Woman*). There was a phone call but I was too far. She read many books. Shakespeare and Tolstoy, *The Tale of Genji*. As a child I read the books she read. I knew her by the books she read. My parents didn't talk to each other very often. Very few words existed between them. But so many words in the books she gave me. So many.

Time rewinds only slightly.

B (*Lady Sarashina*). Why are you leaving? Don't you love my father anymore?

C (*Stepmother*). He has other wives. I'm tired of wanting and waiting.

B (*Lady Sarashina*). You raised me more than my own mother.

C (*Stepmother*). You are already a lady. See the plum tree in front of the house? When it blooms again, I will be back to see you.

A (*Contemporary Woman*). I'll be back to see you.

B (*Lady Sarashina*). I long for her. I wait for a year to pass. The plum tree blooms again, but she does not come.

A (*Contemporary Woman*). I was too late. I didn't know what to say. I didn't know what she had been reading before her death.

B (*Lady Sarashina*). The petals scatter. It is too late now. I write her a letter.

Lady Sarashina is sixteen years old. A (Contemporary Woman) reads from the book as Lady Sarashina writes.

A (*Contemporary Woman reading from the book*). "You promised. The flowers are fragile. When will you come? I turned sixteen before the bloom."

B (*Lady Sarashina*). (*Overlapping*) When will you come?

C. (*Stepmother*) (*a response letter*). Be patient, my dear. Perhaps someone will surprise you.

B. (*Lady Sarashina as an adult*). I never see her again.

Time flows.

B. (*Lady Sarashina*). My sister brings news.

C. (*Sister*). Have you heard the daughter of the Chamberlain Major Chancellor died?

B (*Lady Sarashina as a girl*). I have her calligraphy book! Father gave it to me.

C (*Sister*). She was only twenty.

B (*Lady Sarashina*). I hear she was very beautiful.

C (*Sister*). People say her husband is grieving terribly. He tries nightly to recall her spirit back.

B (*Lady Sarashina*). Has she come to him?

C (*Sister*). No. Her husband cries and cries, people say.

B (*Lady Sarashina*). How sad.

C (*Sister*). Why are you crying?

B (*Lady Sarashina*). It's very sad.

C (*Sister*). You didn't know her.

B (*Lady Sarashina*). I'm remembering Nanny.

B (*Lady Sarashina*) and A (*Contemporary Woman*) (*sadly*). Her calligraphy was excellent, and I heard she was beautiful.

B (*Lady Sarashina as an old woman*). At certain times of my life, sadness overwhelmed me. I hid in books and poetry, until enough time had passed so that I could pretend that my world contained no loss. (*Returns to the sixteen-year-old persona.*) I sit on a pillow behind the curtain and read the books of *The Tale of Genji* one after another. I place the lamp close to me and read as late as I can into the night.

A (Contemporary Woman) and B (Sarashina) sit side by side and read the same book silently. For A, the book is the diary. For B, it's The Tale of Genji.

A (*Contemporary Woman*). This diary was written a thousand years ago in Kyoto by a woman. Her name is lost, but her diary has been translated from old Japanese to modern Japanese to English. I found it in a local library. The librarian said that I was the first person ever to check out the book: *The Sarashina Diary*.

The past. Lady Sarashina is eighteen years old.

B (*Lady Sarashina as a teenager*). I spend my days reading the books of *The Tale of Genji*. I am eighteen. Someone just like Prince Genji will come into my life soon. I wait. I wait for my prince.

The Tale of Genji *Episode*

B (*Lady Sarashina, reading from the book*). "On his way to visit one of his lovers, the elegant and older Lady Rokujyo, Price Genji discovered a mysterious secluded house behind white evening-flower bushes. The house seemed to belong to a lower-class family but the rumor was that a beautiful lady lived there. He visited the house in disguise, concealing his royal status."

C (*As Prince Genji*). I don't know who you are, who your family is. Who is my new lover? What name shall I call you?

B (*As Yugao*). Call me Yugao, the white evening flower.

C (*Prince Genji*). Don't you want to know who I am?

B (*Yugao*). You must be an important gentleman of a high rank. But I don't need a name. What's in a name? That which we call a rose by any other name would smell as sweet. Don't tell me who you are. It will only burden us.

C (*Prince Genji*). This house must be a temporary lodging. If you disappear, how can I ever find you again? Yugao, I cannot bear to lose you.

A (*Contemporary Woman*). She is hiding from someone. Hiding from the consequences of having been someone else's lover. Her life was threatened. (*Reading from the book*) "In the meantime, Lady Rokujyo has sensed Prince Genji's heart receding from her. Still, she waits for his visit."

B (*Lady Sarashina, reading from the book*). "On this one early summer night, Genji was restless for an adventure and carried Yugao off to a deserted hideaway."

IMAGE 1.5-6 **Prince Genji and one of his lovers, reenacted by Lady Sarashina reading the tale.**

Anna Wilson (left), Sophia Skiles (right).

Photograph by David Altman.

    Genji takes Yugao away.

A (*Contemporary Woman*). She was frightened. The inescapable fate
    was closing in on her.

C (*Prince Genji*). I want to spend time with you alone, away from
    the intrusions of the world.

B (*As Yugao*). The world is temporary. We are temporary also.
    I fear, too early; for my mind misgives
    Some consequence, yet hanging in the stars,

A (Contemporary woman) joins in.

Shall bitterly begin his fearful date
With this night's revels; and expire the term
Of a despised life, closed in my breast,
By some vile forfeit of untimely death.

A (*Contemporary Woman*). "That night as they slept, the air turned
icy in the house and woke Prince Genji."

C (*Prince Genji*). Yugao, wake up. The house is haunted.

A (Now Lady Rokujyo) hovers over sleeping B (Yugao).

A (*As Lady Rokujyo*). How dare you neglect me for a low-class
woman? I have a daughter by the Crown Prince. You cannot
treat me like a common woman. You cannot leave me for
someone without a name.

C (*Prince Genji*). Lady Rokujyo! Your jealous spirit has left your
body to come here to do harm to my new lover. Leave us!

B (*Yugao*). I can't breathe.

C (*Prince Genji*). Someone help! Oh, Yugao, please hear me. You
have my eternal devotion.

A (*Lady Rokujyo*). I'm tired of wanting and waiting.

Yugao dies.

End of The Tale of Genji *episode.*

B (*Lady Sarashina to herself*). Lady Rokujyo had no knowledge of
the harm her spirit caused in her sleep. She was suffering from
the nightmare of not being loved. She is not to be blamed.
She is to be pitied.

*C (Sister) runs in. B (Sarashina) joins her. A (Contemporary
Woman) keeps reading.*

C (*Sister*). Look, Sister.

B (*Lady Sarashina*). A white cat!

C (*Sister*). Shh . . .

B (*Lady Sarashina*). It's lovely. Let us keep it.

C (*Sister*). Pretty cat.

B (*Lady Sarashina*). The cat follows us everywhere until my sister becomes ill. (*Pause.*) My sister sleeps and sleeps.

A (*Contemporary Woman*). Another death?

B (*Lady Sarashina*). She is pale, her breath thin, on her forehead, little drops of perspiration resembling rhinestones. I put the cat in the servants' room to keep it from disturbing my sister.

C (Sister) awakes from a dream.

C (*Sister*). Where is our cat?

B (*Lady Sarashina*). Rest, my sister. Do not worry.

C (*Sister*). Bring the cat to me. I had a dream. She is the reincarnation of the daughter of the Chamberlain Major Chancellor, the beautiful lady who died so young.

The cat appears.

B (*Lady Sarashina*). Pretty cat.

C (*Sister*). Pretty cat.

B (*Lady Sarashina*). I wish I could let your grieving husband know that you are with us.

A (*Contemporary Woman*). Pretty cat.

I once named a squirrel that showed up every time I was with my lover in Central Park. I was convinced that it was the same squirrel that followed us. I named it Romeo. It was my first love. I still look for Romeo in Central Park. How long do those small animals live? Can I expect to still find him in this park?/

B (*Lady Sarashina*). Dream/

A (*Contemporary Woman*). After so many years/

B (*Lady Sarashina*). Moons?

A (*Contemporary Woman*). How is it possible that time keeps passing without seeing Romeo in the park?

B (*Lady Sarashina*). Her husband cries and cries, people say.

A (*Contemporary Woman*). Pretty cat.

Time passes. The fall. Night.

B (*Lady Sarashina*). On the thirteenth night of September, the moon is orange and grand. I sit on the veranda with my sister to watch the moon.

C (*Sister*). What do you think happens after death?

B (*Lady Sarashina*). Why are you thinking about it?

C (*Sister*). I don't know. I feel lonely.

B (*Lady Sarashina*). Hold my hand, Sister.

Sister does not take Lady Sarashina's hand, not because she is ignoring her but because she is caught up in her own thoughts.

C (*Sister*). You may not even notice it when it happens to you. You inhale the scent of pine trees, and when you exhale you may already be dead. The pine scent is engraved somewhere deep in your soul. In your next life, the scent will follow you everywhere. That's how you know about the moment of your previous death.

A (*Contemporary Woman*). In your next life, you look for answers to unknown questions. And, one day, you come across a diary written in another time in another country in another language. You gain some answers even though you still don't know what the questions are.

B (*Lady Sarashina*). It's still far, far away. We have many moons to see before we part.

C (*Sister*). The only sad thing is: you won't remember anything else. If we meet in the next life, we won't know that we were sisters once. We will be different people.

B (*Lady Sarashina*). That's not how it happens. We'll be the same people, only in a different place.

C (*Sister*). Where? (*Giggling*) The moon?

B (*Lady Sarashina*). Somewhere like the moon, gentle and beautiful. Hold my hand.

Instead of taking Lady Sarashina's hand, Sister moves her arms as if they are wings.

C (*Sister*). I'll fly away to the moon!

B (Sarashina) gasps in fear and reaches over to her sister as if to prevent her from flying away.

A (*Contemporary Woman, reading from the book*). "The street merchant's voice echoes in the lateness of the night. (*In a sing-song voice*) Oginoha. Oginoha."

c (*Sister*). Let's sit up all night until dawn.

B (*Lady Sarashina as an old woman*). A year later, our cat died.

A (*Contemporary Woman*). The cat died?

Time flows.

A (*Contemporary Woman*). Spring again.

B (*Lady Sarashina*). We climb the Eastern Mountain!

They climb.

c (*Sister*). Look, a well. By the temple.

Lady Sarashina and Sister drink water from the well.

c (*Sister*). So sweet.

B (*Lady Sarashina*). I shall never have enough of it.

c (*Sister*). Never enough.

B (*Lady Sarashina*). Sweet sweet water.

c (*Sister*). I can drink it forever.

B (*Lady Sarashina*). I'll never be tired of it.

c (*Sister*). Look at the sun setting over the city.

Pause. They look at the city far away. Stillness.

B (*Lady Sarashina*). Do you think anyone down there in Kyoto is thinking of us?

A (*Contemporary Woman*). With each lover, I made myself think that he was the one. But then, I never knew how his memory worked. When I'm not with you, do you have an image of me in your eyes? Do you have my voice in your ears? Or do I cease to exist until I am with you again?

B (*Lady Sarashina*). Not knowing makes me sad.

c (*Sister*). Being away is like a small death. We are transitory clouds in each other's memory.

IMAGE 1.7 **Lady Sarashina and her sister enjoy a spring day, as Contemporary Woman watches.**

Sophia Skiles, Margi Sharp, Anna Wilson (from left to right).

Photograph by David Altman.

A (*Contemporary Woman*). Sweet sweet water. I'll never have enough.

Time passes.

B (*Lady Sarashina*). I read *The Tale of Genji*. I am plain and unattractive, but someday . . . I know this in my heart. I'm twenty years old.

A (*Contemporary Woman*). I have a steady job and a pleasant, small apartment. I basically do the same thing every weekend. Laundry, dinner with someone, a movie or maybe a museum, reading. I'm an ordinary person, but I live in this extraordinary city. Where everything is. Where you are allowed to be no one.

B (*Lady Sarashina*). This extraordinary city is where you can meet your prince. You are lucky if you get to live in Miyako. In Kyoto.

A (*Contemporary Woman*). I live in Miyako. The city of my heart.

The Tale of Genji *Episode*

B (*Lady Sarashina, reading from the book*). "Lady Rokujyo decided to leave Miyako. Prince Genji had not visited her in some time, and she could not bear being an older woman abandoned by a young lover. When Prince Genji heard of this news, suddenly, he was filled with a renewed longing for Lady Rokujyo."

IMAGE 1.8–9 **Prince Genji and his lover. In this production, this lover was played by a puppet performed by Makaya Kiritake.**

Anna Wilson.

Photographs by Theresa Squire.

A (*As Lady Rokujyo*). A woman is able to leave her lover when she is certain that she is loved by him. It is when she does not know his heart, severing the tie is painful.

C (*Prince Genji*). Lady Rokujyo, I cannot believe that you will leave me, that you will leave Kyoto.

A (*Lady Rokujyo*). Prince Genji, I have already become part of your past.

C (*Prince Genji*). I cannot bear to lose you.

Lady Sarashina urgently reads from the book.

B (*Lady Sarashina, reading from the book*). "Lady Rokujyo was tired. Tired of waiting for his touch, days of impossible anticipation and nights of heart-wrenching disappointment. She had no way of assuaging the violence and fire in her heart."

A (*Lady Rokujyo*). People are laughing at me. I am humiliated.

C (*Prince Genji*). We will start over.

A (*Lady Rokujyo*). Some things are not possible to start over.

B (*Lady Sarashina, reading from the book*). "Lady Rokujyo was one of the most refined ladies at court, her poetry was excellent and her beauty radiant. He could not imagine the emptiness of his heart in her absence."

C (*Prince Genji*). I was foolish. I should never have left you alone for so long. Please reconsider. You have my eternal devotion.

A (*Lady Rokujyo*). It is better to stop the history so at sometime in the future you are able to visit it in your mind without grief. It is nearly dawn. You must go now.

End of The Tale of Genji *episode.*

A (*Contemporary Woman*). You should go now.

B (*Lady Sarashina*). I want to be like a character in *The Tale of Genji*. A prince will hide me in a mountain village. He will spend exactly one year with me. After he leaves, I will wait for his letter for the rest of my life there, gazing at spring flowers and autumn leaves, moon after moon. Life will be sorrowful and beautiful.

Lady Sarashina dances. A dream dance.

B (*Lady Sarashina*). While I was reading *The Tale of Genji*, other women around me went to serve at court, attended glamorous parties, played music, and married. I kept reading.

A (*Contemporary Woman*). While I was reading her diary, the rice got burned, the sheets went unwashed, the old-fashioned LPs got all scratched, and the way back was being erased. I kept reading.

B (*Lady Sarashina*). I'll wait for my lover until my death, counting the moons.

A (*Contemporary Woman*). The New York sky is lit with man-made stars. I'm not able to count the moons anyway. I don't want sorrowful and beautiful. I want something else.

Time flows.

B (*Lady Sarashina*). When I am twenty-two, it is determined by the family that I am too old to be staying home and reading tales all day long. I am to be sent to serve at court. My father is saddened by this family decision.

A (*Contemporary Woman as Father*). "I'm old. What if I become ill while you are at court? I may never see you again."

B (*Lady Sarashina*). He is a gentle and quiet soul. He is very attached to me. But I want to experience the glamor of court life. I want a chance to meet someone like Prince Genji.

At court.

B. (*Lady Sarashina*). At court, I am given a beautiful lady companion who teaches me the etiquette of being a lady-in-waiting. We play cards and music, write poetry, and in the evenings, wait for romantic visits.

C (*Lady Companion*). Here comes a gentleman.

B (*Lady Sarashina*). You entertain him. I'll wait here.

C (*Lady Companion*). He speaks softly. There is no need to be shy. Come.

A (*Contemporary Woman, speaking as the Gentleman*). "I have not known a lady like you at this palace."

IMAGE 1.10 **Three women traveling through time.**
Margi Sharp, Sophia Skiles, Anna Wilson (from left to right).
Photograph by David Altman.

B (*Lady Sarashina looking back*). Moonless night of charm and secret. He lingered. We exchange poetry.

A (*Contemporary Woman as the Gentleman*). "What is most beautiful in the world?"

C (*Lady Companion*). The misty spring moon.

A (*Contemporary Woman as the Gentleman*). "The moonlight reflected on snow."

B (*Lady Sarashina*). The autumn moon that falls on my heart.

A (*Contemporary Woman as the Gentleman*). What is most sorrowful in the world?

C (*Companion Lady*). The misty spring moon!

A (*Contemporary Woman*). A slow cry of a bamboo flute.

B (*Lady Sarashina*). Morning frost on the last chrysanthemum.

A (*Contemporary Woman as the Gentleman*). What is most mysterious in the world?

C (*Companion Lady*). The misty spring moon?

A (*Contemporary Woman*). The voice of a new lady on a moonless night.

B (*Lady Sarashina*). Time passing while you are dreaming . . . He compliments the elegance of my language. I will think about him from this day on, filling the spaces between his words with fantasies and hopes, even though he leaves without asking my name.

A (*Contemporary Woman*). The blood of dreaming and storytelling runs through us. As Prince Genji's heart faded, all his lovers were still telling the story of forever and ever. After he was completely gone, they recounted their memories of him. (*To Lady Sarashina*) If you don't watch out, the same thing will happen to you.

B (*Lady Sarashina*). Has it happened to you?

A (*Contemporary Woman*). Yes.

The Tale of Genji *Episode*

In this scene, time is split. The conversations between Prince Genji and Lady Lavender and Prince Genji and Lady Akashi take place in different times in different places, though merged in the scene.

B (*Lady Sarashina, reading from the book*). "Lady Wisteria's illicit son became the Emperor. But no one suspected that Genji is the real father of the new Emperor. Only Lady Wisteria suffered a guilty heart. In the meantime . . ."

C (*Prince Genji*). Lady Lavender, my official wife, I have a proposition to make.

A (*As Lady Lavender*). What is it, my love?

C. (*Prince Genji*). While I was away from the capital three years ago, I met the monk of Suma. He was eager to give his only daughter, Lady Akashi, to a nobleman, so she and I were united.

A (*Lady Lavender*). I see.

C (*Prince Genji*). I hesitated for your sake. But I was far from Kyoto then, and I knew you would understand if I should confess my affair to you.

A (*Lady Lavender*). I see.

C (*Prince Genji*). Lady Akashi had a daughter shortly after. Now she is a beautiful girl. According to the fortune told, I am to birth an emperor and an empress. This girl could well be the future empress.

A (*Lady Lavender*). I see.

C (*Prince Genji*). Lady Lavender, you know you have my eternal devotion. But we are childless. I thought perhaps you would like to raise this child as your own. (*To B*) Lady Akashi, I know you love your daughter very much. But you are of a lower class. Let my wife adopt your daughter.

B (*as Lady Akashi*). It would break my heart to give her up. She is all I have.

C (*Prince Genji*). Do not forget that you have my eternal devotion. And it would be best for her future at court.

B (*Lady Akashi*). Perhaps I could sacrifice my love. Perhaps I could give up my daughter for the sake of her future.

A (*Lady Lavender*). Perhaps I could raise this woman's child. Perhaps a beautiful little girl will ease my loneliness.

C (*Prince Genji*). Lady Lavender, I kidnapped you from your rightful guardian when you were only a little child to raise you myself. Because you were such a beautiful girl. I wanted to make you into my ideal wife. You did not fail me.

A (*Lady Lavender*). I see.

C (*Prince Genji*). I was very fond of your aunt, Lady Wisteria, my father's wife. I was eighteen when . . . You resemble my stepmother whom I adored as a young man.

A (*Contemporary Woman*, *to herself*). On and on and on. Countless numbers of ladies-in-waiting and male relatives made it

possible for Genji to sneak into the bedchambers of numerous women.

c (*Prince Genji*). I must have you. I cannot bear to lose you.

a (*Contemporary Woman*). The women were behind bamboo blinds, nights were dark, so most of the time they didn't even know what each other looked like until the morning. Some women waited for him after that, some became nuns, and some married other men or simply stayed where they were if they were already married. But they all longed for Genji.

c (*Prince Genji*). You have my eternal devotion.

a (*Contemporary Woman*). *The Tale of Genji* is a collection of broken hearts caused by one maniac.

b (*Lady Sarashina*). Prince Genji was heartbroken too. All his life, because he was never satisfied. Finally, when his beloved Lady Lavender died, he left court and became a monk. If I were his lover, I would have gone with him. I would have become a nun and gone with him. I would have loved him with a pure heart.

a (*Contemporary Woman*). Won't you regret later?

b (*Lady Sarashina*). I won't. I won't regret.

a (*Contemporary Woman*). Are you sure, my lady?

Back to Lady Sarashina's life. Another night at court.

b (*Lady Sarashina*). I pushed open the sliding door to let the moon in one night. The gentleman from the other night surprised me.

a. (*Contemporary Woman as the Gentleman*). "I think of you on that moonless night every moment of my life."

b (*Lady Sarashina*). It was a dream.

a (*Contemporary Woman as the Gentleman*). "The next moonless night, I will play the flute for you."

IMAGE 1.11 (*Facing Page*) **As Lady Sarashina reads** *The Tale of Genji,* **Contemporary Woman re-enacts a love scene.**
Margi Sharp, Anna Wilson, Sophia Skiles (from left to right).
Photograph by David Altman.

B (*Lady Sarashina*). Why a moonless night?

A (*Contemporary Woman as the Gentleman*). "A moonless night has charm and secrets. Waiting for it gives us a special bond."

B (*Lady Sarashina*). I waited for that night. It never came. I never saw him again.

Time passes.

B (*Lady Sarashina*). I've wasted my life away in fantasies. No prince came. I marry my husband. I'm thirty.

A (*Contemporary Woman*). I've lived my life thinking there is no end to time. I get divorced. I'm thirty.

Time passes while you are counting blessings. Time passes as you are laying out items from your closets on your bed to decide what to keep, what to throw away. Time passes despite your dreams, or because of your dreams.

Sister's visit. They are middle-aged now.

B (*Lady Sarashina*). My sister has taken leave from her husband to visit me. It's good to see you again, Sister.

On the thirteenth night of September, the moon is orange and grand. I sit on the veranda with my sister to watch the moon.

C (*Sister*). What do you think happens after death?

B (*Lady Sarashina*). Why are you thinking about it?

C (*Sister*). I don't know. I feel lonely.

B (*Lady Sarashina*). Hold my hand, Sister.

C (*Sister*). I have something to tell you.

B (*Lady Sarashina*). It's still far, far away. We have many moons to see before we part.

C (*Sister*). I have something to tell you.

B (*Lady Sarashina*). Hold my hand.

Instead of taking Lady Sarashina's hand, Sister moves her arms as if they are wings.

C (*Sister*). I'll fly away to the moon!

IMAGE 1.12 **Lady Sarashina's sister's death.**
Anna Wilson, Sophia Skiles, Margi Sharp (from left to right).
Photograph by David Altman.

> *B (Sarashina) gasps in fear and reaches over to her sister as if to*
> *prevent her from flying away.*
>
> *C (Sister) disappears.*

B (*Lady Sarashina*). After I lost my sister, I began dreaming about her. In the dream, we are little girls traveling through white dunes. But I always wake up and lose her again.

A (*Contemporary Woman*). But won't you find her again?

B (*Lady Sarashina*). After I left the glamor of court life, I cared for my husband and children. Time passed. I occasionally dreamed about the moonless night.

My husband became ill and faded away like a dream one October day. My father was very old when one morning he simply did not wake up. My children grew up and left. Still time kept passing. I have lived too long.

(*Lady Sarashina is now an old woman.*)

October comes again bringing back memories of deaths. I heard the gentleman I met on the moonless night many years ago also died in October. I don't know what year. I live alone back in my old house. The first house I lived in, in Kyoto with father.

A (*Contemporary Woman as Father*). "I'm old. What if I become ill while you are at court? I may never see you again."

B (*Lady Sarashina*). I wanted to experience the glamor of court life. I wanted a chance to meet my prince.

A (*Contemporary Woman*). There is no such thing.

B (*Lady Sarashina*). How could it be?

A (*Contemporary Woman*). You're the one who told me that.

B (*Lady Sarashina*). But was I to lose everything? My nanny, my stepmother, my cat, my sister, my father, my husband, my October night?

A (*Contemporary Woman*). Where're your children?

B (*Lady Sarashina*). They will have their own losses to recount.

A (*Contemporary Woman*). I've been waiting for you for a thousand years.

B (*Lady Sarashina*). Memories come back to me. Of people who are gone. I write them down. Write down regrets of my life lived in tales and fantasies, waiting for my prince.

A (*Contemporary Woman*). It is said that all her diary entries were made toward the end of her life. She wrote it from memory. My memories are as old as hers. Her memories are someone's future memories. I go back to her diary. Back to *The Tale of*

IMAGE 1.13 (*Facing Page*) **Lady Sarashima remembers her sister's death.** Sophia Skiles.
Photograph by David Altman.

IMAGE 1.15 **The dance with the traveling performer.**
Sophia Skiles, the puppet, Anna Wilson (from left to right).
Photograph by David Altman.

Genji. Back to all the memories that make us human. (*Confidently*) Don't worry. I'll catch up.

Time rewinds fast. They are young girls again. Sister comes back.

c (*Sister*). We are moving to Kyoto/

B (*Lady Sarashina*) Destiny/

A (*Contemporary Woman*). New York City.

c (*Sister*). Look! Traveling performers. How did they find us?

B (*Lady Sarashina*). Please, Father, let them come sing for us.

The traveling performer's music from the past.

Blackout.

CHARACTERS

TIME	A woman. Preferably played by a woman of color. Any age.
CAROLINE HERSCHEL	The first recognized woman astronomer. She ages from 22 to 72 during the play. In one flash-back scene, she is 7 years old.
WILLIAM HERSCHEL	A renowned astronomer. Caroline's brother. He ages from 34 to 84.
MOTHER	Caroline and William's mother. She is in her 50s when she appears in the play.
MARY	William's wife. She ages from the early 30s to late the 60s during the play.

SETTING

1772 to 1822 CE

Hanover, Germany
Bath, England
Slough, England

COMET HUNTER

PROLOGUE

A tall, slender woman stands in a simple dress. Beside her, Caroline Herschel, a small woman of thirty-six, dressed in a conservative dress typical of the 1780s, is looking into a telescope. Stars are projected all around them.

TIME. I am *Time*. I walk with you the distance between birth and death; history observes me but leaves me unchanged; I have no meaning other than the marks you place on me—confirmations, weddings, funerals, discoveries—your transitory human heart. I am eternally missing. I am a void. Yet I exist. (*Turns to Caroline.*) August 2, 1786, Slough, England.

CAROLINE. There was a motion since last night! It *is* a comet!

TIME (*affirming*). It is.

CAROLINE. I have discovered a comet! *I* have discovered a comet.

TIME and CAROLINE. I exist.

Lights change; stars disappear.

In writing this play, I worked with a science consultant, Dr. James Lattis, Director, UW Space Place, Department of Astronomy, University of Wisconsin–Madison.

ACT I

SCENE 1

Hanover, Germany, 1772.

Caroline is twenty-two. She and her mother are in their modest home. Time is present throughout, but only Caroline can see her.

MOTHER. Your brother did not even come home for your father's funeral. After his seizure, I was certain he longed to see William once more.

CAROLINE. Mother, they said goodbye to one another when William last visited. After that, Father never asked for him.

MOTHER. I wrote William about his paralysis.

CAROLINE. Father left us five years ago. Let us not remind ourselves of the sad times.

MOTHER. Caroline, your brother has not set foot in this house in eight years. I don't know what he is coming for all of a sudden. He might as well have waited for my death.

CAROLINE. He simply did not notice how much time had passed. He has been terribly busy with his music career, and England is far.

MOTHER. You have always loved him too much and forgiven him too easily. All that science education and music lessons that your father allowed him have only kept him away from Germany. And Jacob and Alexander, even little Dietrich, are constantly leaving Germany for visits to England to play the organ or violin with William. Who can I depend on?

CAROLINE. Mother, please. William is coming for a visit. Jacob and Alexander and Dietrich always come back. Their stay in England was prolonged last time because they waited for an audience with His Majesty. It was a great honor to play for the King and Queen.

MOTHER. I know all that. They have informed me more than once.

CAROLINE. And I am here to take care of you.

MOTHER. You? You have a tendency to dream up useless activities while your household linens are not adequately made.

CAROLINE. I have been making all the linens and stockings for everyone for fifteen years, since I was seven.

MOTHER. After your father died, you wanted to learn dressmaking! Always dreaming up something.

CAROLINE. Jacob gave me permission to take some lessons.

MOTHER. Only to make your own dresses. For no other purpose. You understand that Jacob forbade you to attempt to make a career in dressmaking.

CAROLINE. Yes, and I have yet to use my skill to make one dress. I have been busy keeping the house. I am as uneducated as you wished.

MOTHER. Pardon?

The moment with Mother pauses, but time flows.

CAROLINE (*to Time*). I am desperately uneducated. (*Pause.*) I have not done much besides knitting in my life. Oh, I also wash, cook, clean, all that. I am very dependable. But there is no meaning.

TIME. What would you like to do?

CAROLINE. Leave. Go far away from here so nothing will remind me of this time and space.

TIME. Why?

CAROLINE. I do not understand why as I stand still, my loved ones disappear. If I stand still any longer, I shall lose everyone.

TIME. You have many people. Three brothers. A sister. And your mother.

CAROLINE. My father was a good man. He wanted to give me an education, but Mother was always absolutely against it, and he was too gentle to defy her wishes. He used to steal a little time on Dietrich's violin for me. Some evenings when his pupils gathered for a concert, he would call me to the parlor and say—

TIME. "Lina, play the second violin for us."

CAROLINE. And William. Oh, I adored him as a little girl. He is most like my father out of all the brothers and the only person left who calls me Lina. I remember when I was seven, William took me out of the house on one frosty night into the streets, and we stood and watched the constellations. Mother was unhappy because she thought the night air was bad for our constitutions. William ignored her, and we stayed out a good half hour, holding hands, looking up at the heavens. He left for England the next day.

TIME. But he isn't really gone, is he?

CAROLINE. While time moves forward and William leaves and becomes a very accomplished composer, I stand still, and Father dies. I continue to stand still.

TIME. Would you like to have children?

CAROLINE. I shall never marry.

TIME. Why?

CAROLINE. Because I am ugly.

TIME. No, Caroline, that's not why.

CAROLINE. Because I had typhus when I was eleven, I never grew any taller. My body is strangely stunted, terribly small. When I recovered from the illness, my father said not to expect to marry when I grew up.

TIME. He told you that you were ugly?

CAROLINE. No, not exactly. He was kind. He regretted that I was so dreadfully uneducated.

The moment goes back to Mother with a knock on the door. William enters.

WILLIAM. Hello, Mother. Hello, Lina.

CAROLINE. William!

She runs to him. He sweeps her small body off the floor and they embrace for a long moment. Then they separate.

TIME. Rewind time to 1757. During the French occupation of Hanover. Caroline is seven years old.

We hear a knock on the door though William has not moved. He stands still at the place where he entered previously. He is now nineteen. Seven-year-old Caroline runs to him again. They embrace.

CAROLINE. William!

WILLIAM. How is my little Lina?

CAROLINE. Mother says you are going away again.

WILLIAM. Yes, I am, but I will be back to fetch you.

CAROLINE. Fetch me? To where? Why?

WILLIAM. You will know why in the near future. Not too near, I hope. But when you realize that you wish to be fetched away from this place, you must remain patient.

CAROLINE. Why do you have to leave?

WILLIAM. There is a war going on, little Lina. That is where our father is. That is where I was last year.

CAROLINE. Mother and I were terribly worried when you were at war because of your *delicate constitution*.

WILLIAM. Is that what Mother said?

CAROLINE. She cries all the time. William, are you going back to war? She will be heartbroken.

WILLIAM. No, Lina. I am going to England.

CAROLINE. Because of your *delicate constitution*?

WILLIAM. Partially, yes. But more than that, I cannot go back to war because it is not my life's purpose.

CAROLINE. What is your purpose?

WILLIAM. I am not certain yet. I only know what is not. I must go search for my purpose. What is yours, Lina?

CAROLINE. I am a girl. I have *duties*.

WILLIAM. Is that what Mother said?

CAROLINE. She thinks I shall marry a prince someday. There are things I must learn to prepare.

WILLIAM. Such as?

CAROLINE. Knitting!

WILLIAM. Good, good. But Lina, remember two things. Everyone has a purpose. And I will be back to fetch you.

For a moment, Caroline is confused and sad.

WILLIAM. Now, shall we go out and see the constellations?

CAROLINE. Now? In this cold night?

WILLIAM. Yes, now. Hold my hand.

TIME. Fifteen years later, a knock on the door. The beginning of your purpose.

The time is restored to 1772. William and Caroline embrace.

CAROLINE. William!

WILLIAM. How is my little Lina?

CAROLINE. Oh, my dear William. Fine. Just fine. Mother, William is here.

MOTHER. I can see.

William goes to Mother and kisses her cheeks.

WILLIAM. You look well, Mother.

MOTHER. You too, William. You look fine. The journey was not too difficult, I hope.

WILLIAM. Not too difficult.

MOTHER. Sit down. Are you hungry?

CAROLINE. We have tea prepared for you.

WILLIAM. That would be nice, Lina. Some tea.

Caroline goes to get the tea set. Time follows.

CAROLINE. Is he not handsome? Is he not splendid? He is the only one.

TIME. There is greatness to come. You love him not because he under-stands you, but because you sense an important future in him.

CAROLINE. What I long for is not his past which is missing from my present. I long for his future which I am afraid that I will miss. I baked his favorite cake.

The moment goes back to Mother and William. Caroline serves tea and cake.

CAROLINE. William, see this cake? I—

MOTHER. It is your favorite. I hope you like it.

WILLIAM. It looks divine, Mother. Thank you for remembering.

MOTHER. Of course I remember. That is what mothers do.

(*Caroline continues to serve, now in silence.*)

What news do you bring? Are you well?

WILLIAM. I am, Mother. The last few years, I have not even had a cold.

MOTHER. England must be agreeable to you. When you were a young boy, you had a delicate constitution. That is why your father sent you to England in the first place. He did not think you could survive the military service.

WILLIAM. I could not have survived it. The little experience I had in the military told me that plainly. It was not entirely for physical reasons. My mind was too fragile for that kind of life.

MOTHER. Nonsense. Your father was a brave soldier. All his sons inherited his bravery. He did not deserve such a painful death. He had lost the entire function of the left side of his body after his first seizure. He could no longer play the violin and grew more and more melancholy over the last three years until he finally gave up.

WILLIAM. Mother, he had a good life.

MOTHER. He gave all of *you* a good life.

WILLIAM. Very true. He knew all his children loved him and were grateful. He enjoyed music. And he had a wife who was devoted to him. You made him a happy man.

MOTHER. I suppose so. What are your plans, William? You are thirty-four years old. When do you plan to marry?

WILLIAM. I have not given it much thought.

MOTHER. Perhaps you would like to meet some German ladies during your visit. It would be nice to make a marriage with someone from your homeland.

WILLIAM. I am extremely busy. As the organist at Octagon Chapel, I have to compose for the choir and the orchestra and be responsible for every concert. I have no time for leisure.

TIME. He has no time for his true purpose.

MOTHER. Are you compensated well?

WILLIAM. Enough.

TIME. Not enough for the lost time for watching the stars, trying to fill in the blank space in the sky that the ancients had no knowledge of. His purpose.

CAROLINE (*urgently*). How can I help?

MOTHER. Caroline! Stop your nonsense.

WILLIAM. Actually, Mother, I wanted to talk to you about taking Lina with me to England. I was not planning to approach this subject until later, but since it came up, let us address it now. I would like her to keep the house for me and assist me in copying music. My life would be bearable if I had Lina to help me. She could also sing in my winter concerts after taking some lessons. She is a good, natural singer.

MOTHER. Absolutely not! What an outrageous idea to make her into a career singing girl. Caroline, did you know William was coming here with this ridiculous proposal? Have you had a letter from him?

WILLIAM. Mother, Lina is also hearing this for the first time.

MOTHER. Your brother wants to make you into a glamorous singer and not to have to do the honest, hard work of a woman keeping a house.

WILLIAM. Lina will have more work than now. She will keep house for me and assist me at the church. It will be demanding work; she will not stay idle, I promise you.

MOTHER. And my house? Who will keep my house in her place? Who will do all the work? Do you expect your brothers to do it?

WILLIAM. We will arrange for hired help for you.

MOTHER. I have a daughter. I should not have to have hired help.

TIME. Lina, you're going to travel.

MOTHER. I refuse to let her go. She stays with me.

TIME. You will leave Hanover on August 16, 1772 on an open vessel from a quay at Heluotslsis to get to a packet boat to cross the ocean to Yarmouth. From there you will take an open wagon to London, then to Bath. You will arrive at the other end of your fate on 27 August. Eleven days will have passed. Eleven days will be in between this time and space you want to forget and the time and space yet to be formed in your mind.

MOTHER. No, she stays here. There is work to be done here. She is responsible for her family.

WILLIAM. Mother, be reasonable. Lina took care of Father for the three years of his steady decline. She has managed the household for you since she was a little girl.

MOTHER. She deserves a medal for meeting the basic duties of a daughter?

TIME. Medal? What a wonderful idea! Lina, you shall have a medal!

CAROLINE. Please be quiet.

MOTHER. I beg your pardon?

CAROLINE. I did not mean . . .

WILLIAM. Mother, I came prepared to provide a small annuity for you to hire someone in Lina's place.

MOTHER. I object to the insinuation that I was a bad mother. I taught her everything she needed to know to be a wife and a mother.

TIME. You will travel.

WILLIAM. Of course. You were right to do that. But you know Lina will never marry. It is a safe and respectable choice for an unmarried woman to reside with her brother.

MOTHER. I could never get her interested in considering marriage. It is not for the lack of trying on my part that she is not married. I did not wish her to become a spinster.

WILLIAM. Of course not.

MOTHER. Just a little while before you arrived, I was reminiscing about how beautiful she looked on her first communion. And she is a capable housekeeper. No man would complain about how she keeps a house. And a decent cook. She made the cake especially for you today.

WILLIAM. She did?

MOTHER. I do not know how she got to be twenty-two and unmarried. We are a good family. Not wealthy, but our reputation is unblemished. There is no reason at all why she should not have married.

WILLIAM. I agree, but she will be most valuable for my bachelor's life.

MOTHER. I suppose there is no hope of marriage for her now.

WILLIAM. Agreed, then?

MOTHER. I have always been afraid for her, she being so small. The safest place for someone like her is home. Without money or a father or a husband, how would she have survived in society?

WILLIAM. Times are changing, Mother. She will be fine.

MOTHER. Protect your sister, William. A woman who knows too much of anything is prone to danger and pain.

TIME. Get ready, Lina.

CAROLINE. I will travel.

Starlights come up all around them for a brief moment. Lights down.

SCENE 2

March, 1781, Bath, England. Caroline is thirty-one, William is forty-three. They are in a room which looks like a workshop with a turntable for grinding glass, but it is actually their parlor. Caroline is seated at a desk working beside William who is playing sections of the Messiah *on the piano. This goes on for a moment. Then he stops playing.*

WILLIAM. I would rather be polishing a mirror for my telescope.

CAROLINE. The Easter concert is fifteen days away. After that we will have more time.

WILLIAM. This is a waste of time.

CAROLINE. Music?

WILLIAM. Yes. Music. I wish I could be freed from music.

CAROLINE. It is not easy to copy the *Messiah* for an orchestra of nearly one hundred people.

WILLIAM. I know, Lina, I appreciate it. But I would rather if you helped me make the tube for my large telescope. A two-and-a-half-foot Gregorian telescope is not adequate for what I wish to see. I want to build a twenty-foot telescope. I have ordered the glass from London already. Can you start making the tube with pasteboard?

CAROLINE. As soon as I am finished with copying. Please, William, concentrate on music for fifteen more days. You are a wonderful organ player and composer. We are fortunate to be able to rely on your talent.

WILLIAM. It is a burden. An injustice. I am not satisfied with observing the universe that other men have seen and know already. I want to make new discoveries. I want to rewrite the map of existence. For that, I need time. I will make such telescopes, and see such things!

CAROLINE. You have made discoveries. You unearthed the nature of a true nebula.

WILLIAM. I will run out of time before my eyes will have gazed the deep sky from corner to corner.

TIME. Time seems to be a very big issue here.

CAROLINE (*responding to Time*). These are serious matters. You do not understand because you have no sense of time.

TIME and WILLIAM. I beg your pardon?

CAROLINE. Being a musician is a noble profession.

WILLIAM. Composing or playing music is a small act. It does not tell us why we are here. It does not teach us the profundity of the parallel lives of the stars and ours. It neither confirms nor denies God.

CAROLINE (*appalled*). William!

WILLIAM. Lina, when you see the mirrors after they are polished to perfection, what do you see? What is it for?

CAROLINE. It is for gathering light.

WILLIAM. What do you see?

CAROLINE. When it is just finished, I see myself. When it is in its place in a telescope, I see the stars.

WILLIAM. They are the same thing. In both cases, you are seeing yourself. Stargazing is an intimate act of searching for your own soul's history.

CAROLINE. I do not think that my soul is worth such an extensive searching. I must copy this music. It is nearly dark and the sky is clear. I assume we will be soul-searching this evening.

William goes back to playing the piano.

TIME. You'd rather be polishing your seven-foot mirror, too, wouldn't you?

CAROLINE. I made it from the rough into the finished. When I am done polishing it will be beautiful. It is for Sir William Watson.

TIME. I see.

CAROLINE. My first mirror.

TIME. But not for William. For Sir Watson.

CAROLINE. Sir Watson is very kind to William. And he is a member of the Royal Society. He is going to present William's astronomy work to His Majesty.

TIME. When you finish the mirror for him, will you see yourself in it?

CAROLINE. Seeing myself has no meaning. I do not have the ability that a woman with beauty has to look at her own image and see the universe in it. When I look in the mirror, I can only hope to see the possibility of a continuum, beyond myself, beyond time, beyond meaning.

TIME. Do you hope to lose yourself in the continuum?

CAROLINE. An unmarried woman is a defective element in society, unless she has a title. I am not a full member of society. When

I am at a dinner, I wait for all the married women to enter the dining room and take their seats before I proceed. I keep silent when told in insincerity that my life must be a luxury without a husband and children to look after. But these are rare occasions. I have so little time for dinners and friends. I copy music and keep the house by day, assist William observe the sky by night, and sing and keep accounts somehow in between. I have no choice but to be lost in the continuum.

TIME. And Sir Watson?

CAROLINE. He is a gentleman, a kind soul. You know he and William met here in Bath when William had his telescope on River Street one night, and Sir Watson happened to pass by and asked William if he could take a look. The next day he came back and introduced himself as a fellow astronomer.

TIME. He's married.

CAROLINE. I am aware of the facts of his life and mine. I have no illusions. My fantasies are temporary.

TIME Are you unhappy?

CAROLINE. I am only unhappy because I cannot do more for William. He rescued me from despair and gave me the beauty of music and light. He deserves my complete devotion.

TIME. Are you lonely?

CAROLINE. I have decided to live my life with a genius, lover of luminous beings, dreamer of origins, thinker, traveler, musician, my brother.

TIME. There is greatness to come. You love him not because he understands you, but because you sense an important future in him.

CAROLINE. Father said that perhaps when I was old, someone might marry me on account of my worth. I still do not know what he meant. What could be my worth?

William's piano goes on for a while and then stops. Pause. Caroline looks up from her copying.

WILLIAM. I have something to tell you, Lina. (*Pause.*) . . . Your singing has improved a great deal. You are an excellent singer

now. I receive many compliments for your performance after
every concert.

CAROLINE. Thank you, William.

WILLIAM. Do you enjoy it then?

CAROLINE. Yes, I do. It feels like an extension of stargazing to me.
When I am singing, I imagine faint waves of my voice going
out to space and traveling through the empty space between
earth and the nearest star. I know this is silly, but I still think it.

WILLIAM. So you enjoy it most of all? Of course, more than household chores or keeping the accounts. But more than sweeping
the sky? More than cooking or those sorts of activities?

CAROLINE. I have not thought about it. It is simply one of the things
that I do to serve you.

WILLIAM. But you do not have to sing only for me. You could most
certainly get engagements elsewhere.

CAROLINE. William, whatever for? And how would I ever manage
everything?

WILLIAM. I have an offer for you from the Birmingham Festival to be
the first singer. (*Pause.*) You should not be concerned with me.
I can get hired help for the house and a student to assist me in
music and another student to assist me in my astronomical pur-
suits. (*Pause.*) That is if you should decide that this engagement
is an important one. (*Pause.*) Certainly it is an impressive offer.
You should consider it most seriously. (*Pause.*) You are thirty-
one years old. It is certainly time that you decided on your true
calling, your purpose. I know this because I was your age when
I realized that I was meant to be an astronomer.

TIME. "Lina, remember two things. Everyone has a purpose. And I
will be back to fetch you."

WILLIAM. Once you realize your mission, nothing should distract
you from your path. Of course, in normal cases, a woman's
mission is to be a wife and a mother, but you are not an ordinary woman. I hope you know that I hold you in the highest
esteem of any woman I know.

CAROLINE. William.

WILLIAM. Yes?

CAROLINE. Please decline the offer.

WILLIAM. It is not only this offer you would be declining. This may be the first step to becoming a professional singer. If you accept Birmingham, surely other offers will follow.

CAROLINE. I have no interest in singing when you are not the conductor. I shall only sing when it is your concert. And when you are freed from music and no longer have to conduct, I shall stop my singing as well.

TIME. But would you not like to sing?

The stars come up all around them.

CAROLINE. Oh, I *am* singing. (*Pause while they stand under the stars.*) Come, William. It is time.

They are now outside. They move to the telescope, where William looks and Caroline is ready to take notes.

WILLIAM. Eta Coronae Borealis. Double. A little unequal. Whitish. Less than ¼ diameter. Position 59° 19′ North following.

CAROLINE. Flamsteed 2. Inclining to red or blue?

WILLIAM. Neither. White.

CAROLINE. Four hundred and sixty magnification?

WILLIAM. Yes. (*Pause as he watches the sky.*) The dim star in Corona Borealis. Double. Equal. Both dusky. About 1¾ diameter.

CAROLINE. Very small. The smallest between Theta and Delta?

WILLIAM. I think so.

CAROLINE. They are not contained in Flamsteed.

WILLIAM. Position 21° 0′ North proceeding. (*Pause.*) Lina, do you remember long ago when I was sent to England with the regiment from Germany?

CAROLINE. Why are you thinking about that tonight?

WILLIAM. The restlessness of the heart makes me reminisce about the time I was longing for something.

CAROLINE. What were you longing for then at age seventeen?

WILLIAM. I was not clear. I brought back Locke's *On Human Understanding* from England. I was thinking about his theory of man's natural rights—life, liberty, and property. The idea of a government as consent of the people. Something was stirring in me, but my ideas did not converge until I began stargazing. After that, I knew. I was longing for a purpose, and it was my right to have it.

CAROLINE. I remember your return. I was five years old. There was an earthquake that same year in January. It destroyed Lisbon, and we felt the tremor all the way in Hanover. I was frightened. I thought the threatening ground movement was the war I was feeling, and it worried me sick for your safety.

TIME. It was 1755.

CAROLINE. Two years after that, you were gone, never to come back to Germany.

TIME. "When you realize you wish to be fetched away from this place, you must remain patient. Now, shall we go see the constellations?"

WILLIAM. And here you are. (*Looks in the telescope.*) Sigma Coronae Borealis. Triple. The two nearest pretty unequal. The third very faint. The two nearest both white. The third dusky. The large star two diameters. Position 77° and 32′ North proceeding.

CAROLINE. Flamsteed 17.

Pause as he watches the sky.

WILLIAM. Lina, look at this.

She looks in the telescope and tries to determine what it is William wants to show her.

CAROLINE. The comet? The one we saw last month.

He takes the telescope and gets increasingly excited.

WILLIAM. The orbit has declined but very little from the ecliptic.

CAROLINE. That is strange.

WILLIAM. It is perfectly sharp upon the edges. Extremely well defined.

IMAGE 2.1 **William Herschel's telescope, with which he discovered planet Uranus.** *Image courtesy Hap Tivey.*

TIME. He will name it Georgium Sidus in honor of King George III and call it so for the rest of his life, though it was renamed Uranus later.

CAROLINE. William!

TIME. This discovery will give him a place in history and preserve his name for many generations of stargazers, amateur and professional.

WILLIAM. There is not the least appearance of any beard or tail. Lina!

TIME. For now, it will give him great recognition and a meager two hundred pounds a year salary from the King to be Royal Astronomer. And yes, freedom from music.

WILLIAM. It is a planet!

Caroline gasps and clings to William's shoulder. He holds her hand on his shoulder. They stay still for a moment.

TIME. March 13, 1781. In five years, you will leave Bath and move to Slough near Windsor, where William will erect the world's largest telescope.

WILLIAM. Lina, do you know what this means?

CAROLINE. You have looked into the corner of your soul that you have never seen before.

WILLIAM. Yes, and?

CAROLINE. This is the first planet not known to the ancients.

TIME. Uranus is an ancient Greek deity of the heavens, the earliest supreme god.

WILLIAM. I am the first modern man to discover a planet.

They look into each other's eyes. Hold this moment.

SCENE 3

Time stands and, next to her, Caroline is looking into a telescope—stars are all around them—exactly the same image as the opening of the play. 1786. Caroline is thirty-six.

CAROLINE. It is quiet.

TIME. Are you missing William?

CAROLINE. When William is away, melancholy thoughts invade my heart. Perhaps because I was a lonely child. My older sister Sophy's marriage turned out badly, so she came back to Hanover when I was four. She was distraught and did not care to have small children near her, so I was sent outside to play on winter days. I would stand by the lake and watch my brothers ice skate, shivering, waiting, until the boys were ready to go home. It was almost as if no one thought I was there.

TIME. You felt invisible.

CAROLINE. I was delighted when William gave me a Newtonian Sweeper of my own after our very last concert at St. Margaret's Chapel. He wanted to assure me that giving up music was the right thing to do—not just for him, but for me. But when William is home, my own sweeping is often interrupted to write down his observations. When he is away, I have all the hours of the night for myself, but doubt clouds my mind.

TIME. Doubt?

CAROLINE. I am a small person. Without William, the universe is too large. I am not confident that I will someday discover a piece of the heavens yet untouched by the human eye.

TIME. Change is coming.

CAROLINE. I must keep busy and get some paperwork done while William is away. Once he gets home, every moment after daylight is again allotted to observing.

TIME. A starlight night without a single human being near enough to be within call. (*Pause*.) A letter from William.

Time hands Caroline a letter. The letter is in William's voiceover. Time flows faster.

WILLIAM. July 20, 1786. Dear Lina, I am still in Hanover, and find it a most agreeable place.

CAROLINE (*writing in her journal*). July 24—I registered some sweeps in time and Pole distance. I swept from ten to one.

WILLIAM. Mother is perfectly well and looks well. Jacob is a little older, but not nearly so much as I expected.

CAROLINE. July 28—I wrote in part of Flamsteed's catalog in the clear. It was a stormy night.

WILLIAM. In Sophy there is hardly any change, but a few white hairs on her head. Alexander and Dietrich are just the same as before.

CAROLINE. July 29—I paid the smith. He received today the plates for the forty-foot tube. Registered sweeps today and booked in the old register, 564. 563 is marked not to be registered; 560, and 561, I was obliged to pass over on the account of some difficulty. The rest of the day I wrote in Flamsteed's catalog. The storm continued all day, but now, eight o'clock, it turns to a gentle rain.

WILLIAM. The King's telescope arrived in perfect order. This instrument I built as King George's present to the Göttingen Observatory is superior to all other equipment there.

CAROLINE. 30 July—I wound up the sidereal timepiece and made covers for the new and old registers. I find I cannot go fast enough with the registering of sweeps to be serviceable to the *Catalogue of Nebulae*. Therefore, I will begin immediately to recalculate them, and hope to finish them before he returns.

WILLIAM. The Society of Gottingen has elected me as a member. Farewell, dear Lina. I will write again. I shall be back by the August 24. Adieu once more.

CAROLINE. August 1—I counted one hundred nebulae today. I also saw an object. I do not want to say what it might be. It will reveal itself tomorrow night. August 2—not a clear night. It has been raining throughout the whole day. I am waiting for the sky to clear.

Pause. Back to normal flow of time.

TIME. Time flies.

CAROLINE. You are funny. (*Pause.*) It feels good to be working. It feels good to be alone. For a while.

TIME. A letter from William.

Time hands Caroline a letter. She opens it and reads.

CAROLINE. "Dear Lina, All is well with me and everyone. Yesterday and the day before, I saw the Bishop of Osnaburg and Prince Edward. We long very much to hear from you, as we have never had a letter yet. This is the fourth I have sent you, and I hope you received the former ones. I shall be happy to see old England again, though old Germany is not a bad place. Adieu, Lina. We shall see each other very soon."

TIME. No letter?

CAROLINE. I have been busy. Mother understands that.

TIME. It's William, not your mother, who's asking for a letter.

CAROLINE. He shall return in a fortnight. It would make him happy if I finished the Flamsteed catalog by then.

TIME. Do you miss Germany?

CAROLINE. I have been busy. I wonder who knits their socks.

TIME. Socks?

CAROLINE. When Mother agreed that I should leave with William, I was told to knit enough cotton socks for everyone to last two years. I knitted long hours, day and night.

TIME. Your brothers are older. They have children of their own by now. They have wives. Perhaps they buy the socks at a shop now.

CAROLINE. Yes, of course. Hanover stands still in my mind. The day I left, poor Mother looked uncharacteristically frail.

TIME. Don't you resent your Mother for denying you a formal education?

Time rewinds. 1772. Caroline is twenty-two.

MOTHER. Education is useless. Especially for a girl.

CAROLINE. Yes, Mother.

MOTHER. Of course, your ability to read and write is fine. I have been quite lonely at times because I could not read my husband's letters myself during the war, or the Bible, ever.

CAROLINE. I am sorry.

MOTHER. Nonsense. You read them to me, so it was fine. *You* were able to read my husband's letters. (*Pause.*) And the Bible. It was helpful for your first communion. You looked so beautiful in your new black gown with a bouquet of flowers.

CAROLINE. Thank you.

MOTHER. Yes, very beautiful, indeed. William thought so also. He was here visiting that day.

CAROLINE. He did not see me in my new gown. He had to leave early in the morning that day to return to England. He was only here for six days and could not stay for my confirmation. I was miserable in my black gown.

MOTHER. Do not be ridiculous. The gown was not for William.

CAROLINE. Well, he did not see it.

MOTHER. I meant to say your father, not William. Your father thought you beautiful in your new dress.

CAROLINE. Father did not think I was beautiful.

MOTHER. Certainly he did. Perhaps he was restrained in his compliments. A woman needs to be humble. She invites difficulties if she is outlandish in any respect. It is better to live life unnoticed, quietly and protected.

Time is restored. Caroline looks into the telescope. Clouds and faint stars.

CAROLINE. The sky is clearing up. What time is it?

TIME. I walk with you the distance between birth and death; I have no meaning outside of the marks that you place on me. I am Time. I am eternally missing. I am a void. Yet I exist.

CAROLINE. I have been waiting since last night for something. A change.

TIME. A change in what?

CAROLINE. In the order of things I thought were permanent. By that, I mean the order of my life. A change beyond my imagination in the order of things I believed about my purpose.

TIME. August 2, 1786. Slough, England.

The sky becomes bright.

CAROLINE. Let me see . . . There it is!

TIME. Midnight.

CAROLINE. There was motion since last night! It *is* a comet! *I* have discovered a comet!

TIME. Caroline Herschel, Comet Hunter, the first recognized woman astronomer in the world.

CAROLINE and TIME. I exist.

Time and Caroline look into each other's eyes. Stars brighten around them. Hold this moment. Then stars fade.

CAROLINE. I will write Dr. Blagden to announce the comet.

TIME. It's late.

CAROLINE. I cannot rest. I wish time would flow faster. Oh, *you* must know the fate of my comet. Please tell me.

TIME. No.

CAROLINE. Why? You tell me other things I do not ask to know. I want to know this. I cannot wait.

TIME. I get to choose the moments. For your benefit, of course.

CAROLINE (*sighs and writes the letter*). Dear Dr. Blagden—In consequence of the friendship which I know to exist between you and my brother, I venture to trouble you, in his absence, with the following account of a comet—Last night, the 1st of August, about ten o'clock, I found an object very much resembling in color and brightness that 27 Nebula of the Connoissance des Temps . . .

TIME. "I believe the comet has not yet been seen by anyone in England but yourself." Comet C/1786 P1 (Herschel). Lina, your first.

CAROLINE. I suspected it to be a comet; but with the haze coming on, it was not possible to satisfy myself as to its motion till this evening.

TIME. "Madam, you have immortalized your name."

CAROLINE. By the naked eye the comet is between the 54 and 53 Ursae Majoris and the 14, 15, and 16 Comae Berenices, and makes an obtuse triangle with them, the vertex of which is turned toward the south.

TIME. "I wish you joy, most sincerely, on the discovery."

CAROLINE. I beg you, if this comet should not have been seen before, to take it under your protection.

TIME. "You deserve a reward from the Being who has ordered all these things to move as we find them, for your assiduity in the business of astronomy, and for your love for so celebrated and so deserving a brother."

CAROLINE. With my respectful compliments to the ladies, your sisters, I have the honor to be, Sir, your most obedient, humble servant, C. Herschel.

TIME. "Accept my best thanks for your obliging attention in communicating to me the news, and believe me to be, with great esteem, your obedient, humble servant, C. Blagden."

Stars come up all around them.

CAROLINE. How many more nights of stargazing are allowed me in my life? Each time I sweep the heavens, I cannot believe the glory of the gift of lights. I am a small person. How is it possible that I should be part of the enormity of the universe? How much time is allowed me before this dream ceases?

TIME. As your heart races faster and faster and your longing approaches the speed of light, time intervals between points of your memories dilate. You will have endless time to observe the heavens, until finally, there is no time at all, not even the end of time. Your second comet will come on December 21, 1788, around one degree south of Beta Lyrae. You will follow it until February 1789. One hundred and fifty-one years later, on July 28, 1939, Roger Rigollet will discover an eight magnitude comet. The orbital calculations will suggest that this new comet is identical to your comet from 1788. You will have been gone from this planet for ninety-one years. The next return of this Comet 35P/Herschel-Rigollet to the inner solar system will be at the end of the twenty-first century.

CAROLINE. I baked William's favorite cake.

William enters, full of cheer and energy.

WILLIAM. Lina!

CAROLINE. William!

> *William sweeps her off the floor. They embrace for a long time. Stars come up all around them. He puts her down and steps back. Time stands between them. Caroline looks into the telescope. Time rewinds.*

CAROLINE. There was a motion since last night! It *is* a comet! *I* have discovered a comet!

TIME and CAROLINE. I exist.

> *Lights down.*

SCENE 4

Slough, England, 1788. A modest house in the country. Caroline is thirty-eight. William is fifty. Caroline is just getting home and encounters William and Mary, a woman about Caroline's age.

WILLIAM. Here you are, Caroline, where have you been?

CAROLINE. I have been to the market.

WILLIAM. Mrs. Pitt, this is my sister, Miss Caroline Herschel. Caroline, this is Mrs. Mary Pitt.

CAROLINE. How do you do?

MARY. Pleased to meet you, Miss Herschel. Your brother has told me much about you.

WILLIAM. Mrs. Pitt kindly stopped by to give me some books that she thought might interest me. I was about to see her home.

CAROLINE. Will you stay for tea, Mrs. Pitt?

MARY. Thank you, but I must be elsewhere. I would like to have tea another time.

CAROLINE. You are welcome here anytime.

MARY. Very kind of you. Miss Herschel, do you like opera?

CAROLINE. Yes, very much. Though I have very few opportunities to go to the theater.

MARY. Perhaps we can make a date to go to London to see the opera sometime. I go often with my father, and we would be most honored if you could join us.

CAROLINE. Thank you, but William needs me here.

WILLIAM. It will be good for you to have a holiday. Even if it is a short visit to London. I think it is a wonderful offer, Caroline.

MARY. It is decided then. We will fetch you sometime when you are able to leave your brother for an evening. It will be lovely to get to know you, Miss Herschel.

WILLIAM. Well, then . . . I will see you in a bit, Caroline. (*Exits with Mary.*)

Caroline closes the door behind them.

TIME. Change is coming.

CAROLINE. He called me Caroline.

TIME. He usually does, when there is company.

CAROLINE. Yes, but today, it was different. Distancing.

TIME. As time moves, distance alters. Don't worry. This is neither the beginning nor the ending.

CAROLINE. William has talked about that woman, Mrs. Pitt. She is the widow of a wealthy merchant. She is not as beautiful as I imagined.

TIME. And you? Do you think you are as beautiful as she imagined?

CAROLINE. Who am I that she needs to imagine? She will have everything and I will end with a void.

TIME. Why?

CAROLINE. I do not know why.

TIME. Caroline Lucretia Herschel, there will be a planet named 'Lucretia' after you are gone. Lucretia will exist for a long while, even after you are forgotten, into the time and space that you cannot imagine now.

CAROLINE. Why do you have to be so strange and say strange things as if you were Jesus?

TIME (*mock-appalled*). Caroline!

CAROLINE. I have another question. Are you my guardian angel?

TIME. No. I'm *Time*.

CAROLINE. So you have told me. Does everyone have *Time* of his own?

TIME. *His?*

CAROLINE. Why are you with me? Are you my imagination? Are you illusory?

TIME. Ultimately everything is a figment of human imagination.

CAROLINE. Please do not get philosophical with me. I have little time before William returns.

TIME. Why is this so urgent all of a sudden?

CAROLINE. Because I realize that you know about Mrs. Pitt and I do not.

TIME. I'm with you because you need me and I need you. Everyone has something. You have me, not a prizewinning horse or the best hunting dog or visions of Jesus. You need me to understand history beyond what is apparent at this moment. I need you because you will, in turn, move time forward.

CAROLINE. And William? What does he have?

TIME. He has a singular purpose and an understanding of his role in history. He has you. And now he will have Mary.

CAROLINE. You talk endlessly.

TIME. You started it.

CAROLINE. Please be quiet. (*Begins searching the house for something.*) Books. William said she brought books for him. It is not possible she would know what books my brother would prefer. I cannot understand a woman's audacity in choosing books for a brilliant man. Only I know what William likes because he used to have me read to him during long hours of mirror polishing. There were times that I had to put food in his mouth little by little while he went all day grinding without rest. I kept him alive. No one else knows William the way I do.

TIME. There is no dispute.

CAROLINE. I have been taking care of William for sixteen years. I write all his memoranda—in English! Sixteen years ago when

I arrived in England, I had no knowledge of the language. There were a few words I learned on the boat that I repeated like a parrot whenever someone approached me. "Pardon." "I do not understand." "Thank you." The day after I arrived, William started me on lessons in Mathematics and English. Six days after that, he sent me to the market alone. I was terrified. Naturally I had no friends, but I had no time either. By Lent the following year, I was speaking English and at the concert rehearsal a lady complimented me on how I pronounced words just like an Englishwoman. It has not been easy. Mrs. Pitt has no idea.

TIME. What books did you read to William when his hands would not leave the mirrors for long hours?

CAROLINE. He liked *Don Quixote* and *Arabian Nights*. Where are the dumb books that she gave William?

As Caroline searches, William returns.

WILLIAM. Lina?

CAROLINE (*surprised, almost breathless*). What books of interest did Mrs. Pitt present to you?

WILLIAM. Some things by Friedrich Schiller. She acquired them from an acquaintance. They are in German. Are you well?

CAROLINE. I would like to read them when you are done.

WILLIAM. Of course.

CAROLINE. I did not realize that Mrs. Pitt was a good friend of yours. You have not talked much about her before.

WILLIAM. It is an interesting thing, Lina, but I did not really notice her until recently. We were introduced to each other at Sir Watson's dinner almost a year ago. She was delightful company, but it never entered my mind that I should invite her for tea or dinner. I suppose I had acquired a habit of not paying any attention to things outside of the heavens in the past ten years.

CAROLINE. Fifteen. Well, we do not need more people to come for tea. You are quite busy, and we frequently have to entertain important scientists. I am certain that Mrs. Pitt would understand.

WILLIAM. Lina, I am fifty years old.

Caroline starts for the kitchen.

CAROLINE. Shall we have tea?

WILLIAM. Not now. Please sit down. (*Caroline sits and waits for the inevitable change.*) I am getting old. (*Pause.*) You will like Mrs. Pitt . . . Mary. She has a lightness of the heart. I have known her to have absolutely no ill will for anyone. She has no children. And she would like to have one.

CAROLINE (*quickly*). William, how can you even consider such a thing? When have you and I had even an afternoon to relax? You wrote seven papers for the Royal Society last year. When do you even foresee being able to read the books Mrs. Pitt gave you?

WILLIAM. Lina, I am grateful for the many sacrifices you have made for me . . .

CAROLINE. I have made no sacrifices. You are the purpose of my existence. Your work changed the scale of human thought by expanding the size of the solar system. It is an honor that my small life is spent assisting you in any way.

WILLIAM. I have kept you unmarried for selfish reasons.

CAROLINE. William, I am unmarried for reasons that are not yours.

William pauses briefly.

TIME. Would you like to have children?

CAROLINE. I shall never marry.

TIME. Why?

CAROLINE. Because I am ugly.

TIME. No, Caroline, that's not why.

CAROLINE. Because I had typhus when I was eleven, I never grew any taller. When I recovered from the illness, my father said not to worry about getting married when I grew up.

Time continues.

WILLIAM. Lina, I think I would like to have a child.

CAROLINE. I understand.

WILLIAM. I was thirty-five when I first read Ferguson's book, *Astronomy*. I fell in love, and from that day on nothing else mattered. Even when I was still a musician, my heart was with the stars. For fifteen years, I was entangled in a deep love affair. I was never alone. Then suddenly, loneliness permeated my heart. When I took my eyes off the sky, Mary was standing next to me.

CAROLINE. She is quite beautiful.

WILLIAM. You will like her, Lina. She is an amiable woman.

CAROLINE. When?

WILLIAM. When?

CAROLINE. The wedding.

WILLIAM. Oh, later in the spring. Perhaps in May.

CAROLINE. Three months then. I have much to do to prepare the house before I can hand my position over to Mrs. Pitt . . . Mrs. Herschel.

WILLIAM. Everything will be done informally. Do not worry.

CAROLINE. I would like to take a different lodging when Mrs. Herschel moves into the house.

WILLIAM. There is no need for that.

CAROLINE. William, I assure you, it is better this way. Mrs. Herschel will prefer it also.

William pauses again.

TIME. You will travel.

CAROLINE. My traveling is finished. I have nowhere to go.

TIME. I know you're sad now and will be for some time. But this isn't a change in the order of your being.

CAROLINE. Yes, it is. My heart, eternally broken.

TIME. One hundred thousand light years across this galaxy alone. And two million light years to the next galaxy. Your travel continues.

Back to William.

WILLIAM. We have time to settle everything later. I hope you are happy for me.

CAROLINE. My dear brother, you deserve happiness. You are an extraordinary person. Mrs. Pitt and I are both very fortunate to share in your grandeur. Now, shall we have tea?

WILLIAM. That would be nice, Lina, some tea.

Caroline goes to get the tea set. Time follows. The moment goes back to Hanover when Caroline was twenty-two.

CAROLINE. Is he not handsome? Is he not splendid? He is the only one.

TIME. You long for his future which you're afraid you'll miss.

CAROLINE. I baked his favorite cake.

Back to the present moment.

WILLIAM (*calling out from the parlor*). Mary baked a cake for us, Lina. Please serve it with tea. It is my favorite.

CAROLINE. He is the only one I have ever truly loved. I know I am capable of love because I know William. Now I know I am also capable of hate. Because I know Mary.

WILLIAM. Yes, it will be nice. You and I have been alone for too long.

CAROLINE (*to herself*). I could have been alone with you for eternity.

Lights down.

ACT II

SCENE 1

Time and Caroline are in the exact position as the opening of the play. Stars are all around them.

TIME. 1789. William discovers Saturn's sixth moon, Enceladus, on August 28, and seventh moon, Mimas, on September 17, 1790. Caroline discovers her third comet, C/1790, on January 7.

CAROLINE. A brightness of 7th magnitude. The comet's apparition was poor and seen only on three other days, the last being January 21.

TIME. Comet C/1790 H1 (Herschel) discovered on April 18. Caroline's fourth comet.

CAROLINE. By the end of May, it brightened to 5th magnitude and was developing a visible tail. In early June, the comet approached Earth at a distance of only 0.7 AU and brightened to 4th magnitude. The last sighting was on June 29.

TIME. Comet C/1791 X1 (Herschel) discovered on December 15. This broke the twenty-months drought of comet discoveries by anyone in the world. Caroline's fifth comet.

CAROLINE. Despite Perihelion occurring on January 14 at 1.29 AU, the closing solar distance was not enough to compensate for the increasing distance of the comet from Earth, and it faded. The last sighting was on January 28. A brief encounter.

Mary enters. Stars fade.

MARY. Good evening, Caroline.

CAROLINE. Hello, Mary.

MARY. William must be delayed in London. He is attending the King's concert.

CAROLINE. Yes, I know. I had expected to begin sweeping this evening without him. I thought I was coming to an empty house.

MARY. I did not feel well, so I decided not to accompany him today.

CAROLINE. Perhaps you should go inside, away from the night air.

MARY. Oh, there is no need for concern. It feels nice to be outside for a moment. But please do not let me interrupt your work. I will sit here quietly.

CAROLINE. It will not be interesting to you to watch me. Most of my hours are spent without any excitement, in quiet anticipation.

MARY. Would you rather be alone?

CAROLINE. No, please, stay a while.

Awkward pause.

MARY. Caroline, William and I have been married three years now. All this time, you have commuted to the observatory from your small lodging. It was not easy for William to adjust to your absence at the beginning. He was used to things being a certain way.

CAROLINE. You seemed to have been very successful. William looks well, and he seems quite happy with the way things are, as you made them.

MARY. And you?

CAROLINE. Me?

MARY. Are you happy?

CAROLINE. I do not know what you mean.

MARY. It is a rather simple question.

CAROLINE. But why ask me the question?

MARY. No particular reason. We were talking about happiness.

CAROLINE. William's. William's happiness, which I care a great deal about.

MARY. Something we have in common.

CAROLINE. Yes, of course.

MARY. I did not mean to offend you, Caroline. It was simply idle conversation.

CAROLINE. I am not used to idleness.

MARY. Yes, I know. You are very busy. (*Awkward silence.*) . . . Because you are so busy, we thought perhaps you would like to move back to the house and be rid of some of the daily tasks.

CAROLINE. We?

MARY. Yes, William and I.

CAROLINE. He has not said anything to me.

MARY. He thought perhaps it would be better if we had a talk.

CAROLINE. Why?

MARY. A sister talk.

CAROLINE. I do not know what you mean.

MARY. Caroline, I shall make a home that is comfortable for you if you permit me.

CAROLINE. Thank you, but it is really not necessary. I am perfectly fine where I am.

MARY. Are you not . . . lonely?

CAROLINE. My dear, I am always lonely. When I watch the heavens, I am overwhelmed by their magnificence. I do not want to be bound by things like eating, sleeping, writing letters, smiling at people. My heart is elsewhere. So I am always lonely.

MARY. I am not sure if I understand.

CAROLINE. One of the reasons that William is so special to me is that I know he has the same loneliness. That is why he is lost in the stars most of his life. You ought to understand.

MARY. I do not believe it is loneliness that propels him to the heavens. He has different ambitions from yours. He is looking for an answer.

CAROLINE. Answer to what?

MARY. The existence of God. (*Pauses.*)

TIME. "Composing or playing music is a small act. It does not tell us why we are here. It neither confirms nor denies God."

CAROLINE. He said that. When was it? Why have I not been paying more attention?

TIME. There is greatness to come. You've done more than pay attention to him.

CAROLINE. He has achieved greatness.

TIME. You made it possible for him.

CAROLINE. But perhaps Mary could have done the same. She is a smart person. She even had formal education. She could have learned what I learned and assisted William just the same.

TIME. Lina. You're no longer invisible.

CAROLINE. I have carried ill feelings toward Mary for three years. I do not like anything about her. I do not like her new linens. I do not like where she keeps the silverware. Why did she even have to move them? I do not like her perfect hair, the lightness of voice, the special innocent smile she has for William. I do not like the way he looks at her.

Back to Mary.

MARY. Forgive me. I did not mean to offend you.

CAROLINE. I have known William all my life.

MARY. Yes, of course, but perhaps certain things are only understood between a man and his wife.

CAROLINE. What would be those certain things?

MARY. Caroline, we do not have much else in common, do we? Other than the wish for William's happiness?

CAROLINE. That should be enough. We should try not to disturb William with our differences. Please tell him that we had our sister talk, and I was very grateful for the offer, but I decided that the arrangement I have now is convenient and suitable.

MARY. What can I do to be your friend?

CAROLINE. We are perfectly friendly most of the time. This is a strange night.

MARY. We have been cordial to each other, because that is all you allowed me for three years.

CAROLINE. I assure you I have the highest opinion of you, Mary. You are the wife of a brilliant man, therefore, you deserve respect in all societies and by all men and women. I, on the other hand, can only turn to scientists for respect, and they are all men. So fundamentally they lack respect for me on a certain level. Please do not be concerned. You are fine.

MARY. You think I play this role that is expected of me without even being aware of the expectation. You are right in supposing that I could not live the life you do. But I know the price of being inside. I did not have the courage to live outside of the expectation.

CAROLINE. It was not courage that made me choose this life.

MARY. No, not courage alone. But talent. And a longing. Longing for discoveries, not linen-making, not opera, not dinners in high society, but for creating a celestial map. You have a purpose.

CAROLINE. I did everything for William. I simply followed him.

TIME. You made history through him, with him, and finally, without him.

MARY. I have no particular talent. It would have been dangerous for me not to be part of the accepted whole. Do not misunderstand me. I love William and I am proud and happy to be his wife. But I do have moments of longing for something outside myself, something that will connect me to the larger world.

CAROLINE. Remember, as soon as you notice your life out there, you also notice how lonely you are here.

MARY. I do not know that loneliness, but I also do not know the ecstasy of being out there. And once in a while, I fancy that I can give up everything, to have one chance at freedom; freedom from this time and space.

CAROLINE. Are you unhappy?

MARY. Oh, no. I am happy. William is a loving husband. I am fascinated by his work. I enjoy being able to attend the King's concerts and operas in London. Life is very pleasant.

CAROLINE. Good.

MARY. And you?

CAROLINE (*thinks for a moment*). I am. Two years ago when the King gave me a pension of fifty pounds per year to be William's assistant astronomer, I was truly surprised that a woman could do what she loved and get paid for it. I had worked very hard since I was seven years old, but never had any money of my own. I received my first payment of twelve pounds in October that year, and it was the first money ever in all my life that I felt I could spend any way I liked. It made me happy.

MARY. I have never had my own money. What I have is either my father's or my deceased husband's money. I use William's money as well. Most of the time, I do not even think about why I should perpetually rely on men's money. It must be extraordinary to have your own money that you made with your work.

CAROLINE. I suppose it is. Yes, it is extraordinary.

They sit in silence for a little while.

MARY. I am the one who is lonely. I wanted you to move back to the house because I was lonely. We keep the house completely quiet during the day after William has had a long night of sweeping. When he is awake, he has much work to do and often goes to meetings in Greenwich or London. In the evenings, you and he spend many hours in the observatory. I do not know what to do with myself.

CAROLINE. Mary, thank you for the offer, but I should be alone. I am not good at regular woman things like having tea and chatting. I need to work.

MARY. I understand. But I would like us to be friends.

CAROLINE. Why all of a sudden? I am not at all amusing to you.

MARY. Soon, I will need no amusement. I will have a baby. That is why I need your friendship.

TIME. Change is coming.

MARY. The baby will be born in March next year. I would like my child to know its aunt, who is talented, elegant, and strong.

TIME. The first woman comet hunter in the world.

CAROLINE. You are very kind, but I do not know how to behave with children. I did not enjoy being a child myself. I will only displease you.

MARY. Caroline, I do not know how to behave with children either. I shall have to make it up as I go along. So shall you.

CAROLINE. I am not certain if I will succeed, but I shall try my best to be a good aunt to your child. (*Pause.*) I am very happy for you. Truly.

MARY. I am happy for you also. For all the splendor of your life.

CAROLINE (*astonished*). Splendor?

Stars come up around them.

TIME. Comet 2P/Encke is passed down from hunter to hunter. It is first sighted on January 17, 1786, in the constellation of Aquarius by the French comet hunter Pierre Méchain. Caroline Herschel finds it again nearly ten years later on November 7, 1795. It is followed for a period of three weeks. Ten more years will pass before it is sighted again on October 19, 1805, by Jean Louis Pons. 1819, German astronomer Johann Encke calculates its orbit back over time and confirms that the comets seen in 1786, 1795, and 1805 are in fact the same comet. It is named after him, and he predicts the next return of the comet to be May 24, 1822. Life continues. You will travel.

SCENE 2

Hanover. 1792. Caroline is in her old family house. She is forty-two years old.

CAROLINE (*shivers*). It is cold.

TIME. Not yet spring in Hanover.

CAROLINE. The house looks the same as when I left.

TIME. Why have you not come back before?

CAROLINE. I never had a reason to. I was busy. Time passed. (*They look around the house in silence for a little while.*) For twenty years, news between Mother and me was exchanged secondhand. William would write Alexander and tell him about me, which was communicated to Mother. Dietrich would write me and I would know how she was.

TIME. She couldn't read or write.

CAROLINE. Then the letter containing the final news about her came.

TIME. A letter from Dietrich. (*Hands Caroline a letter.*)

Caroline opens the letter and reads. They are in the recent past.

CAROLINE. "Dear sister. You have expected this news for some time now, as you knew Mother had weakened terribly the last several months. She passed away this morning. She missed you toward the end of her life and was full of affections for your memory. Only a few days ago, she was reminiscing about how beautiful you looked on your confirmation day, with your new black dress and a bouquet of fresh flowers . . ." (*Looks up from the letter.*) They were not fresh. The flowers were artificial.

TIME She always thought her daughter was beautiful.

CAROLINE. Yes, but I never believed her. I liked Father better, so I believed him.

TIME. The world must have looked very dangerous to your mother when she thought of you. You being. . . small and unprotected.

CAROLINE. Poor and unmarried.

TIME. Times were different for women in her generation. They will be different still in the future. Humans do make progress. Every decision your mother made for you, she probably understood it to be the safest choice for your life.

CAROLINE (*continues reading*). "Her end was peaceful. She lived a very long life, and I am certain she is happy to join Father in heaven, whom she longed for all these years. I am afraid that the house will remain in disarray for a while. Jacob, Alexander, Sophy, and I are all occupied with our own family matters. I will write more after the burial. Dietrich."

Back to the present moment.

TIME. It's quiet.

CAROLINE. I miss something. Someone.

TIME. The house is old. Everyone's missing. There're only memories.

CAROLINE. Ghosts.

TIME. Do you believe in ghosts?

CAROLINE. The space in the heavens is vast. Anything not visible to telescopes can float there without being detected. Souls can be crisscrossing and we do not know it.

TIME. Do you think about your mother's soul traveling?

IMAGE 2.2 **A portrait of Caroline Herschel in her old age.**
Image courtesy Hap Tivey.

CAROLINE. I cannot grasp her death yet. The last time when I was in
this house, she was here. Now she is not here, yet the house
still stands. There is something mysterious and wrong about
lives that are brief and things that remain.

TIME. Would you have liked to have children?

CAROLINE. The concept was always so far outside of my reality. I
always had people to look after, and by the time William
no longer needed me, it was too late for me to even think
about it.

TIME. You are the same age as when your mother gave birth to Dietrich. Mary is about to give birth and she is older than you.

CAROLINE. It is too late for me. (*Pause.*) My father's prophecy came true. No man asked me to marry him.

TIME. You lived his prophecy purposely. You wanted him to be right.

CAROLINE. Why would I do that?

TIME. What would have happened if your father was wrong?

CAROLINE. I would not have left Germany. I would have probably married someone in Hanover and had a life similar to . . .

Pause.

TIME. Your mother's?

CAROLINE. Possibly.

TIME. And you would have had children. Someone who would survive you and carry your name.

CAROLINE. Not my name. My husband's name. But this is a meaningless exercise.

TIME. Most people's names fade away eventually. Women's names end with the woman. They never go beyond one lifetime. Children or no children. Comet C/1786 P1 (Herschel). Your first. Your second, Comet 35P/Herschel-Rigollet will return at the end of the twenty-first century. Imagine.

CAROLINE. I cannot.

TIME. All this will look very different then. There will be more people. And they will be connected as if they live on the web of a spider. More people will see things, know things, and imagine things. When your comet returns, your name will be carried on the threads of the web around the world.

Pause.

CAROLINE. Then Father's prophecy was a gift. He did not even know it was. I did not know it until now. He freed me from being a small person in human society and allowed me to be a small part of the universe instead.

TIME. A starlight night without a single memory forbidding enough to haunt you.

CAROLINE. This is where I first realized that the stars exist. I knew there were stars in the sky, but I did not know until that frosty night when I was seven, when William and I stood in the streets looking up at them, that they were true, and they existed with us.

TIME. Why have you been lonely then?

CAROLINE. Because I was born lonely. I think people are either born lonely or born with comfort. Two people can have the exact same life from birth to death, but the person born lonely will always have doubt and the person born with comfort will always be confident. William was born with comfort in his heart.

TIME And your mother?

CAROLINE. She was lonely. (*Pause.*) I should try to sort out things that need to be done. I do not even know where to start. I used to know this house very well, but now it is a strange place. (*Begins going through things.*)

A moment passes.

CAROLINE. Something smells familiar. Kind of a funny smell. Do you smell it?

TIME. I'm *Time*. I feel space, light, speed, and emotions. I don't smell things. That would be ordinary.

CAROLINE. I am terribly sorry.

TIME. Fine. What do you smell?

CAROLINE. It is not anything specific, but a general scent that belongs to a place. Rather like a feeling. An unidentified, nostalgic, general feeling about a place and time of your life. I smell it.

TIME. Is it pleasant?

CAROLINE. It is. I suspect it is pleasant because twenty years have passed. It is an old smell for me. Here are some old things. (*Finds an old accounting record for the household.*)

CAROLINE. Old accounts. Meat, sugar, flour, ballroom-dance lessons for Dietrich—he never got to take the lessons, but this shows the lessons were paid for.

TIME. Why didn't he take the lessons?

CAROLINE. Dietrich and I were very close, and Mother was worried that if she let him take the lessons, I would learn from him.

TIME. How do you know this?

CAROLINE. I overheard Father explaining to Dietrich why he would not be taking the lessons. Nothing was said to me, since it was understood I would not take those lessons in the first place. (*Unearths some old letters and looks at them.*)

CAROLINE. Here are letters from Father to Mother written during the war.

TIME. The ones you read to your mother.

CAROLINE. I do not remember the content. I only remember Mother crying. (*Sits and read the letters.*)

A moment passes.

TIME. What's in the letters?

CAROLINE. He was weary of the war and longed for home. He tried to be optimistic but was exhausted in his heart. He loved my mother very much. (*Pause.*) And he thought I was the loveliest child.

TIME. "Lina, play the second violin for us."

CAROLINE. I adored my father.

TIME. You have traveled a long way.

CAROLINE. I wanted to see the old house one more time. I wanted to forgive something. But perhaps there is nothing to forgive.

TIME. A letter from William. (*Hands Caroline a letter.*)

Caroline opens the letter and reads. William's voiceover.

WILLIAM. My dear sister, how is the old house? I hope you are not too melancholy to be there alone. Please give my love to everyone when you see them. Lina, you are an aunt. My son, John Herschel, was born on March 7 . . . .

Caroline sighs in joy. Stars come up all around them. Time rewinds. Caroline looks into an imaginary telescope.

CAROLINE. There was a motion since last night! It *is* a comet! I have discovered a comet!

Stars brighten. Then lights down.

SCENE 3

William's house in Slough. Autumn of 1816. Caroline is sixty-six years old. She is sitting in the parlor. William enters. He is seventy-eight.

WILLIAM. Lina, John has already left. We expected you at breakfast.

CAROLINE. I wanted you and Mary to have some private time with John. Was he in good spirits?

WILLIAM. Remarkably good. He surprised us with the news that he shall return to Slough in a short while. He is leaving the University and the dreaded legal profession. He intends to come under my direction and take up observations of the heavens.

CAROLINE. It will be wonderful to have John at home, assisting you.

WILLIAM. You are not surprised.

CAROLINE. It is the only reasonable option. We knew he was unhappy at Cambridge, but he was too proud to abandon his chosen career. He was a brilliant mathematician at St. John's College. It was only a matter of time before he decided to become an astronomer.

WILLIAM. Did you already know his decision?

CAROLINE. My dear brother, you should recall his paper on that remarkable application of Cotes's Theorem in the Transactions of the Royal Society. It is his fate to continue his father's work.

WILLIAM. Nonetheless, I should have thought you would be as surprised as his mother and I about the news.

CAROLINE. I am surprised.

WILLIAM. When did he tell you?

CAROLINE. Some time ago. During his summer holiday.

WILLIAM. Why did he not tell me?

CAROLINE. He wanted to surprise you.

WILLIAM. I should have been surprised at anytime of the holiday.

CAROLINE. It is because you were so disapproving of him going to Cambridge. He felt an obligation to stay with the decision that he made against your wishes.

WILLIAM. Have I been a difficult father?

CAROLINE. No, William. John has the highest regard for you. He loves you very much.

WILLIAM. I wonder if he told Mary about it before today. (*Looks at Caroline for an answer. Pause.*) He told Mary as well.

CAROLINE. It was meant to be a departing gift to you.

WILLIAM. John is going to pay his bills at Cambridge and pack up his books and return straight away. He will be back in a fortnight. Hardly a departure. Why did Mary keep it from me?

CAROLINE. It is my fault. I convinced Mary to adhere to John's wishes. Remember when he was eight, he had trouble with bullying boys at Eton College? You had said that he was to stay, but Mary removed him from the school. He felt ashamed about it for a long time. I thought it best if, this time, Mary was not the person to tell you about his leaving school. And she agreed. It was a favor to me that Mary kept this from you.

WILLIAM. When did John tell you this?

CAROLINE. During the summer, William.

WILLIAM. No, no, about Eton College.

CAROLINE. When he was eight years old.

WILLIAM. Where was I then?

CAROLINE. You were looking at the stars.

WILLIAM. You?

CAROLINE. I was, too. I was looking at the stars.

WILLIAM. And John?

CAROLINE. He, too. He was looking at the stars at age eight. That is why he is returning home now at age twenty-four.

WILLIAM. It is not because of my aging and wavering health?

CAROLINE. I was almost John's age when I left Hanover to come to England for a life of stargazing. By the time I was his age the stars were in my heart. The stars have been in John's heart since he was born. That is why.

WILLIAM. Lina, I am grateful to you for the work you have done with John's education. And for helping Mary with his upbringing.

CAROLINE. I assure you, it was for my selfish pleasure.

WILLIAM. I have not known you to be selfish. Not ever.

CAROLINE. I love John very much, but I want John to carry on the prominence of your life and work.

WILLIAM. I am afraid that John is easily distracted. He should be able to make great contributions to science if he would only concentrate on one study. He is a smart man, but he lacks a singular mission in life.

CAROLINE. He is the new generation, William. They seem to be able to do more things simultaneously than we ever could.

TIME. John Herschel will publish his first paper in astronomy in 1822, the year of his father's death. His major publication will come in 1824, a catalog of double stars, a continuation of his father's work on the subject. In 1833, he will develop a method to determine the orbits of these stars which circle a common center of gravity. For this work, he will receive a medal from the Royal Society in 1833, a year after his mother's death. But Caroline will be alive through all these events and more of John's accomplishments. Among them, his famous *Discourse on Natural History*.

WILLIAM. Perhaps he will become an important person. I think his love for the heavens is genuine.

CAROLINE. His love for you is genuine as well.

Pause.

WILLIAM (*mysteriously*). Lina, how are you?

CAROLINE. I am well. What is on your mind, William?

WILLIAM. Life is amusing, is it not?

CAROLINE. It most certainly is.

WILLIAM. Perhaps John will become an important person. I shall like him to be happy. As I have been in my life.

CAROLINE. I believe that he shall have very little loneliness in his life. He seems to me a person of comfort.

WILLIAM. A person of comfort?

CAROLINE. He takes after your optimism.

WILLIAM. I am not so completely optimistic. I suspect that perhaps I made a mistake somewhere in my construction of the heavens. And I am seventy-eight years old already. I do not believe that I shall have the time to correct my mistake. But life has been amusing. I am thankful for that.

CAROLINE. You suspect that stars have inherent differences in their brightness.

WILLIAM. I had almost always suspected it. But I was plowing a path on a land that no one had attempted to trek before. It was time for humans to not only imagine the three-dimensionality of the heavens, but to actually survey it, map it, and understand the distribution of the stars. I had to have a method.

CAROLINE. No one before you strove to understand the shape of the universe. We know what we look like because of you. You have shown us God's creation of which we are an integral part. We can no longer live with not seeing.

WILLIAM. I was always interested in the deeper parts of the sky. Even as a teenager, I knew in my heart that Kant was wrong in his imagining of the flattened clouds of stars. I sensed a deeper, uneven sky even then.

TIME. William Herschel divided the sky into squares perpendicular to the Milky Way and surveyed them systematically. This work he called Construction of the Heavens. He based his observation of the depth of the sky on the brightness of the stars. The faint stars gave him a reason to long for far away places. Farther than possible. Farther than imaginable, and beyond. (*To Caroline*) He was partially right.

CAROLINE (*to Time*). Please do not tell me more than I need to know.

WILLIAM. I beg your pardon.

CAROLINE. No, I did not mean you.

WILLIAM. Whom did you mean?

TIME. Time.

CAROLINE. Time. No one. I was thinking how time passes.

WILLIAM. It seems so. We are all getting old. But you know what Kant says. We project time onto the phenomenal world. It is not reality.

CAROLINE. Kant is probably wrong about that also. (*They chuckle quietly.*) In my mind, time is related to knowledge. Or perhaps imagination. The concept of infinity, for example. In the Middle Ages, people looked at the sky and believed that the stars were placed on a fixed sphere, and the other side was heaven. Not enough time had passed for people to be able to imagine infinite space yet. Now enough time has passed that we can think about infinity. Time passing allowed this. Just think what John will know by the time he is your age.

WILLIAM. Where is heaven today?

CAROLINE. Possibly beyond infinity.

WILLIAM. I should think in all the years of stargazing I would have come across some evidence of the location of heaven.

CAROLINE. William.

WILLIAM. I am not saying that heaven does not exist. I think that heaven is a state of mind. It seems to me that being with God is being one with the whole. To return to our original state, before all this began. But time does not seem to flow the other way, so the closest I can be to being one with the whole would be to know what the whole is.

CAROLINE. Hence, Construction of the Heavens. Have you been looking for God in the shape of the universe?

WILLIAM. No. Perhaps. I do not know. I have been simply in wonderment. The more improvement I made on the quality of telescopes, the more intimate the stars became. The secrets were being revealed to me with every degree of magnification. I suppose I have been trying to speed up time so that I can know more. The consequence of that action is that I grew old quickly.

CAROLINE. You are not so old yet.

WILLIAM. Oh, I do not mind it. I find life most amusing. And you think John finds life amusing as well. What do you think of Mary? Do you think she finds life amusing?

CAROLINE. She is your wife. You should know.

WILLIAM. Yes, yes, but there are certain things that cannot be understood between husband and wife.

CAROLINE. What things?

WILLIAM. The concept of happiness, for one. I cannot ask Mary if she is happy—

CAROLINE. Why?

WILLIAM. Because in effect I am responsible for her happiness. Asking about the state of one's wife's happiness can have dreadful consequences.

CAROLINE. What a silly man you are.

WILLIAM. Indeed. It seems I do not know what makes my wife or child happy. They conspire against me about leaving schools.

CAROLINE. I assure you, William. They are happy.

WILLIAM. How do you assess this?

CAROLINE. John has never ceased talking to me since he could talk. And Mary and I had a sister talk once.

WILLIAM. When?

CAROLINE. Twenty-five years ago.

Mary enters the parlor. Her interaction with Caroline is simple but warm.

MARY. Hello, Caroline.

CAROLINE. Hello, Mary.

MARY. We missed you at breakfast. We had a rather pleasant surprise from John.

CAROLINE. William told me. You must be pleased.

MARY. Yes. Would you like to stay for tea? I made William's favorite cake.

CAROLINE. Thank you. That would be lovely. (*Mary exits.*) William, please do not ask Mary about knowing John's decision before his announcement.

WILLIAM. All right, Lina.

CAROLINE. There is no need for you to know everything. You know enough.

WILLIAM. I doubt I will ever know everything. Not enough time has passed for that.

TIME. In time, humans will know about the intrinsic luminosity, the inherent differences in the brightness of the stars. This will render Herschel's celestial diagram obsolete. But his numerous contributions to astronomy will far outweigh his shortcomings, which were due only to not enough time passing.

CAROLINE (*making a face at Time as she addresses William*). I do find life amusing.

WILLIAM. Indeed.

CAROLINE. I do. Truly.

WILLIAM. I know. It is quite amusing.

SCENE 4

Time stands alone in William's library.

TIME (*reads from a note*). "Lina, there is a great comet. Come to dine and spend the day here." (*Looks up from the note*). June 2, 1822. Comet 2P/Encke's return. This was the comet Caroline sighted twenty-seven years ago in 1795. Caroline Herschel is now seventy-two years old. William is eighty-four. His son John is thirty.

William and Caroline enter the library. William is leaning on his sister as he walks feebly.

WILLIAM (*anxious*). You see, the whole library is in disarray. There is a great deal of information here, but no one will be able to make any sense of it.

CAROLINE. William, do not worry. It is not as bad as you think.

WILLIAM. I want you to make memorandums on all the books, papers and letters, do you understand?

CAROLINE. Yes, I understand.

WILLIAM. When?

CAROLINE. Today. I will work on it today until dinner.

WILLIAM. How much time will you need to complete everything?

CAROLINE. Not very long. Most of it is already recorded. I will only have to organize the papers.

WILLIAM. There are some new papers that I have written, and . . .

CAROLINE. I shall take care of those carefully without fail. William, please do not worry. Worrying is not good for your health.

WILLIAM. My life's work is in this library, and no one will be able to make sense of it.

CAROLINE. Your work will not be lost. I know everything about this library. John as well.

WILLIAM. I am tired.

CAROLINE. Please sit down, Brother.

William sits down. Caroline sits beside him. Silence for a moment. William becomes calm.

WILLIAM. Do you remember your first comet?

CAROLINE. Of course. I memorized all the events surrounding my first comet. I still go over them in my mind sometimes when I have trouble sleeping.

WILLIAM. Tell me.

CAROLINE. It was 1786, and you were away in Germany. On August 1, I sighted the comet, at the magnitude of about 7½. The sky condition was poor and I had to wait until the next night to confirm it. There was a naked-eye sighting reported on August 17. The following night, Mr. Messier observed a tail 1½°.

WILLIAM. The night after that, I determined that it was considerably brighter than the globular cluster M3. It was between 5th and 6th magnitude.

CAROLINE. I followed it through October 26.

WILLIAM. Your first. (*Takes a deep breath and closes his eyes.*)

CAROLINE. Have you any pain today?

WILLIAM. It is every day now. I shall get used to it eventually.

CAROLINE. Let us take you to a doctor for bloodletting in the arm again. It helped last time.

WILLIAM. I do not know if it helped. Nothing will help in the end. Time passed.

CAROLINE. Do not say such things. Our time together is not over yet, William.

WILLIAM. Lina, you must prepare yourself. You must try to give me some assurance that you will continue your life in good spirits when I am gone.

CAROLINE. William, what is there to continue when you are gone?

WILLIAM. Days. Years. Time will continue. *You* will continue.

CAROLINE. Let us not be pessimistic. You will feel better again.

WILLIAM. No, Lina. I will not. (*Pause.*) I know Mary and John will be heartbroken, but they will be fine. John has four children already and will have more, I am certain. The grandchildren should keep Mary very busy. They will be sad for a long while, but then they will understand my death as a natural course of the events in their lives. But you, Lina, you are too romantic. Your attachment to me will cause you significant pain if you do not prepare yourself.

CAROLINE. There is no good way to prepare myself, William. How can I be without you? I owe my life to you.

WILLIAM. We are old. Together we unveiled a very small corner of the immense universe. I was very fortunate as a stargazer to be allowed the King's pension and you. I owe my life to you.

CAROLINE. This is too much.

WILLIAM. Lina.

CAROLINE. You cannot prevent my grief, William.

WILLIAM. All right, all right.

CAROLINE. Please do not worry about me. Do not worry about anything. I will start on the paperwork now. I shall be able to show you that everything is in order in a few days.

WILLIAM. Thank you. You are a great help, Lina.

Stars come up around them. Time rewinds. 1789. William is fifty-one, Caroline is thirty-nine. He gets up on his forty-foot telescope. Caroline is at the foot of the telescope.

TIME. Rewind time to 1789. William erects a forty-foot telescope which took the Herschels four years to build. August 28. The world's largest telescope's first light.

CAROLINE. William! Say something!

WILLIAM. Such brilliance! We have been near blind until now. Oh, Lina, the greatness of the heavens is unmistakable.

CAROLINE. And you!

WILLIAM. How strange is fate? Was I always meant to find this brightness? I was just an ordinary boy once.

CAROLINE. You were never ordinary. There was always greatness to come.

WILLIAM. Lina, I am looking at Saturn.

CAROLINE. Yes, I know. You have been wanting to see it closer.

WILLIAM. My suspicion was right. The sixth moon of Saturn exists.

CAROLINE. Are you certain that the sixth is not a star?

WILLIAM. Its ranging is exact as the other four moons and with the ring.

CAROLINE. The retrograde motion should amount to nearly four and a half minutes per day. So in about two hours you should be able to ascertain if it is in fact a moon.

WILLIAM. Will you stay up with me until then?

CAROLINE. Of course, William. I will always stay with you. (*Pause.*) What an exciting night. First light.

WILLIAM. You are a great help, Lina.

William comes down from the telescope and exits. Stars disappear. Caroline sits alone in silence for a while. Forward time. Mary enters.

MARY. Will you not change your mind, Caroline?

CAROLINE. No, dear. Now that William is buried, I would like to leave England as soon as possible.

MARY. Will you come back and visit us?

CAROLINE. No. I am quitting England forever.

MARY. Then John shall visit you from time to time in Hanover. And I will write.

Pause.

CAROLINE. Through my adult life, I was certain that I would die first. It did not matter that he was twelve years older than myself. His life was more valuable. It seemed natural that he should outlive me. (*Pause.*) I had a will, but it was done with a belief that William would survive me. It is useless now. I also had a long letter to him that he would have received after my death. There are things unsaid between us. He did not get to read my last letter.

MARY. I am certain he knew whatever it was that you wanted to say to him.

CAROLINE. Mary, forgive me. I have been caught up in my own grief and so inconsiderate to yours. How can I help you?

MARY. Do not worry about me, my sister. John is taking care of everything.

CAROLINE. How is my dear John?

MARY. He is sad, of course, but fine. He is keeping everything in order. He is a very dependable man.

CAROLINE. Yes. He is a wonderful soul. William was very proud of him. (*Pause.*) Well then, I will say goodbye.

MARY. What will you do back in Hanover?

CAROLINE. Do? I am a person who has nothing more to do in this world.

TIME. You will travel.

MARY. I am certain that the whole of Germany's science community is awaiting your return.

CAROLINE (*to Time*). He is the only one.

MARY. Soon your time will be filled with important visitors. Dignitaries and scientists.

CAROLINE. Mary, do not worry about me. I am grateful to you for having made William very happy. (*The two women look into each other's eyes. Mary exits in silence.*) I cannot bear the blankness of life after having lived within the radiance of a genius.

TIME. You made history through him, with him, and finally without him.

CAROLINE. I destroyed most of my journal. But before doing so, I extracted certain days from it to bring the past once more to my recollection. I saved everything William ever wrote to me. (*Reads.*) "Lina, there is a great comet. Come to dine and spend the day here."

TIME. I have no meaning outside of the marks that you place on me—confirmations, weddings, funerals, discoveries—your transitory human heart.

CAROLINE. I have never been so lonely.

TIME. You will complete William's catalog of two thousand and five hundred nebulae and receive a gold medal from the Royal Astronomical Society in 1828, six years after William's death. You will be the first woman to receive an honorary membership to Britain's Royal Society in 1835, then to the Royal Irish Academy in 1838, and will be awarded the gold medal for science by the King of Prussia in 1846. Your life will end on January 9, 1848. You will be ninety-eight years old. You will hold the record for women comet hunters until 1980.

Stars come up around them. Caroline seems ageless.

CAROLINE. William Herschel, lover of luminous beings, dreamer of origins, thinker, traveler, musician, father, husband, my brother. His amorous heart reflected on the blue-green with faint grey belts paralleling the equator, his name will orbit human consciousness, a longing for knowing something outside of ourselves.

TIME. It's quiet.

CAROLINE. How many more nights of stargazing are allowed me in my life? Each time I sweep the heavens, I can't believe the glory of the gift of lights. I am a small person. How is it possible that I should be part of the enormity of the universe? How much time is allowed me before this dream ceases?

TIME. As your heart races faster and faster and your longing approaches the speed of light, time intervals between points of your memories dilate. You will have endless time to observe the heavens, until finally, there is no time at all, not even the end of time.

Stars brighten.

CAROLINE. It *is* a comet! I have discovered a comet!

Lights down.

LEAVING EDEN

A Chekhovian Tragicomedy

IMAGE 3.1 **Moscow, c.1903. Nadya's adopted brother Sasha suffers from tuberculosis, but dreams of a better future (Act II, Scene 1).**

Kaytie Morris (left), Timothy Pyles (right). *Leaving Eden: A Chekhovian Tragicomedy*, directed by Greg Lemming, Greer Garson Theater, Meadows School of the Arts, Dallas, Texas, 2005. (All subsequent photographs of this play are of this production.)

Photograph by Russell Parkman.

CHARACTERS

ANYUTA	Working-class woman. She appears in her early 20s, early 30s, and late 30s.
STEPAN KOROLYOV	Medical student who becomes a doctor. He appears in his 20s and his 30s.
NIKOLAI FESTISSOV	Young artist. He appears later as a failed artist in his 40s.
SOPHIA	Young woman of 20, an heiress.
PROFESSOR	Older, distinguished doctor.
CHRISTINA DMITRYEVNA	Woman in her 40s, Sophia's governess
VARVARA	Poor but spirited teenager. Later she appears as a chorus girl in her late 20s.
DYUDYA	Father-in-law to Anyuta and Varvara.
THE HUNCHBACK	Varvara's husband.
TRAVELER	Man in his 30s.
LADY	Nikolai's wife in his middle age.
NADYA	Young middle-class woman
SASHA	Nadya's adopted brother, in his 20s.
NINA IVANOVA	Nadya's mother.
ANDREY	Nadya's fiance.
ASIAN WOMAN	Contemporary.
SOPHIA	Contemporary.
MAN 1	Contemporary.
MAN 2	Contemporary.
WOMAN 2	Contemporary.
WOMAN 1	Contemporary.
ANTON	A Russian man.

SETTINGS	Moscow, c.1880, c.1900
	A factory outside Moscow, 1887
	The countryside, c.1890, c.1904–06
	New York City, present

The play is inspired by Chekhov's five unrelated short stories: "Anyuta," "The Heiress," "Peasant Women," "The Chorus Girl," and "The Betrothed." I have taken great liberty with the stories, weaving unrelated stories and fictional and non-fictional accounts from Chekhov's life into one play. I have consulted several different translations of Chekhov's short stories and letters. However, all the dialogue is my original writing.

The several characters are played by seven actors:

Actor 1, Female (20s–30s), plays Anyuta and Asian Woman

Actor 2, Male (20s–30s), plays Stepan, The Hunchback, Sasha, and Man 2

Actor 3, Male (30s–40s), plays Nikolai, Traveler, and Man 1

Actor 4, Male (30s–50s), plays Professor, Dyudya, Andrey, and Anton

Actor 5, Female (40s), plays Christina, Lady, Nina, and Woman 2

Actor 6, Female (20s), plays Sophia and Nadya

Actor 7, Female (early 20s), plays Varvara and Woman 1

LEAVING EDEN

ACT I

SCENE 1

Around 1880. Winter in Moscow. A shabbily furnished room in disarray. Anyuta (in her early 20s) sits on a stool by the window, hunched over her sewing. Stepan Koryolov (in his 20s) paces the room, then goes back to his desk and hunches over his book. There's a pause. Then he looks up from his book.

STEPAN. Anyuta, is there any tobacco left?

ANYUTA. No, Stepan.

STEPAN. Well, why didn't you tell me we were out of tobacco?

ANYUTA. You finished the little there was yesterday. Don't you remember?

STEPAN. I suppose we don't have any money either.

ANYUTA. No, Stepan. (*Pause as they go back to their work.*) . . . Snow is coming.

STEPAN. Don't be ridiculous.

ANYUTA. You'll see. The small finger on my left hand aches every time it's about to snow.

STEPAN. There is no medical basis for your little folk theory. Human fingers do not predict weather.

ANYUTA. My grandmother . . .

STEPAN. Enough, Anyuta. Your grandmother was an ignorant peasant.

STEPAN and ANYUTA. We live in a modern age.

This is something Stepan says often. Anyuta knows when it's coming. They giggle together.

STEPAN. It's certainly cold. How about some tea?

ANYUTA. We're out of tea. (*Stepan is irritated. Anyuta conloses him*) If I finish this embroidery, I'll be paid twenty-five kopecks, and we can buy tea and tobacco.

STEPAN. Sugar?

ANYUTA. We won't be able to manage sugar, but there are still four pieces left.

STEPAN. Four pieces. And supper?

ANYUTA. There is some kasha.

STEPAN. Four pieces.

ANYUTA. Stepan, the man whose coat collar I'm embroidering is a doctor. You see this? How elegant they will look on a distinguished man! He wants to wear the coat this evening when he goes out to a dinner party. No doubt there will be important people there, professors and artists.

STEPAN. You're talking nonsense.

ANYUTA. When you become a doctor, you'll wear a coat with embroidered collars also.

STEPAN. When I'm finally a doctor, I'll put four pieces of sugar in every cup of tea!

ANYUTA. I must hurry to finish this job. Otherwise there'll be no tea and tobacco for us.

STEPAN (*mumbles*). Four pieces.

ANYUTA. You can talk to me while I work if you like.

STEPAN. I have to go back to my studies. I have an important examination next week. We now study living bodies. Diagnostics and obstetrics and gynecology. Humans! Alive! You can't possibly understand, Anyuta, you simple, sweet thing!

ANYUTA. I love it when you talk to me about your studies.

STEPAN. Until last year, before you and I began rooming together, things weren't so bright.

ANYUTA (*hopeful*). Is it true, Stepan?

STEPAN. When we were learning anatomy, every day there was some pickled limb to deal with.

IMAGE 3.2 **Moscow, c.1880. Young Anyuta scrapes by, living with a medical student, Stepan.**

Mark Krawczyk (left), Kate Cook (right).

Photograph by Russell Parkman.

ANYUTA (*disappointed*). Oh . . .

STEPAN. Each of us had a whole corpse to dissect as well. Moscow's poor, hanged or drowned or starved. Sometimes ones that died of drinking or typhoid or tuberculosis. The stench seeped into my clothing and I couldn't get it out. Once I had a corpse of a man who died in such tremendous pain, I could not open his fists or straighten his back. His whole body was rigid.

ANYUTA. Please, my dear.

STEPAN. You asked me to talk to you.

ANYUTA. I'm sorry. Yes, please continue.

STEPAN. I should think it's good for you to learn some things that are not about sewing and washing. Even though you are a woman, I think you're smart. It would not hurt to pay attention and make use of the fact that you room with a medical student.

ANYUTA (*somewhat detached*). I've roomed with two medical students before. They are doctors now.

STEPAN. Yes, yes, you've made your confessions to me. No doubt that those men have forgotten you already.

ANYUTA. I can remember each room—furnished much like this one.

STEPAN. I don't want to remember anything about this cheap room in the future. (*Pause.*) Look. I have to go back to my studies.

ANYUTA. I'm sorry I interrupted. Please talk some more. You rarely tell me anything about your studies.

STEPAN. No, no, I'm nervous now about my examination. (*Goes to his desk and hunches over his book. Anyuta sighs and goes back to her embroidery. Pause. Stepan pulls at his hair, gets up, and paces the room, then goes back to his book. He gets up and paces again. Anyuta is used to this and does not look up from her work.*) The right lung consists of three sections . . . The upper section on the anterior wall of the chest reaches the fourth or fifth rib, on the lateral surface, the fourth rib . . . the spina scapulae in the back . . . (*Looks up at the ceiling, trying to visualize this, then begins to feel his own ribs through his waistcoat.*)

Anyuta shivers and looks at the window.

ANYUTA. The edges of the windows are frosted with white, crinkly ice.

STEPAN. Your ribs are like piano keys. You have to make a mental picture of them to avoid confusion. I need to study them on a skeleton.

ANYUTA. Snow is coming. My left pinkie . . .

STEPAN. Anyuta, come here. I need your body. (*Anyuta gets up from her chair, goes to him, and stands facing him.*) Well, go on,

remove your clothes. (*Anyuta takes off her top. Her chest is bare.*
They sit, and Stepan begins to feel her ribs.) The first rib cannot
be felt. It's behind the collar bone. This must be the second
rib. Yes, and here is the third. Right. And the fourth. (*Anyuta
shivers.*) Be still, Anyuta. I'll lose my place if you fidget.

ANYUTA. Your fingers are cold.

STEPAN. Has your grandmother told you that you could die from
cold fingers?

ANYUTA. No, but you can get terribly ill from shivering too much.

STEPAN. Nonsense.

ANYUTA and STEPAN. We live in a modern age. (*They giggle.*)

STEPAN. All right. One more time. The second . . . the third . . . You
are so skinny, yet I can hardly feel your ribs. I'm getting confused. I have to draw them on you. (*Picks up a piece of charcoal
and draws lines on Anyuta's chest.*) See? Now it's all clear.
Good. Good. Let me sound your chest. Stand up.

*Anyuta stands and raises her chin. Stepan taps her chest and
becomes deeply immersed in the task. Anyuta tries to control her
shivers. In her attempt to cope with the cold, she speaks.*

ANYUTA. Is this helpful, Stepan? I want you to do well in your exam-
inations. (*Pause.*) It's important you do well in your third year.
You are nearly a real doctor now.

STEPAN. Anyuta, be quiet.

ANYUTA. By next winter, our second winter together . . .

STEPAN. Shh . . . (*Continues tapping for a little longer.*) Good. Good.
It's all coming together. You sit there just like that. Don't
touch the charcoal. I need to go over some more things; then
I'll review again. (*Goes back to his books.*)

*Anyuta sits and remains still, with black lines drawn on her bare
chest. There's a sudden knock on the door, and Nikolai Festissov (in
his 20s) enters without waiting for a reply. Anyuta quickly throws
a shawl over her shoulders.*

NIKOLAI. Greetings, Korolyov!

STEPAN. Nikolai Festissov.

Nikolai nods to Anyuta.

NIKOLAI. I've come for a favor. Lend me your beautiful maiden for an hour or two. I'm working on a painting, and I have no model today.

STEPAN. With pleasure. Go along, Anyuta.

ANYUTA. I'd really rather not. I'm tired, and I have to finish this job.

STEPAN. That can wait. What you're doing is merely labor. An artist needs to work on his creation. It's not for some trifling little pastime. He's going to be an important painter someday—Nikolai Festissov. Go help him.

Anyuta begins to get dressed. Nikolai watches.

IMAGE 3.3 **Moscow, 1880. Stepan and young artist Nikolai talk about life.** •
Mark Krawczyk (left), Christopher Domig (right).
Photograph by Russell Parkman.

NIKOLAI. Why don't you light the stove, Korolyov? It's awfully cold in here.

STEPAN. It's not so bad. I don't even feel it when I'm under pressure.

NIKOLAI. Studying?

STEPAN. I have to keep grinding away at it. There is so much information to learn. There is no time to worry about the temperature of the room and that sort of thing.

NIKOLAI. But you live in a pigsty. Pardon me, Korolyov, but only the devil knows how you can live this way.

STEPAN. How do you mean?

NIKOLAI. Your bed isn't made, books and clothes are scattered everywhere, and the basin is filled with dirty water and floating cigarette butts. And here, yesterday's porridge still in the bowls.

STEPAN. I only get twelve rubles a month from my father. It's difficult to live decently on that money.

NIKOLAI. So it is. Still, a civilized man should have aesthetics.

STEPAN (*thinking for a moment*). True enough. (*Pause.*) Anyuta didn't manage to tidy up today. She was busy.

NIKOLAI. Well, I appreciate you loaning her to me.

STEPAN. What are you painting?

NIKOLAI. Psyche. It's a struggle. I have to use different models all the time. Yesterday, I had one with blue legs. Why are your legs blue, I asked her. She said that the dye from her cheap stockings had colored her legs! I can't do any serious work with that sort of comedy going on.

STEPAN. Psyche. That's a wonderful subject. Tell me, are you painting her very beautiful?

NIKOLAI. Of course.

STEPAN. In a European kind of way? Not Asiatic or like a Jewess.

NIKOLAI. No, no. Psyche is pure beauty.

STEPAN (*directing his earlier frustration at Anyuta*). Not like a peasant.

Anyuta is dressed.

NIKOLAI. Well then, I will return your maiden to you in less than two hours.

Anyuta and Nikolai exit. Stepan lies down on the sofa and begins studying, but he can't concentrate.

STEPAN. A civilized man should have aesthetics. (*Pause.*) Four pieces of sugar.

Lights dim on Stepan. At the edge of the stage, lights up on Nikolai and Anyuta.

NIKOLAI. So, precious Anyuta. Lie down on your left side, prop your upper body up on your elbow. Stretch and cross your legs. Here. (*Manipulates Anyuta into an awkward position.*) Good. Now keep still while I paint. I've had such difficult times with models lately. You are a saving grace. (*Paints.*) Why do you room with Korolyov?

ANYUTA. What do you mean?

NIKOLAI. I mean, do you love him? Are you going to marry him?

ANYUTA. Oh no, we won't marry.

NIKOLAI (*teasing*). So you are going to break his heart.

ANYUTA. You know very well that's not how things will go.

NIKOLAI. I heard that you've broken quite a few hearts. Some doctors. An artist, too. I think there was a professor.

ANYUTA. No. They were not those things when I lived with them briefly in furnished rooms. They were students. Just like Stepan, who should not have told you my business.

NIKOLAI. He isn't upset about it.

ANYUTA. Why do you think he should be upset?

NIKOLAI. I don't. You're free then.

ANYUTA. I don't know what you mean.

NIKOLAI. What are your plans?

ANYUTA. I don't have any plans.

NIKOLAI. Everyone has some thoughts about the future.

ANYUTA. More of the same, I suppose. Washing and sewing.

NIKOLAI. Family?

ANYUTA. They're poor.

NIKOLAI. Look, Anyuta, take my advice. Look for a man who owns his furniture.

ANYUTA. I don't know what you mean.

NIKOLAI. Yes, you do.

ANYUTA. You'll own your own furniture someday, no doubt.

NIKOLAI. Yes, some people are meant to. I'm one of them. Korolyov is, too.

ANYUTA. And some people are not meant to.

NIKOLAI. Don't shift your body, Anyuta. Stay still. (*Pause. He paints.*) So, do you love him?

ANYUTA. Why do you ask me so many questions? I don't know you.

NIKOLAI. I'm an artist.

ANYUTA. So you are.

NIKOLAI. What are you? (*Anyuta does not answer.*) Does it matter?

ANYUTA. No.

NIKOLAI. Why?

ANYUTA. Because my stockings don't run color on my legs. Not today anyway.

NIKOLAI. Anyuta, you are free. Think carefully about that.

ANYUTA. Please stop saying things I don't understand.

NIKOLAI. As you wish. Keep your head tilted slightly. Right. (*Paints.*)

Anyuta's position is uncomfortable and her body aches.

ANYUTA. Who is Psyche?

NIKOLAI. She was a Greek maiden. People abandoned their worship of the goddess Venus for this beautiful virgin. Psyche incurred the wrath of Venus for her magnificent beauty. She was punished with loneliness and longing.

ANYUTA. How strange.

NIKOLAI. What do you mean?

ANYUTA. To be so beautiful and still lonely.

NIKOLAI. Are you lonely?

ANYUTA. I'm not beautiful.

NIKOLAI. Well, Psyche got married and lived in a beautiful palace for a time. But her husband would only come visit her during the dark of night and leave her before the morning sun. So she never knew what he looked like. You could say she was in love with a stranger.

Pause.

ANYUTA. He giggles sometimes.

NIKOLAI. What?

ANYUTA. Stepan. He giggles.

NIKOLAI. I see. I've never heard him giggle. (*Continues to paint.*)

Lights dim on Nikolai and Anyuta. Lights up on Stepan, sitting on the sofa and looking around the room. Anyuta comes back to his space. She begins to take off her coat.

STEPAN. I have to tell you something. I mean, this room is disgusting, and well, I will receive patients in my office someday soon, you see . . . So there is no avoiding it further. We have to separate. I don't want to live with you anymore. (*Pause. Anyuta is exhausted.*) You must have known that we would have to separate sooner or later. You are good and kind, and not stupid. Anyuta, you understand, don't you?

Anyuta puts her coat back on and gathers her sewing things. She attempts to straighten the room. She finds four pieces of sugar and places them on his books.

ANYUTA (*softly*). These are for you. Some sugar.

STEPAN. What are you crying for? (*Crosses to the window, awkward and embarrassed.*) You're a strange one. You know we can't be together forever. What's the point of crying about it?

ANYUTA. I'm sorry that there is no tobacco and tea for you.

STEPAN. I'm not talking about that.

ANYUTA. Yes, I know.

STEPAN. A civilized man must have some things, you see: elegance, beauty, and proper china for tea in the drawing room. I can't look to my parents for that sort of thing. It's all up to me.

ANYUTA. I'm free then.

STEPAN (*not understanding what Anyuta means*). It's good that you have embroidery skills. Anyuta, you are good. A good person. You've roomed with four promising young men before. So you know. You know these things. It shouldn't be difficult. (*Pause.*) Have you packed everything you need?

ANYUTA. Yes. Just some clothes. And needles and threads.

STEPAN. Yes, yes, you mustn't forget them. And your scarf. It's going to snow. My left pinkie . . . (*Silence. As Anyuta hesitates, Stepan massages his left pinkie. Then, suddenly*) Well, don't mope around here if you are staying. I have to study. (*Pause.*) What are you standing there for?! If you are going, go! If you don't want to go, take off your coat and stay! Stay!

Anyuta silently takes off her coat and blows her nose quietly. Stepan paces back and forth, and then hunches over his books. Anyuta hunches over her embroidery at her stool. The same image as the beginning of the play.

Lights down.

SCENE 2

Seven years later. Circa 1887. Spring. A country bedroom that shows wealth. Sophia (twenty years old) is reclining in bed. The governess, Christina Dmitryevna (in her 40s), a woman with short hair and a pince-nez, is at her bedside.

CHRISTINA. My darling Sophia, there is a peasant woman here who wants to see you. I've told her that you're not feeling well, but she won't leave. She has come here every day for two weeks now. She is very stubborn, and I'm quite at the end of my patience.

SOPHIA. Can't Mama see her?

CHRISTINA. She has gone out to see the accountants. I must say, this is your father's fault, may he rest in peace; he used to socialize with the workers at the factory, so now every worker and peasant thinks they can visit the heiress.

SOPHIA. What is her name?

CHRISTINA. Anita or Anyuta or something or other. I can't remember.

SOPHIA. What does she want to see me about?

CHRISTINA. Something about her child. Shall I send for the foreman? He can talk sense into her. She wouldn't dare come back again. I haven't done that because she looks so pathetic, and I keep hoping that she'll give up.

SOPHIA. No, no. I'll see her. Briefly.

Christina calls Anyuta. She is seven years older, now in her late 20s. Christina hovers over Anyuta.

SOPHIA. Christina Dmitryevna, please leave us.

Christina exits reluctantly.

ANYUTA. Thank you for seeing me, Miss.

SOPHIA. I'm not feeling very well. Please be brief.

ANYUTA. I've lived here in town for nearly seven years now, since I left Moscow. I saw you when you were still a little girl from afar.

SOPHIA. How can I help you? What is your name?

ANYUTA. Anyuta. My little boy, Grisha, works at the factory.

SOPHIA. Yes?

ANYUTA. Won't you get him back for me? He's too small to be working so many hours every day with rough, grown men and not be able to come home to his mother.

SOPHIA. How old is Grisha?

ANYUTA. Six.

SOPHIA. But who is his father?

ANYUTA. Pyotr Nikanorich.

SOPHIA. You mean the factory manager?

ANYUTA. Yes.

SOPHIA. Does Grisha live with him and . . . in the apartment at the factory?

ANYUTA. No, my Grisha does not live with Pyotr and his mistress.

SOPHIA. I don't understand.

ANYUTA. He was taken from me. I live with my father-in-law and his family.

SOPHIA. But . . .

ANYUTA. Grisha is lost somewhere in those big buildings.

SOPHIA. But who took your son away from you and why? (*Anyuta does not answer*.) I'm very sorry, Madam, but I can't help you. I don't manage the factory. Your husband does.

ANYUTA. You're the heiress.

SOPHIA. I don't even go into the buildings. The smell of the dye bothers me a great deal.

ANYUTA. What should I do?

SOPHIA. Can you talk to your husband?

ANYUTA. No. Pyotr doesn't care about his son.

SOPHIA. How did this all happen? (*Anyuta does not answer*.) I'm very sorry, but I'm not well. You must go now.

ANYUTA. Of course. Thank you, Miss.

SOPHIA. Please don't thank me, I just. . . I'm not well.

ANYUTA. Take care of yourself.

SOPHIA. Please go. Please. I can't breathe.

ANYUTA. I'm going, Miss. I'm going. (*Exits*.)

Sophia cries in her bed.

The location shifts to a doctor's office in Moscow. Stepan is now in his early 30s.

PROFESSOR. Another telegram from Christina Dmitryevna. Stepan, this time I think you should go see this patient.

STEPAN. Who is Christina Dmitryevna?

PROFESSOR. She is the governess of the young heiress of a great big fabric factory.

STEPAN. Do you want me to leave Moscow to make a house call in the country?

PROFESSOR. The young lady has been sick all her life. Occasionally I get frantic telegrams from her governess. The lady is under the care of the factory doctor, but when her condition gets worse, Christina Dmitryevna wants a doctor from the city.

STEPAN. Factories seem to be a futile cause. Thousands of people breathing the same air, the filthy conditions, drinking, vomiting, fighting, eating horrible scraps of food.

PROFESSOR. You won't be treating workers. You don't even have to go near one if they scare you so much.

STEPAN. I pity their dejected lives. I must admit I am afraid of breathing in such glum air.

PROFESSOR. There have been improvements in their lives. Things are not as bad as they used to be.

STEPAN. But I imagine there is still abuse of workers by a handful of managers, squabbling among the workers, and the only person who is protected from misery is this heiress who gets rich without doing anything herself.

PROFESSOR. What a righteous young doctor you've become, Doctor Korolyov.

STEPAN. I'm not, Sir. Obviously it's impossible for everyone to belong to the same class. The world would come to a standstill then. I'm not advocating radical egalitarianism, because it cannot be achieved. But professor, don't we have more useful things to do than taking up a whole day making one house call?

PROFESSOR. The town is only two stops on the train. This young woman, Sophia, has suffered all her life, and now, she is practically bedridden. She may be rich, but she isn't pretty or elegant. Everyone deserves some sympathy.

STEPAN. Very well.

PROFESSOR. There will be a carriage waiting for you at the station. Christina Dmitryevna will greet you at the house. You won't see the mother. She loves her daughter very much, and it frightens her to deal with her illness. You'll be back home with your family in time for supper.

Stephan walks up to the house. Christina opens the door.

CHRISTINA. Please come in, Doctor. We've been expecting you for a long time.

STEPAN. The train was . . .

CHRISTINA. This way, please. Sophia had a very difficult night. None of us got any sleep for the fear that she would die during the night. We had hoped that the professor himself would come

IMAGE 3.4 **The Russian countryside, c.1887. Stepan, now a doctor, makes a house call. The housekeeper, Christina, dominates the visit.**

Mark Krawczyk (left), Jaquai Wade (right).

Photograph by Russell Parkman.

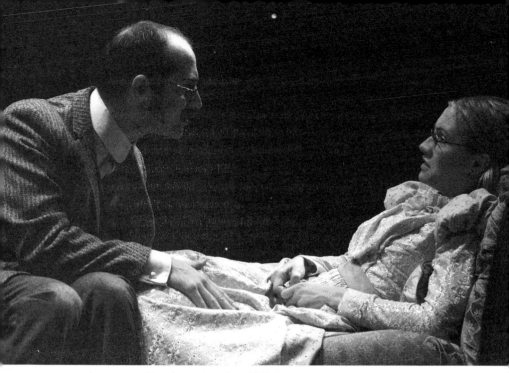

IMAGE 3.5 **Russsian countrysde, c.1887. Stepan talks to Sophia about a future in which she will be well.**

Mark Krawczyk (left), Kaytie Morris (right).

Photograph by Russell Parkman.

early this morning, but well, please sit down. She has always been sickly, since she was a little girl. Now she is twenty, and she doesn't get out of bed because her heart is too weak. She has seen many doctors, of course, and they mostly say it's nerves, but when she was seven she had scrofula and a doctor pushed the lumps inside, just pushed them, and I think she got sick like this right after that and never recovered for thirteen years.

STEPAN. What happened last night?

CHRISTINA. She had violent heart palpitations, and she felt that she was near death. Her face was very pale, and the poor thing was in tears and didn't want her mother or me near her. The servants gave her cold compresses, but she would fling them off her saying that they were boiling hot. Whenever she feels very sick, she can't have people around her, but she can't be left alone either. And she weeps and weeps. And her mother weeps. Her mother, when she was young—

STEPAN. May I see the patient?

CHRISTINA. Please. She has been waiting for a long time to see you. (*Leads Stepan to the bedroom where Sophia lies in bed, distressed.*)

STEPAN. Hello. I'm Doctor Korolyov.

SOPHIA. Doctor Korolyov, I'm not feeling well.

STEPAN. I'll listen to your heart. (*Takes out his instrument and listens to her heart.*)

SOPHIA. It was pounding all night. I was trying to hold it to calm it down. I thought I would die of fright.

STEPAN. Be still for a moment.

SOPHIA. Please give me something to stop the pounding. I can't bear it any longer.

STEPAN. I will, I will. Calm down. (*Takes another moment, then lets her go.*) There is nothing wrong with your heart. It's fine. You got yourself worked up with worries. It's understandable. You should just rest now. What you need is sleep. (*Sophia cries.*) Why are you crying? It's good news that your heart is in good order.

SOPHIA. But it isn't. My heart is in trouble, and if you can't see it, I won't be saved.

STEPAN. Stop crying. You'll upset yourself even more.

SOPHIA. What am I to do now?

STEPAN. Try to get some sleep. I assure you, you're safe. Your nerves played a trick on you. It happens to everyone.

SOPHIA. Will you stay the night?

STEPAN. My family is expecting me home, and I have a great amount of work to do in Moscow.

SOPHIA. I understand.

STEPAN. You're all right.

SOPHIA. I believe you, Doctor. It's just that I'm frightened that something bad will happen again tonight.

STEPAN. It won't. If you're worried, continue taking the medicine that your regular doctor gave you.

SOPHIA. Yes, thank you for seeing me.

STEPAN KOROLYOV (*hesitating for a moment*). I suppose I can stay one night, as long as I get the early train in the morning.

Lights dim. Stillness. Then a voice is heard.

CHRISTINA. Doctor, please come to supper. (*Lights up on the dining table set for dinner. Christina is seated. Stepan sits down to join her.*) This wine is very good. French. I hope you like chicken cutlets and fruit stew. Very good. Please, Doctor, no ceremony. (*Eats quickly and contently.*) Her mother had no education, so she is at a loss about what to think. She adores Sophia and has given her everything, French lessons, dancing, music, tutors. One day Sophia became an invalid, and her mother thought it was because of something that she failed to do. She doesn't understand it's physiological. So now she buys paintings thinking that they'll make Sophia better. I tell her that only a serious medical treatment will do Sophia any good.

STEPAN. I find nothing special the matter with her.

CHRISTINA. Our doctor at the factory gave Sophia potassium bromide. I think it makes her sicker. Shouldn't he prescribe some kind of drops for the heart?

STEPAN. I think the factory doctor is doing a fine job. If Sophia wishes to continue the treatment, she should. There is no need to change the prescription. There is nothing seriously wrong with her.

CHRISTINA. But I must tell you, from my experience—

STEPAN. I'll check her again before I go to bed and let you know how she is.

CHRISTINA. . . . Fine.

STEPAN. How many patients does this doctor look over at the factory?

CHRISTINA. Two thousand employees in five buildings. Sometimes their families also.

STEPAN. He must not have much time to tend to each worker.

CHRISTINA. No one really gets sick. Our workers are healthy and content. Every winter, we have theatrical productions at the factory, and they act in them. They admire Sophia. Last Sunday they sang a song for her during the service. They don't have education, but they have feelings.

STEPAN. I suppose you have education.

CHRISTINA. Yes. It was advantageous for the family to have an educated governess while Sophia was growing up.

STEPAN. I thought Sophia had tutors.

CHRISTINA. I augmented her learning.

STEPAN. I see. Sophia's father passed away?

CHRISTINA. A year and a half ago. Left us three women to fend for ourselves. Since he passed away, Sophia's condition worsened, so we only live here during the summer. We live in Moscow in winter.

STEPAN. You've been with the family for a long time then.

CHRISTINA. I'm a member of the family. Please, have some more fruit stew. Mmm . . . very good.

As lights dim, Stepan leaves the table. Time passes. The striking of the hours is heard loudly from the factory building. Lights up on Sophia's bedroom. Stepan enters and finds her awake in her bed.

STEPAN. How do you feel?

SOPHIA. I'm all right, thank you.

STEPAN. You're not asleep. It's almost three in the morning, and you sit in the dark distressing about something.

SOPHIA. I can't sleep.

STEPAN. Does this happen to you often?

SOPHIA. Yes, I'm afraid of the dark. As soon as the sun begins to set, I feel dread coming over me every evening.

STEPAN. My dear lady, what's the matter? What's the matter with your life? (*The clock strikes three. Sophia shudders.*) Does that sound upset you?

SOPHIA. I don't know why. I've heard it all my life. Everything here upsets me. I thought, perhaps, I could talk to you about it.

STEPAN. Yes, of course.

SOPHIA. It seems to me that I'm not physically ill, but my heart is tormented. And I think it's my fate that I should suffer this way because I was born in the wrong place at the wrong time. I shudder every time I catch the sight of those buildings with tall chimneys casting shadows on the warehouses and the barracks. I'm unable to appreciate things that made my father happy. I can't see any beauty in it. Every night, the smoke from the chimneys chokes me, and I can't sleep.

STEPAN. I couldn't sleep tonight either. I've been walking the grounds. In the dark, someone called out to me, "Who goes there?" which startled me. It was eerie and lonely.

SOPHIA. Oh, Doctor, I'd like to have someone to talk to, a friend who would understand me.

STEPAN. Have you no friends?

SOPHIA. When I was a child, I wasn't allowed to play with the workers' children. I thought when I grew up, I'd have friends, but it seems that my fate is to remain lonely.

STEPAN. Do you talk to your mother about your concerns?

SOPHIA. No. But I love my mother very much. We talk about books sometimes.

STEPAN. I see you read many books.

SOPHIA. I read too many books. I don't know if the books are telling me the truth. I don't know what people really think outside of the books. After the sun sets, I feel something is watching me. Every night I fight the shadows from entering my mind.

STEPAN. Do you mean the Devil?

SOPHIA. I don't know. Do you think the Devil exists?

STEPAN. No. I don't believe in the Devil.

SOPHIA. Do you believe in God?

STEPAN. Yes, but God is in us, not outside us.

SOPHIA. Like the Devil?

STEPAN. If you believe it.

SOPHIA. I'm punished and condemned for something.

STEPAN. Listen. Many people who are in your position of wealth are satisfied and sleep soundly. You're a kind person, so you can't sleep. It's not the Devil that watches you at night. *You* are watching yourself. Sophia, you're not the Devil. Your heart is good.

SOPHIA. What will become of me?

STEPAN. I suspect you'll get up from your bed one day soon, and wear a white dress and put a flower in your hair.

SOPHIA. Oh, how I wish a day like that would come! I shall open the house and invite people to come eat with us, and my mother shall faint seeing so many people in our house!

STEPAN. The fact is our parents didn't have conversations like this. They were ignorant and slept soundly. Our generation sleeps badly and talks a great deal. We're always asking if we have the right to this or that, if we deserve this or that. Perhaps our grandchildren will have the answers; why life is the way it is.

SOPHIA. What will our grandchildren do?

STEPAN. I suspect that they'll leave.

SOPHIA. Leave? Where to?

STEPAN. Why, wherever they like.

SOPHIA. Leave the factory . . .

STEPAN. Do you hear the nightingales?

SOPHIA. Yes. I like them. But I don't like the frogs that croak in the field behind the buildings.

STEPAN. Do you hear the frogs now?

SOPHIA. No.

STEPAN. Now try to sleep. I'll be gone before you awake, so I'll say goodbye now. You're a good, interesting person. I won't see you again, but I'll always be glad that I met you.

He presses her hand in his, then exits. Sophia remains still in her bed, thinking.

Lights down.

SCENE 3

Three years later. Around 1890. Late spring. A country tavern and lodging. A traveler sits and eats his supper. The tavern's owner, Dyudya, sits with him and smokes. Anyuta stands nearby. She is now in her early 30s.

DYUDYA. Have you had a long trip?

TRAVELER. No, just from the town. A day's trip.

DYUDYA. Where're you off to?

TRAVELER. To see about some apprenticeship for the boy. Just to see.

DYUDYA. I reckon that little fellow is your son.

TRAVELER. Sasha? He's adopted. An orphan.

DYUDYA. Have you got a wife?

TRAVELER. No. I had a fine match arranged for me once, but it didn't work out. I had some trouble, and there was this orphan.

DYUDYA. How did you come to be responsible for him?

TRAVELER. It's a complicated story. Seven years ago, I lived next to a young couple, newlyweds. The wife Mashenka was expecting a baby when the husband was called away to duty. He was shipped off to Poland, and Mashenka gave birth to Sasha, the boy I have now. Since she was a neighbor and her husband was serving in the country, I started to look after her, helping her with things a woman couldn't do. It was summer, she was nineteen, and she wore a white dress. I was young and clever. I liked talking to her about theology or politics, and she gave me tea and jam. Before a year had passed, I was possessed with the Evil Spirit, and one morning she opened her gate, let me in, and from that day on, we lived as man and wife.

DYUDYA (*shakes his head gravely*). The Evil Spirit.

The Hunchback rushes into the room, pays no attention to anyone, grabs a handful of sunflower seeds from the bowl on the table, jiggles his pockets to make sure he has some change, and rushes out.

TRAVELER (*startled*). Who's that?

DYUDYA. My son. I have two sons, Pyotr and Alexey. Pyotr is a capable man, the manager at the fabric factory. But Alexey . . . It's God's affliction, his hunchback, so we don't expect much from him. We got him a wife thinking it would improve him. Now we keep another man's daughter for nothing. She runs around like a hussy and doesn't earn her keep.

TRAVELER. We all have our burdens. I had lived with Mashenka for two years when the letter came from her husband that he was coming home. I was relieved. I had a fine match arranged for me, but I didn't know what to do with Mashenka. I said to her, "Thank God, now you'll be an honest woman again." But she was stubborn. She made a scene, she cried and tried to hang on to me. I told her that we had sinned and we must ask for forgiveness. I said to her, "You must wash your husband's feet and drink the dirty water. Be an obedient wife to him." I tried to give her sound counsel. But when her husband came home, she made more scenes and cried. Every day she would run over to my house and scream, "If you don't love me, kill me!"

DYUDYA. Shameless hussy!

TRAVELER. She was married in the church, that little fool. I tried to put the fear of God in her. I tried to make her see that she'd end up in a blazing fire as an adulteress if she didn't stop the repulsive behavior. I did what I could, what any good Christian could.

DYUDYA. Anyuta, the man's supper is done. Clear the table. You're not needed here.

Anyuta exits with plates, moves to the shadow outside the door, and stands still to listen. Lights slowly down on the scene. A moment later, lights up. Anyuta is in bed. Varvara, a teenager, comes in and stands by the bed.

ANYUTA (*whispering*). Is that you, Varvara?

VARVARA. It's me.

ANYUTA. Where have you been? (*Varvara does not answer.*) Dyudya was complaining about you being gone.

VARVARA. Old devil! My own damn hunchback husband doesn't care, so why should he?

ANYUTA. Be quiet, Varvara. You'll only bring about unhappiness for yourself.

VARVARA. I don't care.

ANYUTA. You know your own family can't take you back.

VARVARA. Being poor doesn't make you a slave.

ANYUTA. It doesn't?

VARVARA. Oh come, Anyuta, I'm in a good mood. I had a magical night.

ANYUTA. You're very young. There're things in life that you can't yet imagine. Tonight a man came to Dyudya's tavern with a little boy and told us a terrible story about what happened to the boy's mother.

VARVARA. What happened?

ANYUTA. She died in jail.

VARVARA. Anyuta. Why are you worried?

ANYUTA. You know you can't go back to your own family. You have to earn your worth.

VARVARA. It wasn't my idea to marry the hunchback. I was brought here to keep Dyudya's son company. It's not my fault he's a freak. Besides, people say Dyudya has eight thousand rubles in the town bank. He gets money from the lodgings, the tavern, his honey, his cattle, and his tar trade What's another mouth to feed? Let's stop thinking about the old devil. How are you, Anyuta?

ANYUTA. The same. Same as yesterday.

VARVARA. Nothing changes. At least your husband is not a hunchback. And you don't even have to live with him at the factory. Though I hear his apartment is pretty nice. The big shot at the factory. He's a bore anyway. (*Curls up next to Anyuta and holds her hand.*) You were young not so long ago. You remember what it's like.

ANYUTA. I don't think I want to remember.

VARVARA. I was with the priest's son!

ANYUTA. You're lying!

VARVARA. It's the truth.

ANYUTA. It's a sin.

VARVARA. I don't care.

ANYUTA. Listen, this boy Sasha's mother, Mashenka, was kicked and beaten with reins. She was an adulteress. The same thing will happen to you if you're not careful.

VARVARA. I bet she wouldn't have given up her lover for fear of a beating.

ANYUTA. It was a tragedy.

VARVARA. Tell me, did the man say Mashenka was very beautiful?

ANYUTA. Why ask such a thing?

VARVARA. Because it's much better to have been beautiful and admired once and die young than being stuck for the rest of your life with an ugly drunken hunchback. I thought it was a good deal. Before I got married I never had enough to eat and I always went barefoot. I wanted to get away from all that misery, and the hunchback had money. Now I'm a slave.

ANYUTA. Still, we have some protection.

VARVARA. What're you saying? Your husband kicked you out so he could get another woman. You've seen her, that fat one. She lives with your husband over at the factory. And Dyudya took your little boy and stuck him in a factory somewhere to work like a slave. You work for Dyudya like a slave yourself.

ANYUTA. Still.

VARVARA. I'd rather have a little fun now and be struck dead by lightning later. The priest's son is really sweet. He says he likes his women healthy and strong, like me. I drink vodka with him and his friends. What a funny bunch! They are young government officials, and they make fun of everyone. You should see how they imitate the hunchback. (*Cannot contain her laughter.*)

ANYUTA. *Your* husband.

Varvara laughs harder. Anyuta can't help but laugh.

VARVARA. We drink and dance, then after his friends are gone, he says to me, "Alone at last." By that time he's completely drunk, but amazingly he can do it. Magic!

ANYUTA. It's a sin.

VARVARA. I don't care. Anyuta, have you been in love?

ANYUTA. You're just giddy. Stop saying silly things.

VARVARA. Tell me if you know what it's like to be in love.

ANYUTA. When I was young. Once, I think. A medical student in Moscow. Twice, maybe. There was a philosophy student.

VARVARA. You lived in Moscow? You never told me about that.

ANYUTA. Because I don't think about it anymore. I was very young then.

VARVARA. Tell me about your lovers.

ANYUTA. I think of them as men I roomed with. Not lovers. I was nobody. They all became important men.

VARVARA. How did you end up here?

ANYUTA. I was extremely fortunate to . . . I surrendered to God, and then I was given a husband.

VARVARA. How fortunate! What a husband!

ANYUTA. You're too young to understand.

VARVARA. I want to live in Moscow.

ANYUTA. Varvara, it's time to sleep. Dyudya will be angry if he catches us awake.

VARVARA. This woman, Mashenka, why did she go to jail?

ANYUTA. She murdered her husband. They dug up his grave and opened his stomach, and found arsenic.

VARVARA. You said he beat her.

ANYUTA. One day this man struck her because she wouldn't leave him alone, and then her husband came running like a madman yelling, "Don't you hit her," and beat his wife with his fists, stomped on her, and then got a hold of the reins and gave her a thrashing.

VARVARA. Brutes.

ANYUTA. The poor boy, Sasha. He was in jail with his mother until she died. He's about the same age as my Grisha.

VARVARA. Do you think Grisha remembers his mother?

ANYUTA. How can he? He was taken from me before he turned six. He's almost nine now. Probably starving, sleeping on the floor in a corner somewhere in the factory. Alone, hungry and cold. Three years. How can he remember his mother?

VARVARA. Anyuta, what's the point of crying? He'll be all right. He'll grow up to be just another brute. Just like his father who doesn't care about his own son.

ANYUTA. Sasha, at least, has some protection. My Grisha has no one.

VARVARA. Why does this man have the orphan?

ANYUTA. Sasha is his sweetheart's child. He said he took him in for the salvation of his own soul.

VARVARA. His sweetheart? Think about that. Two people enjoy each other a while, and the woman is beaten and dies in jail while the man lives and comes to the tavern to eat supper!

ANYUTA. Varvara, we have to sleep. Let's forget all this, and promise me that you'll be careful playing around with the priest's son.

They lie in silence for a while.

VARVARA. I can kill the hunchback. I won't regret it either.

ANYUTA. God help you. You're talking nonsense.

Varvara presses close to Anyuta. Anyuta shudders.

VARVARA. Let's kill Dyudya and the hunchback. You want to, don't you?

ANYUTA. People will find out. Like they found out about Mashenka.

VARVARA. Why did they dig up her husband's body?

ANYUTA. The day after the husband beat her, he fell ill with cholera and it only took him one day to die. Mashenka didn't go to the funeral because her face was bruised badly. People became suspicious.

VARVARA. Gossipers. She was murdered by gossiping old devils.

ANYUTA. Just imagine what people would say if the father and the son both died and only us women were left in the house.

VARVARA. Dyudya is old. It's time for him to die anyway. And people will say the hunchback croaked from drinking too much.

ANYUTA. It's impossible.

VARVARA. We'll poison them, just like Mashenka did to her husband, but we'll be cleverer. We'll do it slowly with Dyudya, so it would look like he just died of old age. Then we'll wait for six months before feeding poison to the hunchback. Or maybe we'll make a little accident for him, a little drunken accident.

ANYUTA. Why? What for?

VARVARA. So I can be free. And you can get your boy back.

ANYUTA. God will strike us both dead.

VARVARA. I don't care. (*Pause.*) Are you asleep? Anyuta?

ANYUTA. It's cold.

VARVARA. It'll soon be light. Go to sleep, my dear.

They lie there awake. The early morning light gradually fills the room. Suddenly with a lot of noise, the hunchback comes bursting through the door. He is covered with dust and straw. He flops down on the floor and snores. Varvara and Anyuta watch him from the bed. The traveler's voice is heard offstage.

TRAVELER. Sasha, get up! Time to harness the horses! Get going!

Anyuta and Varvara listen, almost paralyzed.

TRAVELER. Damn it, Sasha, have you lost your cap, you little swine? Where did you put it? I'll rip your ears off, you little brat! Sasha!

VARVARA. For the salvation of his soul . . .

Anyuta sobs. The hunchback snores.

Lights down.

SCENE 4

Ten years later. Around 1900. Moscow, midsummer. A stiflingly hot afternoon in a room cluttered by a mishmash of gift items such as lace and boxes of chocolates. An attempt to make the room attractive and luxurious is evident, but it is in poor taste. Nikolai, now in his 40s, lounges.

NIKOLAI *(calling out to the back room)*. What's taking you so long?

VOICE. I'm making myself beautiful for you. Be patient.

NIKOLAI. I'm lonely.

VOICE. Have you brought me a gift?

NIKOLAI. I brought you my undying devotion.

Varvara, who is now in her late 20s, dressed in a tawdry and colorful dress, enters.

VARVARA. I don't expect you to bring me gifts. You're the stingiest gentleman I know.

NIKOLAI. The port was vile.

VARVARA. I see you drank the whole bottle.

NIKOLAI. I don't feel so good. It's unbearably hot in here.

VARVARA. No one asked you to come and drink a whole bottle of port. I know you're not going to replace it either.

NIKOLAI. I'm here admiring your pretty face, aren't I?

VARVARA. I have plenty of admirers. Ones who bring me gifts.

NIKOLAI. My devotion to you is artistic. I'm an artist. I have insight into beauty, not like those disgusting businessmen who throw money around without knowing your true value.

VARVARA. What's my true value?

NIKOLAI. My dear, you have many good qualities.

VARVARA. Like what?

NIKOLAI. You're still young enough.

VARVARA. Young enough for what?

NIKOLAI. To be an excellent chorus girl.

VARVARA. I'm an actress.

NIKOLAI. No, not right now. Though you may very well become an
actress someday. No doubt you're talented.

VARVARA. I'm an actress.

IMAGE 3.6 **Moscow, c.1900. Nikolai seduces Varvara, the chorus girl.**
Kate Costello (left), Christopher Domig (right).
Photograph by Russell Parkman.

NIKOLAI. An actress would be someone who acts on stage, at the Moscow Art Theater, for example. Plays, you see. You sing at the pub.

VARVARA. I know what plays are. Please don't tell me about my business.

NIKOLAI. All right, Varvara. So you're an actress.

VARVARA. What else?

NIKOLAI. What else what?

VARVARA. What else are my "good qualities?"

NIKOLAI. Oh, yes, well, you seem to come from good, strong peasant stock. Healthy and beautiful.

VARVARA. I am not!

NIKOLAI. Not healthy and beautiful?

VARVARA. I'm not a peasant!

NIKOLAI. I didn't say you are one now, I said you seem to come from—

VARVARA. I'm not a peasant!

NIKOLAI. All right, Varvara. So you're not a peasant.

VARVARA. I'm not that healthy either.

NIKOLAI. Come closer. Let me hold your delicate body.

VARVARA. I thought you weren't feeling good.

NIKOLAI. Marveling at your body has cheered me up. Come on.

VARVARA. It's too hot.

NIKOLAI. If you give in, I'll paint your portrait like you're a lady.

VARVARA. You keep saying that, but you never do. In fact I don't think you paint anything. You're either drinking at the pub or lounging here all the time. Why don't you go paint something?

NIKOLAI. You wouldn't understand this, but I'm working on a major painting right now.

VARVARA. What is it?

NIKOLAI. Psyche.

VARVARA. I heard you say that to your friends at the pub months ago.

NIKOLAI. It's my eternal subject. I've been painting Psyche for years.

VARVARA. How much longer is it going to take to finish it?

NIKOLAI. I don't mean one painting. I have dozens of paintings of Psyche.

VARVARA. You mean you paint the same thing over and over? You can't get it right?

NIKOLAI. Never mind. It's not important.

VARVARA. It seems important.

NIKOLAI. No, not really.

VARVARA. What's Psyche?

NIKOLAI. She was a Greek maiden. People abandoned their worship of the goddess Venus for this beautiful virgin. Psyche incurred . . . Ah, never mind.

VARVARA. Did she have many lovers?

NIKOLAI. She was married. But her husband would only come visit her during the dark of night and leave her before the morning sun. So she never knew what he looked like.

VARVARA. Maybe it was good that she didn't know what her husband looked like. He could've been a hunchback. (*Nikolai laughs uncontrollably.*) What's so funny? People do that. Marry hunchbacks.

NIKOLAI. I don't know why. Such an act seems to be driven by a complete lack of aesthetics.

VARVARA. Huh?

NIKOLAI. Anyway, I didn't think you'd understand the significance of Psyche.

VARVARA. If you don't think I understand anything, why do you call on me?

NIKOLAI. Because despite your sweet ignorance, you're visually pleasing. A gentleman needs beauty in his life.

VARVARA. What's wrong with your wife?

NIKOLAI. Nothing. We won't talk about my wife. She is a respectable lady.

VARVARA. Why don't you paint her then?

NIKOLAI. I'm working on Psyche. I can't ask her to pose for me as if she were a common woman. I will paint her portrait, when I'm ready.

VARVARA. But is she beautiful?

NIKOLAI. Of course, she is. But I'm not discussing my wife with you.

VARVARA. Well then, let's discuss something general. If a man has a perfectly beautiful and high-class wife, why would he call on a common woman, as he puts it, every day?

NIKOLAI. I don't wish to discuss any man or woman or gentleman or lady of any breeding whatsoever.

VARVARA. Fine. What do you want to talk about?

NIKOLAI. My sweet, must we talk more? Why don't you come closer?

VARVARA. I was married to a hunchback once.

Nikolai laughs. Then he realizes that she is not joking.

NIKOLAI. You're serious! What a hoot. Were you in the circus?

VARVARA. No. What would I be doing in the circus?

NIKOLAI. There are a number of things one can do in the circus.

VARVARA. For an educated man, you say a lot of stupid things. At least the hunchback didn't talk so much.

NIKOLAI. When was this?

VARVARA. Not so long ago. I came to Moscow two years ago.

NIKOLAI. Where is your hunchback husband?

VARVARA. He's dead. My sister-in-law had some money saved up and gave it to me for the train fare. She also gave me the name of a person in Moscow, a doctor. When I looked him up and told him who I was, he set me up with this job. He didn't ask any questions. I haven't seen him since.

NIKOLAI (*mockingly*). This is the new Russia. You're a regular feminist in the new century.

VARVARA. I wanted to come to Moscow. I've always wanted to. Good thing that my husband died, or else my dream would have never come true.

NIKOLAI. Is this your dream?

VARVARA. I'm in Moscow, aren't I?

NIKOLAI. "I remember so little; every day I forget more and more, and life passes by and it won't ever come back, and we're never going to Moscow, never, never, never, I understand it all now; we're never going to Moscow."

VARVARA. What're you talking about? Who's we?

NIKOLAI. Do you have sisters?

VARVARA. Just one sister-in-law. Anyuta. She doesn't write me, though. Her son Grisha died when he was thirteen from typhoid. She didn't even know about it until a year later. The last time she saw her son was when he was five. Anyway, she became even more religious after that, like almost a saint or a lunatic. She thinks I'm a harlot living in sin.

NIKOLAI. She didn't want to come to Moscow with you then?

VARVARA. I can't understand her. She lived here when she was a young girl. If you ask me, she left Eden when she left the city for the godforsaken country. I really miss her.

NIKOLAI. Anyuta from Moscow . . . What's the name of the doctor she had you look up?

VARVARA. I'm not supposed to tell.

NIKOLAI. It doesn't matter. Varvara, very soon, you won't be young at all. All the admirers you have today will forget you. Let me feel your legs now, before it's too late.

The bell rings in the hall. Startled, Nikolai gets up on his feet.

VARVARA. Don't get nervous. It's probably the postman. Or one of the girls from the pub.

NIKOLAI. I'll go and stay in the back while you take care of it. Whoever it is, I don't want to be bothered. Go on, answer the door. (*Exits.*)

Varvara opens the door and finds an aristocratic lady, dressed in black.

VARVARA. May I . . . help you? Are you lost?

LADY. Is my husband here?

VARVARA. What husband? Which one?

LADY. My husband. Nikolai Festissov.

VARVARA. No-o-o, my lady, I don't know any Nikolai.

Lady is distraught. She trembles and bites her handkerchief. Varvara stands paralyzed by the unfamiliar sight.

LADY. So you deny that he is here?

VARVARA. He who? I don't know what you mean.

LADY. I think you do. Have you any idea what it means for someone like me to knock on your door?

VARVARA. Are you sick? Would you like some water?

LADY. Never!

VARVARA (*confused*). Never what?

LADY. You disgusting, deceitful creature!

VARVARA (*startled and confused*). What? What?

LADY. I'm glad that finally I have the opportunity to tell you what I think of you and your kind. You're repulsive.(*Varvara frantically tries to get a strand of her hair that has fallen on her forehead to go back and stay up with the rest of her hair.*) I want to know where my husband is. What are you doing?

VARVARA. Nothing. My hair . . . It's not so easy, you know. I don't have the money for fancy clothes like you. And I have to wear powder on my face, for the pub, because—

LADY. Money? Let me tell you about money. My husband has been discovered embezzling funds entrusted to him. The police were notified. He is going to be arrested for this. Do you see what you have done?

VARVARA. Me? I never even talked to the police!

Lady gets up and paces the room in violent agitation.

LADY. He will be arrested today, and you brought this misfortune and dishonor upon him, upon my children and me. (*Varvara is speechless. She does not comprehend what is happening.*) God will punish you in the end. He knows every tear I have shed, every sleepless night I have passed. I may not be your concern now, but the day will come when you will regret what you have done to me. (*Paces the floor, wringing her hands. Varvara is still dumbfounded and terrified*.) You manipulate men and make them betray their wives. Haven't you ever pondered upon your immoral life? How you destroy good families and good names?

VARVARA. Listen, my lady. You're a proper lady and his wife. Why don't you keep him home?

LADY. So you admit to seducing my husband.

VARVARA. I have plenty of visitors. I don't have to seduce anyone.

LADY. I have known about you all along. Nikolai has come here every day for the last month.

VARVARA. Is that my fault? He comes here of his own free will. I don't force him. This is my place!

LADY. And a fine place it is for a chorus girl.

VARVARA. I'm not a chorus girl. It took me long, terrible years to get to my dream city to become an actress. I came from *somewhere* to Moscow. You didn't, did you? You've always been here. You're not from *anywhere*.

LADY. Have you heard anything I said? My husband is accused of embezzlement! He has taken money that does not belong to him to spend on you, a lowlife woman. Oh, if I can find nine hundred rubles today, it will save us. Only nine hundred rubles.

VARVARA (*alarmed*). What're you saying? I didn't take any money.

LADY. I'm not asking you for money. I know you don't have any. Even if you had nine hundred rubles, I don't want anything that belongs to you. I only want back what is rightfully mine. All I ask is that you give back the gifts my husband has given you.

VARVARA. He has never given me anything!

LADY. Please don't lie to me. He has squandered his own fortune, my dowry, even other people's money. Where has the money gone if not to you?

VARVARA. I'd like to know.

LADY. I was upset just now and said some unpleasant things. You must hate me, but please try to understand how I suffer. You took my husband away from me, and now only you can save our respectable name and prevent our innocent children from lunging into poverty. I implore you to give back all the jewelry he has given you.

VARVARA. Jewelry! I should save your good name with pleasure, only I swear to God, he's never given me a single thing.

LADY. Have you no pity?

VARVARA. Wait a minute. I remember now. He did give me two little things. I'll fetch them for you if you want them. (*Pulls out a drawer and gets a narrow gold bracelet and ring and hands them to the woman.*) Here they are.

LADY. What is this? Don't insult me. I'm not here for charity but for things you extracted from my unhappy husband with your deviant power.

VARVARA. Please stop saying dreadful things. Those little gold bracelet and ring you're holding are the only things Nikolai has given me. And some little cakes.

LADY. Little cakes? His children do not have anything to eat, but he brings you little cakes! If I can't get nine hundred rubles by the end of the day, we will be ruined. Can you really allow my innocent children to eat bread and water?

VARVARA. What can I do? I've never reaped any benefits from your husband. I receive him because we can't pick and choose callers. I've always been poor. I live on bread and water, too.

LADY. I have a deep desire to kill you.

VARVARA. Don't be crazy. Do you really want to go to jail for your lame husband?

LADY. I will kneel down before you for the sake of my family. I beg you, give me the jewelry.

VARVARA. What? What? What?

LADY. I will kneel down before you.

VARVARA. What're you saying? Are you threatening to kneel down in order to humiliate me? The proud and highbred lady kneeling down before a poor singer? Is that the game you're playing?

LADY. I'll sacrifice my pride to save my husband. I will happily kneel before a chorus girl if that's what it takes.

VARVARA. All right! I'll give you the jewelry, but I swear they didn't come from your husband. I got them from other admirers of mine. You can have them, only don't kneel down, for God's sake! (*Pulls out a diamond brooch, a string of corals, more rings and bracelets from the bureau and hands them to Lady, who stares at them.*)

LADY. This cannot be all. There isn't even five hundred rubles worth of jewelry here.

Exasperated, Varvara runs around snatching other items from various locations in the room.

VARVARA. Here. Take this gold watch, and this cigarette case, and these necklaces, too. Now you've cleaned me out! Do you want to check and see it for yourself? And for your information, I'm an actress.

LADY. You, my dear, are what you have always been.

Lady wraps the jewelry in her handkerchief and exits. Varvara stands there breathless. Nikolai comes out from the back dejected.

VARVARA. I'd like to know what gifts you ever gave me!

NIKOLAI. Gifts? Gifts are meaningless. Trivial. I'm an artist.

VARVARA. Artist! Artist! Artist! How does that benefit me? I'm asking you, what have you ever given me?

NIKOLAI. My wife, she wept in front of you. Who are you? She was ready to fall on her knees before *you*, a worthless chorus girl. I shall never forgive myself.

VARVARA. I gave her everything. Why did I do that? I gave her beautiful things I had never even seen before I came to Moscow. And they were mine. Now they're gone.

NIKOLAI. Whatever happened to the past when I was young and hopeful, when I dreamed wonderful dreams and thought important thoughts, when my work was promising and my life was filled with enthusiasm? What happened to it? I'm bored and lazy and useless. I never amounted to anything. The port was vile. It's stiflingly hot. I don't feel good.

VARVARA. Nikolai . . .

IMAGE 3.7 **Moscow, *c*.1900. Nikolai regrets his failed career as an artist in the presence of Varvara.**

Christopher Domig (left), Kate Costello (right).

Photograph by Russell Parkman.

NIKOLAI. Get away from me, you whore. No, excuse me. You're free. Think about that. (*Exits.*)

Varvara is left alone in her devastation.

VARVARA. Oh, I understand it all now, Anyuta—we're never going to Moscow.

Lights fade. Blackout.

ACT II

SCENE 1

Three years later. Around 1903. Early summer. A wealthy household in the country. The family and the fiancé are drinking tea after supper. Sasha, the orphan talked about in Act I Scene 3, is now in his 20s.

NINA. Sasha, you didn't eat enough. You must eat more. You look dreadful.

SASHA. There was too much food. You had too much food prepared.

NINA. You lost weight since we saw you last summer. I remember one year when you were still little, you refused to eat cake on your name day. Every year after that, you didn't want cake at your party. Tonight, you didn't eat any pie.

SASHA. Eating cakes and pies is immoral.

ANDREY. So, Alexander Timofeyich, you're an artist.

SASHA. No, I studied art. I painted for ten years.

ANDREY. What do you paint?

SASHA. I don't anymore.

ANDREY. What did you paint then?

SASHA. It's not what that's important. I can't remember what I painted.

NADYA. My dear Sasha, what do you remember?

SASHA. What's important is not what, it's why. I work at a printing house now.

NINA. The air in the printing shop is terrible for you.

NADYA. Mama, you've never been there.

NINA. Sasha passed the examination to be an architect. But he didn't want to practice.

ANDREY. It must be exciting to live in Moscow.

SASHA. Yes. Nothing happens in the country. People here live in ignorance of how the world history is shaping itself for the future. (*To Nina*) But it's nice here.

NINA. You should stay until fall. For your health.

SASHA. You're right, Nina Ivanovna, I'll stay until September.

ANDREY. Perhaps you'll take up painting again. The country around here is beautiful, despite the fact, of course, of the ignorance of its inhabitants.

SASHA. What did you study?

ANDREY. I graduated with a philosophy degree from the university, but that was ten years ago.

SASHA. Do you have an occupation?

NADYA. Andrey sometimes plays the violin at charity concerts.

SASHA. I see.

NADYA. He has been overseeing the new house. It's a two-story house, and in the drawing room there is a large oil painting in a gold frame. You may know the painting.

SASHA. What does it look like?

NADYA. It's a picture of a naked woman beside a lilac vase with a broken handle.

SASHA. I have no idea.

ANDREY. It's by Shishmachevsky.

SASHA. I don't know who Shishmachevsky is.

Awkward pause.

NINA. Sasha came to live with us when he was ten.

ANDREY. Were you orphaned?

SASHA. They say my mother poisoned my father to death. She died in jail.

ANDREY. Goodness!

NINA. The important thing is that he was adopted by a thoughtful man. When Sasha was ten, his adopted father left him with us to work at a stall in the marketplace. He wanted Sasha to become a merchant. You know we own a row of stalls, and we're in constant need of help.

SASHA. I haven't seen the bastard since. I don't know if he's dead or alive.

ANDREY. Goodness!

SASHA. It's not a problem. We didn't like each other. He was the cause of my mother's demise, but he kept telling me what a great charity he was performing by beating me daily.

ANDREY. Goodness!

SASHA. What does "goodness" mean? I don't know why people say things that mean nothing. Anyway, Nina Ivanovna was very kind to me.

NINA. I dreamed about Sasha two weeks before his adopted father came by.

NADYA. That's my favorite story.

NINA. In the dream, I was walking on a long muddy road with two suitcases. I was alone, and the suitcases were heavy. I realized that I had to leave one of them behind if I were to make it to the end of the road. They were identical in size and weight except that one was grey and the other was red. I decided to take the red one. When I got to the end of the road, a woman took the suitcase from me and gave me a key. I ran back to the grey suitcase that I left on the side of the road. It was still there. I opened it with the key, and Sasha came out.

ANDREY. What did you think it meant?

NINA. It meant that I had a gift coming to me, and I had to be careful not to miss it when it came. Things that look nicer are not always what you should keep. Sasha was to come out of a grey suitcase. When he arrived, he was a skinny little boy.

NADYA. I think the woman at the end of the road was his mother.

ANDREY. Do you remember what she looked like?

NINA. I remember her face clearly. I can still see it in my mind. She had large, dark eyes.

NADYA. Like Sasha.

SASHA. I'm sure my mother looked nothing like me. I'm sure I don't look like anyone.

NADYA. People often think that we're real brother and sister. You look like me.

ANDREY. You don't really believe in prophetic dreams, do you, Nina Ivanovna?

NINA. I don't know. But there are things in life that we just can't explain. Mysterious things.

ANDREY. I don't think life needs to be explained. Some things are God's will.

SASHA. You think that because you do nothing with your life.

NADYA (*quietly*). Sasha.

SASHA. You're a healthy man. There is no reason to be so idle, physically or mentally. This evening, the turkey was enormously fat. Why did we have to have such a large turkey?

ANDREY (*calmly*). What does that have to do with anything?

SASHA. What's important is why. Why turkey and not porridge? Why do we have to have marinated cherries?

NADYA. Sasha, Mama wanted to do something special for you, and Andrey has been looking forward to meeting you. He sent for marinated cherries for us.

SASHA. Nadya, you're smart, beautiful and healthy. And now, you're engaged to be married. That's fine. Still, you shouldn't sit around getting fat from fat turkeys.

NINA. We should all go to bed. Sasha, you need rest. You look dreadful.

ANDREY. Don't get yourself all worked up, Alexander Timofeyich. The situation is not dire.

SASHA. Not for you.

ANDREY. Apparently not for you either.

SASHA. You can't compare yourself to me.

NADYA. Sasha, we can talk more tomorrow.

SASHA. Yes, yes, I am glad to see my family.

NADYA. We'll all have tea tomorrow. Andrey, too.

SASHA. Right. Anyway, please forgive me if I have offended you. I'm not used to idleness.

NINA. That's all right. Will you go to bed now?

SASHA. I'll stay a while and have my tea.

NINA. Sasha drinks tea, Moscow style. Very slowly, late into the night, seven cups in one sitting.

ANDREY. Good night.

SASHA. Good night.

> *Exit all except Sasha, who sits and drinks tea. He has a coughing fit. When it subsides, he drinks tea again. Pause. Lights dim.*
>
> *Lights up. Next morning. Sasha is in the same place at the table, drinking tea. Nadya enters.*

SASHA. You're up early.

NADYA. You, too.

SASHA. I always get up early and read.

NADYA. You need more rest.

SASHA. I don't think it's necessary to rest as much as some people seem to think they need. Look at your servants. They hardly get any rest.

NADYA. Please don't start.

SASHA. All right, Nadya. Did you sleep well?

NADYA. No. I was miserable. I heard you coughing in the middle of the night. Oh Sasha, are you going to be all right? Have you seen a doctor?

SASHA. Never mind my coughing. Why were you miserable?

NADYA. I don't know. I just want to cry. Since I was sixteen, I dreamed of marriage. I was very glad that a wedding was arranged for me at last. But suddenly, I'm not happy.

SASHA. It's because you live a meaningless life. You do nothing. Your mother does nothing. Your fiancé does nothing. Other people have to work so you can be idle. Don't you think it's immoral? You're devouring other lives so you can have leisure.

NADYA. My mother is a sensitive and unique woman.

SASHA. Is she?

NADYA. The other morning, she came to me in tears because she had started reading a novel and got to a place where she could not help but cry.

SASHA. Nadya, she's a kind woman. She is very kind to me. But look at how her maids live. Four of them sleep on the floor in the kitchen, no beds, just bedbugs. Your mother speaks French, for God's sake.

NADYA. I wish you would say something new sometime. Every summer it's the same.

SASHA. Because nothing changes.

NADYA. I know. But what can I do about it? Why do you blame me?

SASHA. Nadya, you should go away from here and study.

NADYA. I can't. I'm getting married.

SASHA. Yes, and Andrey has installed running water in your house.

NADYA. I didn't ask for the house. I don't feel anything for it.

SASHA. But you'll live in it. Year after year. Until you die perhaps.

NADYA. How can I change things now? I'm twenty-three years old.

SASHA. Go to St. Petersburg. Many women are studying there, studying science and mathematics to better human kind. You must join them.

NADYA. I've heard about those bohemian women. They dress unattractively. They smoke cigarettes.

SASHA. At least they're doing something.

NADYA. I'm exhausted. I have to go and rest. There will be guests for lunch, and I have to entertain them.

SASHA. You have to smile, listen to the violin, listen to all kinds of idiocies, and talk about the wedding.

NADYA. Sasha, you should rest, too. You look ill.

SASHA. I'm just bored. I don't think I can stay here the entire summer.

NADYA. The wedding is on July 2.

SASHA. Go and rest, my dear Nadya. Before your mother gets up and fusses over you.

NADYA. Why have you stopped painting, Sasha?

SASHA. Because it wasn't useful. At the printing shop, I'm useful. There will be changes, Nadya. Someday, all this will look different. I want to show you the pamphlets I print. If you come to Moscow with me, you can go from there to St Petersburg alone. Be brave.

NADYA. I used to love your paintings. (*Pensively exits.*)

Sasha goes back to drinking tea. Lights dim.

Lights up on a grey day. Nadya and Andrey in the garden.

NADYA. The summer has turned damp and cold.

ANDREY. The weather will recover by July 2. You'll see.

NADYA. And then?

ANDREY. What do you mean?

NADYA. Nothing. How is your father, Andrey?

ANDREY. He's well. What a good man! God, I really love him.

NADYA. That's nice.

ANDREY. You could, too.

NADYA. Love him?

ANDREY. I mean you could consider him as your father. He wants you to. It must have been difficult for you to grow up without a strong head of the household, someone who represents the family to society. He has great sympathy for you. God, I love that man.

NADYA. That's nice.

ANDREY. Do you remember when Sasha reproached me for living an idle life?

NADYA. Andrey, don't mind Sasha. He can be difficult.

ANDREY. No, my dear, I was about to say he was right. I don't do anything, and I can't do anything. I'm repulsed by the idea of having to do something. He is absolutely right about me.

NADYA. Let's not talk about it.

ANDREY. But you understand that we're all born into a fate. Ranting and raving about other people's fates is useless. We must simply live the life we are given.

NADYA. I have a headache.

ANDREY. My poor Nadya. It'll be all right. We're going to have a great life. We can travel to Europe if you like. Now that's not being idle, is it?

NADYA. Sasha says that the Europeans are primitive. They don't have a profound soul like Russians.

ANDREY. That's ridiculous. Which European country has he traveled to?

NADYA. He says they're all the same. Superficial and materialistic. He reads all the time. All kinds of books.

ANDREY. He didn't even know who Shishmachevsky is. I admit he isn't very famous yet, but I've made an investment in his future by purchasing his painting for the house. He's talented, even you can see that, Nadya. For another painter not to know him—

NADYA. Sasha doesn't paint anymore. He's too busy with his work.

ANDREY. Nadya, I know you care a great deal about him, but he's not a good influence on you. You take him too seriously. After all, he's not your real brother. He wasn't meant to be here with us. I mean, of course fate brought him here . . . well, thank goodness for your mother's kindness.

NADYA. I used to think Mother was the most extraordinary woman.

ANDREY. What do you mean you used to?

NADYA. I just can't remember why I thought that about her. She doesn't seem extraordinary anymore.

ANDREY. Have you had an argument with your mother?

NADYA. I don't think so. Last night I told her I couldn't sleep, and she said to me, "Close your eyes and imagine yourself as Anna Karenina." What does that mean? She didn't ask me why I couldn't sleep.

ANDREY. My dear, she is a very nice woman.

NADYA. I know that. But it's humiliating for me to have to attend all those dinner parties and luncheons. She doesn't understand me.

ANDREY. I don't know what you are saying.

NADYA. I used to think she was really interesting. The novel she is reading now is about an old man and his daughter. The man works in an office, and his superior falls in love with his daughter. She was crying about it. What is so moving about that?

ANDREY. Nina Ivanovna is very sensitive. This is not like you. You've never had an unkind word to say about your mother before.

NADYA. She is sensitive about characters in novels. But our servants don't really like her, even though she smiles all the time and never raises her voice at them. I don't think she loved my father either.

ANDREY. I must protest, Nadya, as your fiancé—

NADYA. Never mind, Andrey. I'm irritated today for some reason.

ANDREY. Oh, my darling, you're just nervous about the wedding. It'll be a big party with champagne and music. You'll look beautiful, and Nina Ivanovna will be very happy. There is no need to worry, Nadya.

NADYA. I'm sure the wedding will be very nice.

ANDREY. After we're married, if you don't want to go to Europe right away, that's fine. We'll go to the country and buy a piece of land with a garden and a river. We can work there if you

like. We can grow flowers and vegetables. We'll be regular
farmers! Would you like that?

NADYA. That'll be fine. I've always dreamed of being married, especially since Father died. Andrey, I'd like to have many children.
I was a lonely child before Sasha came to live with us. We all
need the security of people who will love us for the rest of our
lives. No matter what. No matter how we live and no matter
how we decide to die. I'd like to have four children. So they
can team up, if they want to.

ANDREY. My dear, sweet Nadya. I'm so happy. You'll be my little
wife very soon.

Lights dim.

*Two years later. Early summer. The house. Nadya enters in her
traveling clothes to find her mother.*

NADYA. Hello, Mother.

NINA. Nadya. You've come home.

Nina holds her daughter and weeps.

NADYA. I'm here to visit for the summer. Let's not be unhappy.

NINA. I'm glad to see you again, that's all. You look fine, just fine.

NADYA. Thank you. And you? How are you?

NINA. It was difficult at the beginning, of course. Andrey Andreyich
is still angry. I don't go out to the market anymore for fear of
running into him.

NADYA. It has been two years. I hear he's engaged.

NINA. It was terrible to have to cancel the wedding and explain to
all the guests what happened. I didn't know what to say to
them, but Andrey Andreyich insisted on telling the truth.

NADYA. It was the right thing to do.

NINA. When you didn't return from the train station from seeing
Sasha off, I got sick with worry. Five days later when the letter came from Petersburg, I fainted.

NADYA. It happened two years ago. We've gone over all this in our
letters.

NINA. I know. All is forgiven. I'm glad to see you. You'll stay for the summer. Stay until September.

NADYA. I stopped in Moscow and saw Sasha on my way here.

NINA. He's the one to blame. He hasn't the nerve to show up here anymore because he knows he ruined everything.

NADYA. Nothing is ruined, Mother. I couldn't have married Andrey. I would have been miserable in that house.

NINA. Why?

NADYA. I explained it in my letters.

NINA. I didn't understand any of it. Something about how life is going to be wonderful in the future, hundreds of years from now after we're all dead—

NADYA. We don't have to discuss this. I'm happy, so please don't be angry at Sasha.

NINA. You like Petersburg.

NADYA. I like Petersburg.

NINA. What is it that you are studying again?

NADYA. Biology.

NINA. Biology.

NADYA. Yes, biology.

NINA. Don't you think it's nice here in the country?

NADYA. Yes, Mother.

NINA. Can you believe that Andrey Andreyich is planning to live in the house he got for you? And his new fiancée doesn't come with any dowry. I mean, hardly any.

NADYA. You didn't come to Father with much either, did you?

NINA. I was a good wife to him.

NADYA. I'm sure, Mother, but he fell in love with you because you were beautiful, and he didn't mind that you didn't have a large dowry.

NINA. He loved me, that's true. And I took care of him and his mean old mother. I didn't run away.

NADYA. Did you love Father?

NINA. Of course, I did.

NADYA. Did you really?

NINA. What're you asking?

NADYA. I always had a strange feeling about it ever since I was little. Even when Father was still alive.

NINA. I don't know what this conversation is about. You've become difficult since you left home. You remind me of Sasha.

NADYA. Sasha and I talked for a whole day in Moscow. He was constantly coughing. He said he was going to the Volga in a few days to drink koumiss.

NINA. What's koumiss?

NADYA. It's mare's milk, I think. Supposed to cure consumption.

NINA. Oh, Sasha.

NADYA. You knew he had it, didn't you?

NINA. He never told me.

NADYA. He never told anyone. But we all knew, didn't we?

NINA. I knew no such thing.

NADYA. Mother.

NINA. Well, he could have told me. I wouldn't have stayed angry with him for so long if he had told me.

NADYA. He couldn't admit it to himself. But when I saw him this time, he was so ill, he had to tell me the truth. His legs were so thin; I didn't know how he could stand up.

NINA. He should come here for the summer. The air in Moscow is killing him.

NADYA. I want to tell you, Mother, he's very proud of me. He thinks that I've revolutionized myself with education.

NINA. Nadya, please don't frighten me. What will happen to you now?

NADYA. I'll become a doctor or a teacher of medicine. Make a contribution to humankind.

NINA. But my dear, you will marry, won't you?

NADYA. I'm not thinking about it right now. I have to finish my studies first.

NINA. It'll be too late by then.

NADYA. A lot of women don't marry these days. Now that we're allowed to travel without a man's permission, we don't need men. It's the new century.

NINA. I feel faint.

NADYA. Do you remember the dream you had before Sasha came to us? When I visited him on my way home, he told me that he recently had a similar dream. In the dream, he had two cups of tea. The tea looked identical, just as strong and with sugar, but he knew one of them was poisonous. One tea was in a red cup and the other in a grey one. He tried to remember in his dream which suitcase he came out of in your dream.

NINA. Did he? Did he remember?

NADYA. Not in the dream. He remembered when he woke up.

NINA. What happened in the dream?

NADYA. He drank the wrong tea. (*Nina gasps.*) It means nothing, Mother. It's not an omen. Sasha and I agree that we should disregard all forms of superstition. But all the same, he wanted me to tell you about it. I think it scared him a little.

NINA. Oh Nadya, why didn't you bring him home with you? Poor Sasha. I've been so lonely since that rainy morning you insisted on seeing him off at the station two years ago. The chilly rain continued for the rest of the afternoon and evening, and the servants were out looking for you until dawn. I remember everything so clearly. The feeling of doom has never left me since that day. And now you tell me Sasha has consumption and he's dying.

NADYA. Mother, you knew about Sasha just like you knew that there would be no wedding.

NINA. How could I have known about you leaving Andrey Andreyich without even saying a word?

NADYA. You knew Sasha had consumption. You always said that it was important for you to love him like he was your own because he wasn't long for this world.

NINA. I never believed it entirely. A mother must not believe much in anything, otherwise life torments you.

NADYA. You must face the truth someday, like that day I went to the train station.

NINA. You're not a mother yet. You don't understand how your children can make you into an old woman.

NADYA. Please, let's not quarrel. I'll write Sasha and tell him to come here straightaway once his treatment is finished.

NINA. He should stay until autumn. The clean air and rest will cure him. All is forgiven. All is forgiven. (*Exits.*)

Flashback to Nadya's recent visit to Moscow. Nadya and Sasha talk intimately in the printing shop.

SASHA. I've always felt there was inherited poison lurking in me all my life. I know it isn't logical. I was born long before my mother poisoned my father. But I always thought I'd die from the same poison.

NADYA. Sasha, why don't you take care of your health instead of fantasizing about your poisoned blood? Why do you smoke so much? Tobacco is terrible for you, and you hardly eat any food.

SASHA. I'm not fantasizing. It's a deep feeling. Perhaps I acquired it during the time I was with my mother in jail. I was two, but I think she was still breast-feeding me. A woman's milk cannot be healthy when she is crazed by a betrayal by her lover, beaten by her husband, and murderous at heart for revenge.

NADYA. Do you remember her?

SASHA. No. In the end, no one will remember you or me. That's the natural course of life. There are things that are inherently important in human life. But the rest, no matter how significant they feel to us now, the time will come when they'll be regarded as petty and silly. That's why we have to break out of the precious lifestyle we're so proud of, because in a hundred years, people will look back and consider us barbaric and stupid anyway.

NADYA. Dearest, what precious life? You have nothing but contempt for comfort. You're wearing the same coat and trousers that you've worn for the last five years, the samovar is completely cold, and look at the flypaper on the broken plate. You should clean up the dead flies once in a while. This kind of neglect to your personal well-being is unnecessary.

SASHA. Nadya, none of this is important. We're merely temporary entities whose lives are to become foundations for the future life that is astonishing, beautiful and just. (*Coughs violently.*)

NADYA. Sasha, please. See a doctor.

SASHA. No, no, I'm going on the trip down the Volga in a few days to take koumiss. I'll be all right. A friend of mine and his wife are going with me. The wife is a smart woman. I'm trying to persuade her to go away and study. To revolutionize her life, just like you did.

NADYA. What does your friend say about that? Her husband.

SASHA. I'm sure he'd agree. It's the right thing to do.

NADYA. Sasha, what about happiness and love? What makes you happy? Is there someone who loves you? Besides Mother and I?

SASHA (*laughs uncomfortably*). Happiness doesn't exist yet. That's what I've been saying. It's not for us. Your great-great-grand-children may achieve happiness.

NADYA. I won't have any children. I can't imagine it. It's enough to have a mother. But I don't think it's wrong to want happiness.

SASHA. Why should you be happy when your servants are eating nothing but porridge while cooking poached fish in sour cream for your mother?

NADYA. I'm eating porridge. I want everyone to have poached fish or roasted pheasant. I want that for everyone. I want you to be happy. I want you to be well.

Time splits between the past and present. Nina enters into the present. She does not see or hear Sasha. Nadya talks to Nina, but keeps her eyes on Sasha.

NINA (*distraught*). Nadya, a telegram came from Saratov this morning.

NADYA. Yes, Mama. Sasha got sick there on his way back from the Volga. He lost his voice and was admitted to the hospital.

NINA. Why didn't you tell me?

NADYA. I got his letter only yesterday.

NINA (*weeping*). The poor little boy died alone just like his mother who died alone in jail . . .

NADYA. In the future, no woman is going to die in jail, because men will no longer be brutal and cause women to suffer.

SASHA. My sweet Nadya, right now, there aren't too many people like you. Smart and good and hardworking. There will be more people like you in the next generation, and more in the following generation.

NINA. Aren't you sad about Sasha? Won't you even cry for your adopted brother?

NADYA. I'm going back to Petersburg. A new, bright, meaningful life is coming, Mama. We'll all be free. Your servants will be free too.

NINA. Everyone leaves. There was a time that no one left. Nadya, this house is yours.

NADYA. Soon no one will remember this house even existed.

NINA. Look how beautiful the country is. This is as close to Eden as we can get in this life.

SASHA. The time will come when the entire world has changed because of you, and everyone will be smart and good and hardworking. And finally, you will become part of the past, and people who are even better than you will be born. See Nadya? Happiness is coming. For everyone.

NINA. Stay, my dear.

NADYA. No, Mama. I'm leaving. Tomorrow morning. I'm going back to Petersberg.

Nadya is full of determination. Nina weeps. As lights fade on Nina, Nadya takes off her dress. Underneath she is wearing a contemporary dress. She walks into the next scene and becomes Sophia, a young American woman.

SCENE II

Long Island, New York. Present. A large, festive wedding reception. On the stage a large table with seven people seated at it. The table is facing the audience à la The Last Supper. *It is assumed that when the characters are not involved in the main conversation at the table, they are either talking among themselves or listening to the reception speeches. Some of them may get up and dance—this can be improvised.*

WOMAN 1. I'm a friend of the groom. A really good, intimate friend.

MAN 1. This is the farthest table away from the wedding party.

WOMAN 1. I'm sure that's because I came single, you know. This is a table for seven people, so.

MAN 1. What?

WOMAN 1. He was my boyfriend once. I lived with him for two years. He took the best towels when he moved out.

MAN 1. Goodness!

WOMAN 1. When we moved in together, I took cooking classes so I could make special meals for him. I cooked Indian curries, Thai noodles, Vietnamese sweet rice and chicken, fondue. Every night, I prepared something exotic and elaborate for dinner. But he didn't eat. I mean he stopped eating completely. It was weird.

MAN 1. Goodness!

WOMAN 1. I would spend hours looking for purple mint leaves in Chinatown and make these exquisite rice-paper rolls with shrimp and mint and lettuce and cellophane noodles, and then make homemade peanut sauce, and then decorate the plate with curved radishes to serve the rolls, and he would look at them and say, "No, thank you."

MAN 1. Goodness. Honey, did you hear that?

WOMAN 2. I heard.

WOMAN 1. I realized that I was wasting my life. So I switched to meat and potatoes. But by that time, he was bypassing the dinner table altogether. He didn't even look at the food anymore.

MAN 1. How did he sustain himself?

WOMAN 1. I don't know. He lost lots of weight. He looked anorexic. He slept sitting up. That was weird, too. He would be sitting with his back straight up against the headboard all night. I couldn't sleep with him doing that.

MAN 1. He looks healthy and normal.

WOMAN 1. He didn't eat for a year and a half.

MAN 1. I guess he's eating now.

WOMAN 2. I think it's strange that there is no hint of food being served at his wedding reception.

MAN 1. They're still making speeches. I'm sure the food is coming.

WOMAN 2. Everyone must be starving by now.

WOMAN 1. He likes colored towels. Personally, I like white towels. But he likes colored ones, so I gave him a really nice set of towels as a wedding gift.

WOMAN 2. Why did you do that?

WOMAN 1. I guess I still love him.

WOMAN 2. You stop doing that. It'll only make you crazy. Some things in your life are gone, and you have to accept it. You know how you wake up some mornings remembering your dream, and by the time you're having your breakfast, you've already forgotten your dream? Even though nothing memorable happened between when you remembered your dream and when you forgot it, the dream is gone forever. No matter how hard you try to remember, it'll never come back to you.

MAN 2. This is a strange, random table.

MAN 1 (*turning to Asian Woman at the table*). Hello. I'm a friend of a second cousin of the bride. Where are you from?

IMAGE 3.8 **Long Island, New York, the present. A wedding reception.**
Kaytie Morris, Kate Costello, Mark Krawczyk (from left to right).
Photograph by Russell Parkman.

ASIAN WOMAN. Do you mean who do I know?

MAN 1. OK. Who do you know and where are you from?

ASIAN WOMAN. I'm not sure. (*To Sophia*) Are we at the right wedding reception?

Sophia shrugs to indicate she does not know.

MAN 1. The dress you're wearing, it's so . . . so *delicate*.

ASIAN WOMAN. . . . Thank you.

MAN 1. I once watched a documentary on kimono making. You know, right? You're Japanese, right?

ASIAN WOMAN. Well . . .

MAN 1. In the documentary, they showed these . . . *delicate* silk pieces being hand-painted by craftsmen. Hand-painted.

There were six people working on one small section, and it must have taken them twenty hours to do that.

ASIAN WOMAN. This dress? This wasn't hand-painted. This was mass-produced. Polyester. I got it at an outlet for sixty per cent off.

MAN 1. But you know what I'm talking about, right? Are you from Japan? I love Japan.

ASIAN WOMAN. You've been there, then?

MAN 1. No, but I know a lot about the culture. Many of my friends are Japanese. The women, they are so . . .

Asian Woman and Man 1 speak simultaneously.

ASIAN WOMAN. Delicate?

MAN 1. Proper.

ASIAN WOMAN. I see.

MAN 1. A friend of mine who lives in New Jersey is married to a Japanese woman. She has the most *delicate* things at their home. Her teapots are beautiful.

ASIAN WOMAN. They must have been hand-carried from China on the Silk Road by her great-great-grandfather.

MAN 1. You have those, too?

ASIAN WOMAN. . . . Yes, I have one in my bag. I'll show it to you later.

MAN 1. Yukiko. My friend's wife's name is Yukiko. Do you know her? It means Flower Child.

ASIAN WOMAN. Actually, Yukiko may mean Snow Child. It doesn't mean Flower Child. That would be Hanako.

MAN 1. No, no, it means Flower Child. Yukiko.

ASIAN WOMAN. Fine.

MAN 1. Your dress reminded me of something she would wear. She's smaller than you.

ASIAN WOMAN. Is she like a lotus flower?

MAN 1. She is a wonderful cook. She makes beautiful dishes. I love Japanese food.

ASIAN WOMAN. I'm a lesbian.

MAN 1. What?

ASIAN WOMAN. You know, a lesbian. No flower. This is my date.

MAN 1 (*doubtful*). Are you from Japan?

ASIAN WOMAN (*ignores Man 1's question*). Meet my date. Sophia.

Asian Woman and Sophia kiss tenderly.

MAN 1. Oh, sure, good. Nice to meet you.

SOPHIA. I'm from Brighton Beach. But my grandparents are from Russia. Are you from somewhere?

MAN 1. What do you mean?

SOPHIA. Good for you!

ANTON (*confused*). I'm from Russia.

ASIAN WOMAN. You don't have to be from anywhere. You can just be here, like this other person. Jack.

MAN 1. My name isn't Jack.

ASIAN WOMAN. It isn't?

Man 1 does not quite grasp the situation and, peeved, turns away.

ANTON. I'm really from Russia.

SOPHIA. Are you a friend of the bride or groom?

ANTON. Neither. I'm just visiting. This seemed an inviting party, and there was an unoccupied chair. Are they going to serve food?

ASIAN WOMAN. I assume so, but they have to do a lot of things before then. Speeches and toasts. It'll be a while before we get to eat. You can have some bread if you like.

ANTON. American bread is dreadful.

ASIAN WOMAN. Yeah. It isn't really bread. It's an amalgamation of complex chemicals and bleach. That's why it lasts for months. It's comforting to people to have the assurance that the food they consume won't rot in their stomach before they digest it.

SOPHIA. I've never heard anything like that about any people. Where did you hear this?

ASIAN WOMAN. I don't have to hear it somewhere. It's my opinion.

SOPHIA. Then you have to qualify it as your opinion. You can't pontificate your opinions as if they're facts.

ANTON. In my opinion, Russian bread is better. They also have nice bread in France. The bread is really good in Germany, in my opinion.

SOPHIA. Are you traveling the world eating bread?

ANTON. I've done some traveling.

ASIAN WOMAN. What do you do?

ANTON. I'm a doctor. And a writer. Doctor first. What do you do?

ASIAN WOMAN. I'm a teacher. I teach high school in the city.

SOPHIA. I haven't done much yet.

ASIAN WOMAN. She's a writer.

ANTON. *Chto vy pishete?*

SOPHIA. I don't really speak Russian. I'm sorry. I'm not a writer either. But I'm writing a short story about my great-great-grandmother. She became an heiress to a large fabric factory in Russia in the late nineteenth century. Her name was Sophia. I was named after her.

ANTON. I met an heiress to a fabric factory once. I met a great many people. They're all dead now.

SOPHIA. I think my great-great-grandmother was gay. She never married, but adopted five children. Apparently she wanted to make sure that she had many grandchildren. But when the revolution happened, her property was confiscated, so her grandchildren didn't inherit her legacy. Everyone in the family gradually left her in her old age. The only friend she had was the town doctor. I think she was Sophia's lover. Her name was Natasha or Nadya, something like that. She began living in Sophia's house when she came to town after her studies in St. Petersburg. My parents think somehow they caused me to be gay by naming me after Sophia.

ANTON. Why wouldn't your parents want you to be gay? Gay is good.

SOPHIA. Yes, gay is good. (*Confused pause.*) Gay—homosexual.

ANTON. Oh yes, yes, of course.

ASIAN WOMAN. Do you practice medicine in Russia?

ANTON. I do. I treat mostly peasants. I've treated prisoners in Sakhalin Island.

ASIAN WOMAN. Where is that?

ANTON. Near Japan.

ASIAN WOMAN. I'm not really from there.

ANTON. No, truly. It's next to Japan. I saw Japan from a ship before I returned to Moscow. I wanted to go to Japan, but there was a cholera epidemic going on there.

ASIAN WOMAN (*doubtful*). A cholera epidemic?

SOPHIA. So Sakhalin. What did you see there?

ANTON Starving children, concubines of prison guards who were as young as thirteen, pregnant girls no older than fifteen. Girls there begin prostituting at twelve, sometimes before they start menstruation. The children were filthy, covered with rashes and were neglected altogether. Is life better for the oppressed and the poor now? Here?

ASIAN WOMAN. I think there is progress. We don't think about it very much because most of us are not the people who make the real difference in the world. Most of us don't notice anything because we're not trying to change the world. We're just benefiting from the changes other people have made.

SOPHIA. That's because as soon as you leave school, you're frantic, involved in buying real estate or thinking about buying real estate—

ANTON. Involved with the peasants, scientific farming—

SOPHIA. Reading the *New York Times*—

ANTON. Reading *Herald of Europe*—

SOPHIA. Trying to stop telemarketers from calling you and marching in the gay pride parade—

ANTON. Making speeches and writing to cabinet ministers—

SOPHIA. Making decisions to have babies or not to have babies before the time is up—

ANTON. Fighting evil and applauding good—

SOPHIA. After a while, you get weary.

ANTON. I think what is most strange is that instead of thinking about death, we live doing absolutely everything else as if we're never going to die. Yet, everything we do is driven by the fear of death. We eat and drink, talk about morality and literary criticism, fall in love, get married, have children, have name-day parties, have wedding receptions, all because we are afraid to die.

SOPHIA. But what else can anyone do?

ANTON. I don't know. I thought you might have the answer.

SOPHIA. Me?

ANTON. I don't mean *you*. I mean you, this century, this generation.

ASIAN WOMAN. We all strive to delay death as long as possible. We absolutely refuse to let our grandparents die. If one of them dies at age ninety-nine while undergoing a surgery for the fifth hip replacement, we sue the hospital.

SOPHIA. Do you know that medical malpractice is the sixth leading cause of death in this country? Even if a person is two hundred, the medical profession has no right to harm her.

ANTON. What do you mean, malpractice?

Anton is ignored during the argument.

ASIAN WOMAN. I don't disagree with that, except people who live to be two hundred are not the homeless people with no health insurance. While the rich greedily extend their lives, the entire economy is conspiring to trim the life expectancies of the poor. Capitalism is killing the poor with fake American Dreams, sweet and fat ones they can eat at their neighborhood McDonald's, next to a toxic dumpsite.

SOPHIA. Is this your opinion or is it based on facts?

ANTON (*trying to interrupt*). What are the other five causes of death?

ASIAN WOMAN. You can see the truth about humanity if you really look. I just think we have not earned the right to be extending specific individual lives. We have to first think about caring for society as a whole. Before we invent immortality for the rich, I think the poor need to get their hearing aids.

SOPHIA. You're so extreme. It's unavoidable that the privileged will first benefit from societal advances, but everyone will eventually benefit from progress.

ASIAN WOMAN. Is this your opinion or a fact?

ANTON (*trying again*). Consumption?

SOPHIA. I agree that it's not fair. But would you rather have equal but mediocre medical care for every person, or would you rather have the most excellent medical technology available in the hopes that someday everyone will have access to it?

ASIAN WOMAN. The trickle-down theory. The American Dream: you don't have it, but the fact that there are others who have lots means you can have it too in the future. So hold off on a revolution and go out and buy happiness at Walmart. Equality and a better future should not be mutually exclusive.

SOPHIA. I wish you'd say something new sometime. And you're very *indelicate* to be ranting and raving. It's not proper behavior for a Japanese woman.

ASIAN WOMAN. You're a prick.

SOPHIA. Thank you, my love. (*A gesture of humorous affection.*)

ANTON. We all need access to a dignified death. I was forty-four. I had a glass of champagne in my hand.

MAN 1 (*suddenly excited about what he heard*). Champagne! Do you have champagne in Russia?

ANTON (*in good humor*). Of course.

MAN 1. What about mixed drinks, like Long Island Iced Tea?

ANTON. That too. In Russia is everything. Here in America is nothing.

MAN 1. What about steaks? Do you have big steaks in Russia?

ANTON. Of course. Russia—everything.

MAN 2. I don't think they're going to serve steak. These days, educated people are more sensitive than that. Usually they serve chicken. The least offensive option.

ASIAN WOMAN. I don't eat chicken. They're abused. They grow up and spend their entire life standing in a little box until they're slaughtered.

WOMAN 2. I hope they serve lobster. I'm in the mood for lobster. It's very good.

MAN 1. Lobster! I bet you don't have lobster in Russia!

ANTON. Russia. Everything.

MAN 1. Mafia, you have. Are you aware that the New York City Taxi Association or whatever it's called is controlled by the Russian Mafia?

WOMAN 1. Russia seems very romantic. I love *Doctor Zhivago*.

WOMAN 2. I hope they serve food. Any kind of food.

MAN 2. What do people who attend wedding receptions usually expect?

WOMAN 2. I would say a five-course meal. They'll probably serve chicken cutlets and fruit stew.

MAN 2. Fruit what?

WOMAN 2. Fruit cup. What did I say?

WOMAN 1. So first we have salad, then soup. Minestrone soup, then an appetizer, something like baked clams or stuffed mushrooms, and then an entrée, which should come with rice pilaf or some fancy potatoes and string beans or something thin and long like that. I'm so hungry.

SOPHIA. Here, have some bread.

WOMAN 1. Oh, thank you. I love bread. (*Eating, almost moved to tears, to Sophia*) I used to bake bread for him. This is nice bread.

SOPHIA (*sympathetic*). I'm glad you like it.

ASIAN WOMAN (*to Sophia and Anton*). So what were we talking about?

Sophia and Anton speak simultaneously.

SOPHIA. How to live.

ANTON. How to die.

SOPHIA. How to let live.

ANTON. My dears, there is only one way to live, that is to live as a free person and let others be free. We must press the slave out of us one drop at a time until we wake up one morning and realize finally that in our veins flows not the blood of a slave but of a free person. Sophia, your great-great-grandmother was a slave once, a slave to her guilt.

SOPHIA. Guilt?

ANTON. It was a hard time for common factory workers. Sophia was responsible for their misery, not directly, but indirectly, and she felt powerless to change things. She had to wait for the times to change.

SOPHIA. But the times changed brutally.

ANTON. I imagine she was relieved and hopeful when the factory was taken away from her. She was probably vilified for having been wealthy once, but it was better than carrying a stone in her heart. She thought Eden was coming, a fair world was coming.

SOPHIA. It was all a lie. Bloodbaths came.

ANTON. I believe that an enormous proportion of property vested in a few individuals is dangerous to the rights and is destructive to the common happiness of mankind. They believed this. Not all was a lie. Then later, yes, lies and violence. Failures. My heart eternally broken.

SOPHIA. I'm sure Sophia's heart was broken to find out that she had to wait still, for a fairer world, and she would not live to see it.

ANTON. But freedom was in her by then, flowing through her blood. And now, here you are, a descendant of a free person. Four generations later. How does the world look to you? (*To Asian Woman*.) And to you?

ASIAN WOMAN. Most of the time, I feel powerless to change things, too. If I'm making any impact on the high school kids, I can't see it.

They still watch movies in which women wear no clothes, or are slapped around, or wear no clothes while being slapped around.

SOPHIA. I think that in a hundred years, people will look back at us and be horrified of the wars we fought, the discriminations we practiced, and the junk we collected.

ANTON. I see Eden is farther away. Ladies, we must continue to live, even though we're dying and won't live to see the day when our great-great-grandchildren reach Eden.

ASIAN WOMAN. I'm not a Christian.

SOPHIA. It's a metaphor.

ANTON. You're both smart and good and hardworking. And the time will come when the entire world has changed because of you, and everyone will be smart and good and hardworking.

SOPHIA. It's kind of you to say that.

WOMAN 2 (*referring to the ongoing party*). I think this one is the last speech. I see the waiters getting ready back there to bring out the food.

MAN 1. Attention everyone! It's the last speech!

WOMAN 1. I hope they'll be very happy.

MAN 2. Why?

WOMAN 1. I don't know. It seems like the right thing to wish.

WOMAN 2. Don't wish. It'll only make you crazy.

MAN 1. It's nice of you to wish that. We need nice women in the world. We're surrounded by a hostile, anti-democratic world now—we need personable people at wedding receptions.

ANTON. You think the world is hostile?

MAN 1. Oh, no. You guys are cool. That's in the past. We have bigger fish to fry over there in the Middle East.

ANTON. What?

WOMAN 2. Honey, don't get excited.

MAN 2. The word "personable" doesn't mean what you think it means.

MAN 1. What do you mean?

MAN 2. Do you know the meaning of the word?

MAN 1. You don't think I know what "personable" means?

MAN 2. How are you using it?

MAN 1. How do you think I'm using it?

WOMAN 1. Please stop asking questions.

ASIAN WOMAN. "Personable" means physically attractive. The word is often misused to mean friendly.

MAN 2. I was just about to say that!

WOMAN 1 (*in awe*). I didn't know that.

MAN 2. Yep.

MAN 1. I did.

WOMAN 1. You did what?

ASIAN WOMAN. He's saying that he knew the meaning of the word.

MAN 1. Of course, I knew. I was born here.

SOPHIA. Here? Good for you!

WOMAN 1. I don't feel very personable right now. I'm so very sad.

MAN 2. Maybe the groom will come over to say hello to you.

WOMAN 1. I don't think so. I don't think anyone is coming to this table. We're on the outer fringe of happiness. We are forgotten.

ASIAN WOMAN (*turning away from the rest of the table*). How has your visit been?

ANTON. My trip has been amusing. I expect I'll have two or three days that I'll remember forever with rapture or bitterness. Then it will have been all worthwhile. I will remember that we exchanged thoughts and I was comforted.

SOPHIA. Just think. Conversations like ours are taking place all over the world. I think my great-great-grandmother had a conversation like this with her lover. I like that.

ASIAN WOMAN (*to Anton*). What will you do now? After the wedding reception, I mean.

ANTON. Leave.

SOPHIA. To where?

ANTON. Why, wherever I like.

MAN 1. Here we go. Cheers!

MAN 2, WOMAN 1, WOMAN 2. Cheers! Cheers!

ANTON. I'll say goodbye now.

ASIAN WOMAN. Not waiting for the food? And the cake?

ANTON. I must go. You are both good, interesting people. I won't see you again, but I'll always be glad that I met you.

MAN 1. Everyone, raise your champagne glass!

PEOPLE. Cheers! Cheers!

ANTON. It has been a long time since I tasted champagne.

He clinks glasses with Sophia and Asian Woman and then savors a sip. The three look into each other's eyes.

Lights fade.

CHARACTERS

KATE CHOPIN	The author of the novel *The Awakening*
EDNA PONTELLIER	A mother of two boys, 26 years old
LÉONCE PONTELLIER	Edna's husband
ADÈLE RATIGNOLLE	A model wife and mother; a friend of Edna
MADAMOISELLE REISZ	An eccentric pianist, in her 40s
ALCÉE AROBIN	A young man with a reputation for being a playboy

SETTING

Always, and 1899

Everywhere, and Grand Isle and New Orleans

IMAGE 4.1 **With her book in hand, Kate Chopin looks back on her own life (Scene 27).**

Dale Soules. *Awakening*, Co-production by Crossing Jamaica Avenue, Dance Theater Workshop, and Performance Space 122, directed by Sonoko Kawahara, New York City, 2000 (All subsequent photographs of this play are of this production.)

Photograph by Sonoko Kawahara.

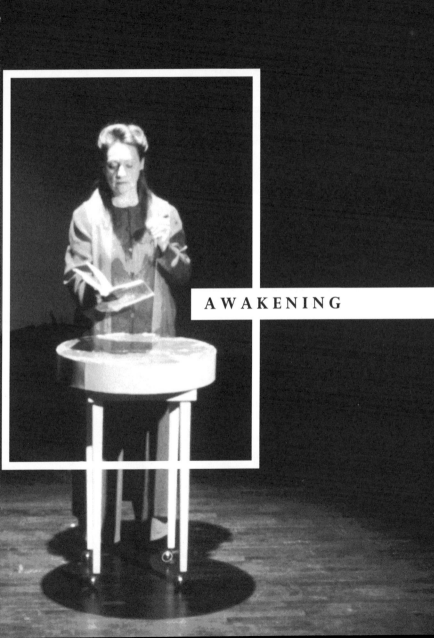

AWAKENING

The play functions on two levels: Kate Chopin contemplating her book *The Awakening*, and the narrative in the book. Both are real. Kate's presence is constant, then as well as now.

Some elements of the theatrical language that should be used to tell the story are not on the pages—music, movement, etc.—and are up to the director to imagine. There is about 50 minutes of text, but the performance should be about 75 minutes. The non-text time is open to visual elements, dance, and music/sound integrated with the text.

Original music has been composed for the songs by Daniel Sonenberg. The director may choose to use the existing music or commission a different composer.

AWAKENING

With Lyrics by Mark Campbell

PROLOGUE

Directed at the audience. Edna and Kate are not in the same place or time, but they share a universe. Throughout the play, the novel is both being written and already completed. Kate's presence is constant.

KATE. Let me prolong this moment,
before the last word is written,
so that I can know you without fear.
Let me postpone my doubt today.

EDNA. Let me prolong this moment,
my last moment of illusion.
I am a melange of things lost
things that cannot be obtained—
but with this act, I will return to the present,
to who I am now,
and release the memory of everything,
all that I suffered,
all that I am yet to suffer.

Another time and place, suspended in future memory.

EDNA. Robert, what have you been seeing and doing and feeling?

ROBERT. I've been seeing the waves and the white beach of Grand Isle. I've been working like a machine and feeling like a lost soul. There was nothing interesting. (*Pause.*) What have you been seeing and doing and feeling, Edna?

EDNA. I've been seeing the waves and the white beach of Grand Isle. I've been working like a machine and feeling like a lost soul. There was nothing interesting.

KATE. When I look up, one hundred years will have passed.

Robert disappears. Time travels to the past. The beginning of summer.

SCENE 1

Grand Isle. Summer. Léonce and Edna's cottage. Léonce is reading the paper on the porch. Edna and Robert come back from the beach.

LÉONCE. You are burned beyond recognition.

> *Looks at Edna as she holds up her hands and surveys them critically, drawing her sleeves up above the wrists. She silently reaches out to her husband Robert and he, understanding, takes her wedding ring from his vest pocket and drops it into her open palm. She puts it on.*

LÉONCE. I'm going over to Klein's Hotel to play a game of billiards. Come along, Robert.

ROBERT. I'd like to stay here and talk to your wife.

LÉONCE. Well, send him away when he bores you, Edna.

EDNA. Léonce, take the umbrella. Are you coming back for dinner?

> *Robert looks back, but is not sure. He does not answer. Edna understands. She fans herself; Robert smokes. Pause.*

ROBERT. What is it like where you come from?

EDNA. Beautiful. Old bluegrass country. When I walk into the ocean, it reminds me of a green meadow, a summer day in Kentucky.

KATE. The grass was higher than her waist, and walking through the field, the little girl threw out her arms as if she were swimming. Swimming endlessly.

EDNA. You?

ROBERT. I was born in New Orleans.

EDNA. It seems so far away. Life there . . . long ago.

ROBERT. It has only been two weeks. Summer in Grand Isle has just begun.

EDNA. Soon it will be autumn, and we will all be back in New Orleans.

ROBERT. Not so soon. Anyway, I'm going to Mexico. Fortune awaits me there. I will be free and independent in Mexico. No longer a clerk in New Orleans.

EDNA. When are you going?

ROBERT. Very soon.

Pause.

ROBERT. To find something. In Mexico. Something of my own.

Time passes. Edna and Robert are comfortable. There is no deep thought between them, just the laziness of the summer.

EDNA. I see Léonce is not coming back for dinner.

SCENE 2

Late at night. Léonce returns.

LÉONCE. Are you asleep already?

EDNA. It's late, Léonce.

LÉONCE. I forgot the bonbons and peanuts for the boys.

EDNA. They won't remember your promise in the morning.

LÉONCE. Are you asleep already?

EDNA. It's late.

LÉONCE. Already?

EDNA. Late.

Pause.

LÉONCE. I'm going to check on the boys.

Léonce Exits. There's a pause. He comes back.

LÉONCE. Raoul has a fever.

EDNA. Léonce, he has no fever.

LÉONCE. If it's not a mother's place to look after the children, whose on earth is it? I have my hands full with my brokerage business. I can't stay home to see that no harm comes to my children.

EDNA. He has no fever.

Léonce lights a cigar.

LÉONCE. You don't pay enough attention to the boys. Your children should be your first thought and your last.

Edna sits up on the edge of the bed, leaning her head on the pillow. Pause. Léonce puts out his cigar, gets into bed and falls asleep. Edna gets up, blows out the candle, and goes out to the porch. She stands still for a while. She then swats a mosquito off her arm, suddenly, violently. Kate goes through the same motion of swatting a mosquito.

KATE. I have a premonition, a sacrifice of my voice for one hundred years to come.

IMAGE 4.2 **After an argument with Léonce, Edna contemplates on her feelings of alienation. Kate is present though invisible to Edna.**
Margi Sharp (left), Dale Soules (right).
Photograph by Sonoko Kawahara.

The next morning.

LÉONCE. I'm returning to the city for business. I'll come back to the island on Saturday.

Léonce Kisses Edna's forehead tenderly, exits.

Time passes. Adèle enters. She is the picture of a perfect, beautiful wife–mother. Edna opens a box of chocolates and hands it to Adèle. She carefully chooses one and eats it.

ADÈLE. From your husband? Mr. Pontellier is the best husband in the world.

EDNA. I know.

Adèle sits in the rocking chair. Robert enters. Adèle takes out sewing materials. Time is stretched, and small events are omitted. Before and after Robert's entrance, an hour or more may have passed.

EDNA. . . . Winter clothes for your children? Adèle, it's still summer.

ADÈLE. You must think of the future.

EDNA. It's summer.

ADÈLE. Think of your children.

Adèle sews. Robert and Adèle speak to each other teasingly.

ROBERT. I was so in love with you last summer, and you treated me cruelly.

ADÈLE. I didn't want to make my husband jealous.

ROBERT. You knew I adored you, and you let me. It was "Robert, come, go, stand up, sit down, do this, do that."

ADÈLE. I never had to ask! You were always there under my feet like a troublesome cat.

Edna begins sketching Adèle. Robert watches. After a while, he rests his head against Edna's arm. Edna pushes him away. Edna continues sketching. Adèle is sewing. Again Robert rests his head against Edna's arm. Pause. Edna pushes him away.

ADÈLE. . . . May I see it?

Adèle and Robert look at the drawing.

ROBERT. Beautiful, isn't it?

ADÈLE. Yes. But it does not look like me.

EDNA. I know.

ROBERT. It's beautiful.

ADÈLE. Yes. I adore it.

Edna crumples the drawing—not, however, a violent act. Time passes. Adèle exits—not a realistic exit. Again, small events are omitted preceding her exit. The exit is already a memory in Robert and Edna's minds.

ROBERT. Are you going swimming?

EDNA. No.

Pause.

EDNA. I'm tired.

ROBERT. The water must be splendid. It won't hurt you. Come.

Edna and Robert walk away together.

SCENE 3A: Time Break Scene

In these "Time Breaks," moments from the future or the past invade the present. Some of the text is projected on a wall as well.

EDNA. Let me see the letter.

REISZ. No.

EDNA. Let me see the letter.

REISZ. What time do you have to be home?

EDNA. Time doesn't concern me.

REISZ. It's growing late.

EDNA. Let me see the letter.

Another day at Grand Isle.

EDNA. Let's go down to the beach. Leave the children.

ADÈLE. Leave the children?

EDNA. Just this once.

ADÈLE. Shall we invite Robert?

EDNA. No. Just you and me. Alone.

> *They walk down to the beach and sit. Edna fans both herself and Adèle. Pause.*

ADÈLE. Blinding.

EDNA. The sun is reflecting off the ocean.

ADÈLE. The heat.

EDNA. Yes.

> *Silence. Fanning.*

ADÈLE. What are you thinking?

> *Edna looks at Adèle surprised, as if her question is the strangest thing.*

EDNA. Nothing.

> *A slight pause.*

EDNA. No, not nothing.

> *Pause.*

> *Dialogue directed at the audience. Edna and Kate stand next to each other, though they are not in the same space in reality. Their dialogue is not interrupted but continuous.*

EDNA. I was thinking of a summer day in Kentucky long ago—

KATE. A summer day in Kentucky—

EDNA. Remembering a meadow that seemed as big as the ocean—

KATE. The grass was higher than her waist—

EDNA. I was little then. I could see only the stretch of green before me—

KATE. Walking through the field, the little girl threw out her arm as if she were swimming—

EDNA. I felt that even if I walked forever, I would never come to the end of it—

KATE. Swimming endlessly.

ADÈLE. Where were you going?

EDNA. I don't remember.

ADÈLE. Were you frightened or pleased?

EDNA. I don't know.

Pause. Adèle senses a disturbance in Edna's heart.

ADÈLE. Edna, are you enjoying yourself at Grand Isle?

EDNA. Yes. Very much.

Adèle holds Edna's hand and caresses it tenderly. Edna is at first apprehensive about her affection, but soon feels coaxed to reveal a secret.

Pause.

EDNA. . . . I was also thinking about an actor I admired before I married Léonce. A tragedian with sad eyes. I haven't thought about him in many years. I was very young then. I had his picture framed on my desk, and every night before going to bed, I would kiss the cold glass with great passion. Then I heard he became engaged. I was just one of many women who loved him from afar. I was nothing, nothing, nothing to him. There was no hope. That summer I met Léonce. In time, I stopped thinking about the actor.

Edna rests her head on Adèle's shoulder, almost intoxicated.

KATE. In time I stopped thinking about disappointments.
I write down the true parts of love,
but the words run away from me
off the pages into the next century
will they find you?

Robert approaches Edna and Adèle.

ROBERT. There, I found you.

IMAGE 4.3 **Adèle is content with devoting her life to her husband and children, and she is concerned about Edna's unfeminine nature. Kate is present.**
Sophia Skiles (left), Dale Soules (right).
Photograph by Sonoko Kawahara.

SCENE 4A: Time Break Scene

ADÈLE. Blinding.

EDNA. The sun is reflecting off the ocean.

ADÈLE. The heat.

EDNA. Yes, the heat.

ADÈLE. What are you thinking?

EDNA. Blinding.

SCENE 5

Immediately after. Adèle and Robert walk back from the beach. Adèle is leaning on Robert's arm.

ADÈLE. Do me a favor, Robert.

ROBERT. Granted. As many as you like.

ADÈLE. I only ask for one. Let Edna alone.

ROBERT. Why?

ADÈLE. She is not one of us. She is not like us. We come from French ancestry. She is only American. She might make the unfortunate blunder of taking you seriously.

ROBERT. Why shouldn't she take me seriously? Am I a comedian, a clown, a jack-in-the-box? I hope she does take me seriously.

ADÈLE. Enough, Robert. If your attention to any married woman here were convincing, we would not think of you as a gentleman.

ROBERT. I'm just a man.

ADÈLE. You're not thinking about what you're saying.

They walk in silence. Robert becomes serious and melancholy.

ROBERT. You made one mistake, Adèle. There is no possibility of Mrs. Pontellier taking me seriously. You should warn me against taking myself seriously.

SCENE 6

At an evening gathering. Mademoiselle Reisz is an eccentric artist. People are at the same time suspicious of and intimidated by her.

ROBERT. Would you play the piano . . .

REISZ. I don't play for idiots.

ROBERT. For Mrs. Pontellier?

REISZ. . . . For Edna, yes.

She plays the piano. This moment is expressed with movement. Edna is greatly moved.

REISZ. Well, my dear, how do you like my music?

Edna is speechless. Everyone is moved by Mademoiselle Reisz's piano playing.

ROBERT. Let's go to the ocean, everyone! Let's swim under the mystic moon at this mystic hour!

*Léonce and Edna walk, followed by Adèle and Robert. Edna enters the
water and swims.*

EDNA. How easy. It is nothing.
    The water shields my solitude,
    dissolves into my body and emerges again
    again and again
    as I reach for the unlimited and lose myself.
    She swims.

KATE. As I reach for the unlimited and lose myself,
    A wave of loneliness threatens to keep me in a haunted chamber.
    I read over my words. I know this is my best work.
    Edna has a vision of death.

EDNA. I have come too far from the shore.
    What if I can't go back to the people I left there?
    Black salt, bitter nausea, memory all consuming my heart.
    Death devours you, your insides burning,
    your tears starved, your hope withered.
    She struggles back to the shore, leans on Léonce.

EDNA. I thought I was going to perish out there alone.

LÉONCE. You were not so very far, my dear. I was watching you.
    Edna prepares to leave the beach.

ADÈLE. You are not going, my dear?

EDNA. I am. Good night.
    She leaves.

ADÈLE. Sometimes I think Edna is capricious.

LÉONCE. I know she is. Sometimes, not often.
    *Robert runs after Edna. Edna is edgy, affected by the earlier piano
    music and her vision of death.*

EDNA. Did you think I was afraid in the dark?

ROBERT. No, I knew you weren't afraid.

EDNA. Then why did you come?

ROBERT. I didn't think of it.

EDNA. Think of what?

ROBERT. Of anything.

EDNA. I'm very tired.

ROBERT. I know you are.

EDNA. You don't know anything about it. Did you hear Mademoiselle Reisz's piano?

ROBERT. Of course. I asked her to play.

EDNA. I mean really hear it. Really hear it.

Pause.

EDNA. I wonder if any night on earth will ever again be like this one.

She gets into a hammock.

IMAGE 4.4 **Edna wants to stay outside on a summer night, while Léonce tries to coax her to come to bed.**

Charles Parnell (left), Margi Sharp (right).

Photograph by Sonoko Kawahara.

ROBERT. Shall I stay with you until Mr. Pontellier comes home?

EDNA. If you wish.

Robert smokes in silence. Long pause. The sound of field frogs swells. The first felt throbbing of desire. Voices are heard approaching. Robert gets up.

ROBERT. Good night.

Edna does not answer. Robert exits.

KATE. I write down the tingling of fingertips
candlelight's burning desire
heart's tremors
a night marked with a thirst
wishing to touch
wishing to touch
wishing to touch
come with me, come with me,
across the ocean and time
Come with me/

EDNA (*overlapping*). Come with me.

SCENE 8

Immediately after. Léonce enters.

LÉONCE. What are you doing out here, Edna?

Edna does not reply.

LÉONCE. Are you asleep?

EDNA. No.

LÉONCE. Do you know it's past one o'clock?

He goes into the house.

LÉONCE. Edna!

EDNA. Don't wait for me.

LÉONCE. You will catch a cold out there.

EDNA. I'm not cold.

Pause.

LÉONCE. Are you coming in soon, Edna?

EDNA. No. I'm going to stay out here.

LÉONCE. I can't permit you to stay out there all night. You must come into the house instantly.

EDNA. Léonce, go to bed. I don't want to go in. Don't speak to me like that again.

Pause. Léonce comes out with wine.

LÉONCE. Would you like some wine?

EDNA. No, thank you.

Léonce sits on the rocker and drinks his wine. He smokes a cigar. He pours another glass of wine. It is at the same time awkward and peaceful.

LÉONCE. Would you like some wine?

EDNA. No, thank you.

Léonce drinks the wine and smokes another cigar. Pause. Edna gets up and walks toward the house, turns around and speaks to Léonce as if nothing is wrong. He in turn answers her affectionately.

EDNA. Are you coming in, Léonce?

LÉONCE. Yes, dear. Just as soon as I finish my cigar.

SCENE 8A: Time Break Scene

EDNA. I'm becoming an artist. Think of it.

REISZ. An artist? You have pretensions.

EDNA. Why pretensions?

REISZ. Are your wings strong?

EDNA. Do you think I cannot become an artist?

REISZ. Are your wings strong?

EDNA. Not become an artist?

REISZ. You have pretensions.

Sunday morning. Edna goes to get Robert at his cottage.

EDNA. Robert, let's go to Chêniére for the church service. The boat is waiting. Hurry.

ROBERT. I haven't even had my morning coffee yet. You lack forethought, Edna.

EDNA. Isn't it enough that I thought of taking the boat to Chêniére with you?

They are in a boat crossing the bay. Long pause.

ROBERT (*flushed and excited, whispering eagerly*). Let us go to Grande Terre tomorrow.

EDNA. What shall we do there?

ROBERT. Anything. And the next day or the next we can sail to the Bayou Brulow.

EDNA. What shall we do there?

ROBERT. Anything.

EDNA. Where else can we go?

ROBERT. Anywhere.

Time jumps. At Chêniére, some events—getting to the church, the service, a fatigued Edna leaving the church—are omitted.

EDNA. My eyes ache. I couldn't have stayed through the service.

ROBERT. Come over to Madame Antonio's. You can rest there.

At Madame Antonio's. Edna loosens her clothes, gets into bed, and sleeps. Time passes. Robert is reading a book. Edna awakes. Gets dressed. Discovers bread and wine. She takes a bite of the bread and drinks some wine. She goes out to find Robert.

EDNA. How many years have I slept? The whole island seems changed. A new race of beings must have sprung up. When did everyone die? When did people disappear from Earth?

ROBERT. You have slept precisely one hundred years. I was left here to guard your chamber. For one hundred years I have been under this tree reading a book.

KATE. *The Awakening* was published one hundred years ago.

EDNA. I wonder if Léonce will be uneasy.

ROBERT. Of course not. He knows we took the boat here for the service.

EDNA. Where is Madame Antonio?

ROBERT. Gone to visit some friends. I am to take you back to Grand Isle in her son's boat whenever you are ready.

EDNA. Shall we go right away?

ROBERT. The sun isn't as low as it will be in two hours.

EDNA. The sun will be gone in two hours.

They sit under an orange tree for a long time.

ROBERT. (*Song*) Waking
I watched you as you slept.
An hour slipped by.
The waves rumbled in and out,
a pair of swallows rose and dove
And never left the sky,
I marveled as you slept
How peaceful you were.
A spider crept across your hand.
A leaf alighted on your brow
And still you did not stir.
And I kept thinking
I must find a way
I must find a way
For you to have that sea
For you to have that sky
I must find a way
For you to have this tree
And all the peace of this day
Forever, forever.

Back at Grand Isle. Adèle has been taking care of Edna's children.

ADÈLE. Etienne was very naughty, but Raoul was a good boy. Mr. Pontellier was uneasy at first, but he was assured by the people at the service that you were only overcome with fatigue. He was about to cross the bay to get you. He is the best husband in the world.

EDNA. I know.

ADÈLE. He went to Klein's to look up some cotton broker. About securities or stocks or bonds or something of the sort. I don't remember. I must go. My husband is alone, and he despises being alone. Good night.

EDNA. Good night.

Adèle exits.

ROBERT. I should be going.

EDNA. Do you know we have been together the whole day, Robert? Since early this morning?

ROBERT. All but one hundred years when you were sleeping.

KATE. All but one hundred years.

SCENE 11

The next evening (takes place without pause after the previous scene). The passage of time is omitted between the interactions. Léonce and Adèle remain on stage frozen during Edna's last interaction with Robert.

LÉONCE. Did you hear that Robert is going to Mexico?

Pause. Edna is bewildered.

EDNA. When is he going?

LÉONCE. Tonight. We shall miss him.

Léonce freezes. Adèle enters.

ADÈLE. We shall miss him. Madame Lebrun would like us to sit with her until Robert departs.

EDNA. No. I don't feel like it.

ADÈLE. It doesn't look friendly, my dear.

EDNA. I hate surprises. The idea of Robert starting off in such a ridiculously sudden way!

ADÈLE. Yes. It was showing us all—you especially—very little consideration.

EDNA. You go on, Adèle. Please tell Robert's mother that I'm not feeling well.

Adèle freezes. Robert enters.

ROBERT. Aren't you feeling well?

EDNA. Are you going right away?

ROBERT. In twenty minutes.

EDNA. How long will you be gone?

ROBERT. Forever perhaps.

EDNA. In case it shouldn't be forever, how long will it be?

ROBERT. I don't know.

EDNA. I don't understand. You never said a word to me about it this morning.

ROBERT. Don't part angrily from me .

EDNA. I've grown used to having you with me.

ROBERT. I've said all along that I was going to Mexico.

EDNA. Robert.

ROBERT. You won't completely forget me, will you?

EDNA. Write to me.

ROBERT. Goodbye.

Robert Exits.

KATE. Silence on my path, memory at my back, all the sorrows and grandeurs, discoveries I make, glorious insignificance, dreams imprinted on strangers' history, I write down. I am a traveler.

ALCÉE. Tomorrow?

EDNA. No.

ALCÉE. Day after?

EDNA. No, no.

ALCÉE. Please don't refuse me.

EDNA. Good night. I don't like you.

ALCÉE. Can you forgive me?

EDNA. I wish you to go, please.

SCENE 12

The end of the summer. Edna runs into Mademoiselle Reisz at the beach.

REISZ. Do you miss your friend greatly?

EDNA. Mademoiselle Reisz. Yes. I miss Robert very much.

REISZ. When do you leave?

EDNA. In two weeks. You?

REISZ. Next Monday.

EDNA. It has been a pleasant summer, hasn't it?

REISZ. Rather pleasant, if it hadn't been for the mosquitoes, and Madame Lebrun's awful cooking, and Adèle Ratignolle's dreadful piano playing, and her husband's dull conversations.

EDNA. Yes, it has been pleasant.

SCENE 13

The story moves to New Orleans.

KATE. My editors ask me: What is the plot what is the plot? What is the plot? I'm not interested in the social realism practiced by men. I'm interested in human impulses, the history between women and men and the journey to gain knowledge about one another that we have been on since the beginning of time.

My second novel, *Young Dr. Gosse and Theo*, was turned down by nine publishers. When the tenth rejection letter arrived, I destroyed the manuscript.

It's fall. Edna and Léonce are having dinner.

LÉONCE. Have you had many callers today?

EDNA. Yes. I found their cards when I got back. I was out.

LÉONCE. Out! What could have taken you out on Tuesday, your reception day?

EDNA. I felt like going out.

LÉONCE. My dear, I should think you'd understand by now that people don't do such things.

The following speech by Léonce represents the entire evening's conversation and events—Edna's responses to his comments and the maid coming in to serve different courses are omitted.

LÉONCE. This soup is really impossible. It's appalling that that woman hasn't learned to make a decent soup. The fish is scorched. I will not eat this. The roast is dry. And those vegetables! I spend money enough in this house for at least one meal a day which a man can eat to retain his self-respect. You must look after your household staff better.

He stands up. Back to real time.

EDNA. Where are you going?

LÉONCE. I'm going to get my dinner at the club. Good night.

He exits.

Edna paces. She tears her handkerchief to ribbons. She takes her wedding ring, throws it on the floor, and stomps on it. Pause. Then she picks up the ring and slips it on her finger.

Adèle's house. Adèle is pregnant.

EDNA. Perhaps I will be able to paint your picture someday. (*Shows Adèle her sketches.*) I want to paint again. What do you think of them? Do you think I should take it up again and study some more?

ADÈLE. Your talent is immense, dear. (*Surveys the drawings.*) Immense, I tell you.

EDNA (*realizing the superficiality of this interaction*). You take them.

ADÈLE. Are you sure? Thank you, my dear, they are lovely. Really. Lovely.

Léonce enters. Adèle keeps looking at the drawings, but we are no longer in her house. Léonce and Edna are back in their house.

LÉONCE. You are a wife and mother. Before you spend days in your studio painting you should think about taking care of your family.

EDNA. I feel like painting. Maybe I won't always feel like it.

LÉONCE. In God's name, paint! But don't let the family suffer for it. Look at Madame Ratignolle; she keeps up her music, but she doesn't let everything else go. And she is more of a musician than you are a painter.

EDNA. Adèle isn't a musician, and I'm not a painter. It isn't because of painting I let things go.

LÉONCE. Because of what, then?

EDNA. I don't know.

SCENE 15

At Mademoiselle Reisz's apartment in the city. Edna's first visit since Grand Isle.

REISZ. So you remember me at last. I said to myself, ah, bah! She will never come.

EDNA. Did you want me to come?

REISZ. I sometimes thought: she promised as those women in society always do, without meaning it. She will not come. For I really don't believe you like me, Edna.

EDNA. I don't know whether I like you or not.

MademoiselleReisz likes Edna's honesty. She is pleased.

REISZ. I got a letter from your friend.

EDNA. My friend?

REISZ. Yes, your friend Robert. He wrote to me from Mexico.

EDNA. He wrote to *you*?

REISZ. Yes, to me. Why not? Though the letter might as well have been sent to you. It was nothing but Mrs. Pontellier from beginning to end.

EDNA. Let me see it.

REISZ. No. But he asked that I play for you Chopin's 'Impromptu' if you should visit. It's his favorite.

EDNA. Let me see the letter.

REISZ. No.

EDNA. Then play the 'Impromptu' for me.

REISZ. It is growing late. What time do you have to be home?

EDNA. Time doesn't concern me. Your question is rude. Play the 'Impromptu'.

Mademoiselle Reisz gets up, gives Edna the letter, and plays the piano while Edna reads it. The shadows deepen in the room. While the piano is still playing, Edna drops the letter on the floor and exits silently. Kate picks up the letter. Mademoiselle Reisz stops playing.

REISZ. Poor fool.

KATE. I read over my words. I know this is my best work. In one hundred years, you will know my name.

At Léonce and Edna's house. Léonce is leaving for a long stay in New York.

LÉONCE. I'm sorry you are not coming to New York with me. Won't you at least go to my mother's with the children?

EDNA. I can't stay in the country, my dear. The children will be fine with your mother. And you will be able to concentrate on your business in New York without having to worry about me.

LÉONCE. What will you do alone in New Orleans?

EDNA. I will paint from morning to night.

LÉONCE. Won't you be lonely alone? Perhaps you'll miss me a little.

EDNA. Léonce, if it weren't for me, you'd never have any annoyances in your life, would you?

LÉONCE. You are my treasure. Sometimes I just don't understand you, that's all.

EDNA. You ask for the impossible, my friend.

LÉONCE. Take good care of yourself.

EDNA. Yes, my dear, good friend.

Léonce kisses Edna's forehead. Edna finds it difficult to let him go. Léonce exits. Edna moves into Mademoiselle Reisz's apartment.

EDNA. I am becoming an artist. Think of it!

REISZ. Ah, an artist! You have pretensions, Madame.

EDNA. Why pretensions? Do you think I cannot become an artist?

REISZ. Artists must possess the courageous soul. The brave soul. The soul that dares and defies.

KATE. A moment of fear.
Black letters connecting the disbeliefs of years gone by.
What if they dissolve into air, never to emerge again?
In death, the words driven by the fear of death may die again.
I am Kate Chopin. Do I think I cannot be an artist?

SCENE 17

*Edna is painting. It begins perhaps with realistic gestures and develops
into abstract movement. Alcée comes in like a shadow at the end.*

EDNA. Do I think I cannot be an artist?

SCENE 18

*Edna's house. Night. Edna and Alcée are counting money won from the
races.*

ALCÉE. You won so much money. Our dear friend Mrs. Highcamp
was jealous.

EDNA. The racehorses were intimate friends in my childhood. I live
when I'm at the races.

ALCÉE. Only at the races?

EDNA. No . . . Always. No, not always.

ALCÉE. When, then?

EDNA. You tell me first.

ALCÉE. Now. I live forever, now.

EDNA. No further than now?

ALCÉE. But forever all the same.

Pause.

ALCÉE. My life would have been so different if I met you earlier. I
was a bad boy.

He draws up his cuff to show a scar.

ALCÉE. I got this scar from a saber cut in a duel.

EDNA. When?

ALCÉE. When I was nineteen. In Paris.

Edna touches his scar, then arises hastily and walks away.

EDNA. The sight of a wound or a scar always sickens me. I shouldn't
have looked at it.

ALCÉE. I'm sorry. It never occurred to me that it might be repulsive.

He follows her and stands close to her. They look at each other for a long time.

ALCÉE. I'll say good night now. Would you go to the races again?

EDNA. No. I've had enough of the races. I need to paint when there is light.

ALCÉE. Yes. You promised to show me your work. When may I come to your studio? Tomorrow?

EDNA. No.

ALCÉE. Day after?

EDNA. No, no.

ALCÉE. Please don't refuse me.

EDNA. Good night. Why don't you go after you've said good night already? I don't like you.

ALCÉE. I'm sorry I offended you. Can you forgive me?

EDNA. My manner must have misled you in some way, Alcée. I wish you to go, please.

ALCÉE. Your manner has not misled me, Mrs. Pontellier. My emotions have done that. I couldn't help it.

He kisses Edna's hand, and then exits.

EDNA *(as if to call after him but really to herself)*. Please let me explain myself . . .

KATE. I explain myself to the critics. "I never dreamed of Mrs. Pontellier making such a mess of things and working out her own damnation as she did. When I found out what she was up to, the story was half over and it was too late."—*Book News*, July 1899.

Do I think I cannot be an artist?

SCENE 19

At Mademoiselle Reisz's apartment. A misty afternoon.

EDNA. Mademoiselle, I am going to move away from my house on Esplanade Street.

REISZ. Ah.

EDNA. Aren't you astonished?

REISZ. Passably. Where are you going? To your husband in New York? To your father in Kentucky?

EDNA. Just two steps away. To a little four-room house around the corner. I'm tired of looking after that big house. It never seemed like mine anyway.

REISZ. That's not your true reason. There is no use in telling me lies.

EDNA. The house and the money that provides for it are not mine. Isn't that enough reason?

REISZ. What does your husband say?

EDNA. I haven't told him yet. He'll think I am demented, no doubt.

Mademoiselle Reisz stands up and gets a letter and gives it to Edna.

EDNA. Another letter so soon?

Mademoiselle Reisz plays the piano while Edna reads the letter

EDNA. Oh, unkind! Malicious! Why didn't you tell me? He's coming back!

REISZ. You knew he would be back eventually.

EDNA. But when? He doesn't say when. And why? Why is he coming?

REISZ. I don't have the answers to your questions. Are you in love with Robert?

EDNA. Yes.

REISZ. Why do you love him when you shouldn't?

Edna thinks for a moment.

EDNA. Because I do.

REISZ. What will you do when he comes back?

EDNA. Do? Nothing, except feel glad and happy to be alive.

REISZ. The bird that would soar above the level plain of tradition and prejudice must have strong wings.

KATE. I'm not thinking of any extraordinary flights. I am only writing.

EDNA. It's still summer.

ADÈLE. You must think of the future.

EDNA. It's summer.

ADÈLE. Think of your children.

EDNA. It's still summer.

ADÈLE. You must think of the future.

EDNA. It's summer.

ADÈLE. Think of your children.

SCENE 20

Edna's house.

ALCÉE. I've never seen you in such a happy mood.

EDNA. Oh, Alcée, one of these days I'm going to pull myself together for a while and think.

ALCÉE. About what?

EDNA. What character of a woman I am.

Alcée touches Edna's hair. Pause.

ALCÉE. When do you move to the pigeon house?

EDNA. I'll sleep there after I give my dinner party the day after tomorrow.

ALCÉE. When can I see you again?

EDNA. At the dinner, of course. You are invited.

ALCÉE. Not before? Not tomorrow morning or tomorrow noon or night? Or day after morning or noon?

EDNA. Not an instant sooner.

ALCÉE. May I stay a little longer now and talk?

EDNA. Talk to me if you like.

ALCÉE. I'm jealous of your thoughts tonight. They are wandering. They are not here with me.

He kisses Edna. They continue kissing while Léonce and Adèle appear and speak. When Edna talks, she looks at Alcée and not the others.

LÉONCE. Dear Edna, you must consider the appearance of my financial integrity and must not act upon your rash impulse to abandon your home. Please think about what people would say if you moved into such a small house. Be patient in my absence. I am planning to take you away to Europe this summer. You've always wanted to go.

EDNA. Always wanted to go.

ADÈLE. In some way you seem to me like a child, Edna. You act without a certain amount of reflection which is necessary in this life. Someone was talking of Alcée Arobin visiting you. Of course, it wouldn't matter if Mr. Arobin had not such a dreadful reputation. Be a little careful while you are living alone. And don't neglect me. Promise to come to me for my baby's arrival.

EDNA. Anytime of the day or night, dear.

Alcée and Edna continue to kiss.

KATE. "It is with high expectation that we open the volume, remembering the author's agreeable short stories, and with real disappointment that we close it. The recording reviewer drops a tear over one more clever author gone wrong."—*The Nation* August 3, 1899.

SCENE 21

Edna's letter to Léonce.

EDNA. Dear Léonce, I just got back from visiting the children in Iberville. I was so glad to see them! They told me stories about the pigs, cows, and mules. We spent the whole week talking and picking pecans and fishing in the lake. Your mother is very happy to have the children. I was sad to leave them. I hope your business is going well in New York. Much love, Edna. (*To herself*) I was sad to leave them. All along the journey home, I carried their voices like a sweet song. But by the time

I reached the city, the song no longer echoed in my soul. I was alone again.

KATE. Alone.

SCENE 22

Edna is in Mademoiselle Reisz's apartment. She is alone, waiting for Reisz, having let herself in. A knock on the door. Edna goes to open the door.

EDNA. Robert!

ROBERT. Edna! I didn't expect to see you here. What are you doing in Mademoiselle Reisz's house? Is she home?

EDNA. When did you come back?

ROBERT. I returned the day before yesterday.

EDNA. The day before yesterday! (*Whispers*) Day before yesterday. When were you planning to come visit me?

ROBERT. I've been busy. Mexico wasn't very profitable. So I came back and went back to the old firm.

EDNA. I see.

ROBERT. I was surprised to hear of Mr. Pontellier's absence, and your moving. Shouldn't you go to New York with him or to Iberville with the children?

EDNA. Do you remember you promised to write to me?

ROBERT. I couldn't believe my letters would mean something to you.

EDNA. You're not telling me the truth.

She gets up to leave.

ROBERT. Aren't you going to wait for Mademoiselle Reisz?

EDNA. No.

They walk. They enter her house. Robert looks around. Edna looks at Robert. Finally he meets her gaze. Long pause.

ROBERT. When you are tired of me, tell me to go.

EDNA. You never tire me. You must have forgotten the whole day we spent together in Grand Isle.

ROBERT. I have forgotten nothing of Grand Isle.

Robert takes out an embroidered tobacco pouch, and rolls a cigarette.

EDNA. That's a beautiful tobacco pouch. Did you get it in Mexico?

ROBERT. It was given to me by a Veracruz girl. She embroidered it herself.

EDNA. They are very pretty, those Mexican girls, aren't they?

ROBERT. Some are. Others are hideous. Just as you find women everywhere.

EDNA. What was she like? The one who gave you the pouch?

ROBERT. She was ordinary. She wasn't of the slightest importance.

A knock on the door. Alcée enters.

ROBERT. How do you do, Arobin?

ALCÉE. Lebrun! I heard yesterday you were back. How did they treat you in Mexico?

ROBERT. Fairly well.

ALCÉE. Stunning girls in Mexico. When I was there a couple of years ago, I didn't want to leave Veracruz.

EDNA. Did they embroider tobacco pouches for you?

ALCÉE. Oh no. They made more impression on me than I made on them.

EDNA. You were less fortunate than Robert then.

ALCÉE. I am always less fortunate than Robert.

ROBERT. I've imposed myself long enough. Please convey my regards to Mr. Pontellier when you write. Good night.

Robert exits.

ALCÉE. Fine fellow, that Robert Lebrun.

Pause.

ALCÉE. What do you want to do? Do you want to go out for a walk or a drive or anything?

EDNA. No. I don't want to do anything but be quiet. You go away and amuse yourself. Don't stay.

ALCÉE. I'll go away if I must, but I won't amuse myself. You know I only live when I am near you.

EDNA. Is that one of the things you always say to women?

ALCÉE. I have said it before, but I don't think I ever came so near meaning it. Good night. I adore you. Sleep well.

He exits.

SCENE 22A: Time Break Scene

LÉONCE. Are you asleep already?

EDNA. It's late, Léonce.

LÉONCE. Are you asleep?

EDNA. It's late.

LÉONCE. Already?

EDNA. Late.

LÉONCE. Bonbons and peanuts.

EDNA. In the morning.

LÉONCE. Already?

EDNA. Late.

SCENE 23

Léonce exits and Adèle enters. They are now in Adèle's house.

ADÈLE. I must instruct my maid to be very careful in checking off the list of clothes that were returned from the laundry. To notice particularly if a fine linen handkerchief of Mr. Ratignolle's had been returned. It was missing last week. To be sure to set aside pieces that require mending. I tell you Edna, it is hard work to care for one's family. The children especially. You have to surrender completely to caring for them.

EDNA. I will give up the essentials for my children, but I won't give up myself.

ADÈLE. What are the essentials?

EDNA. Food. Shelter. My life. I would give up my life for them, but not myself.

ADÈLE. What do you mean?

KATE. "The purport of the story can hardly be described in language fit for publication. We are fain to believe that Miss Chopin did not herself realize what she was doing when she wrote it."— *Providence Sunday Journal*, June 4, 1899.

As Adèle exits, Mademoiselle Reisz enters. They are now in Reisz's apartment.

REISZ. Are your wings strong?

EDNA. I'm not planning any extraordinary flight.

REISZ. What are you planning?

KATE. I am planning to talk to women in the next century. *The Awakening* is banned by libraries. From the place of tribulation, I reach for the hope beyond this world with blind faith in time. I know this is my best work.

REISZ. What are you planning?

EDNA. I make small bets with myself all day long. If I finish reading the morning paper before the coffee is brewed, I will hear from Robert. If I manage to paint all day without using the color blue, I will run into Robert. If I do all the insignificant aspects of everyday life perfectly, then Robert will appear at my door.

REISZ (*sympathetic*). And you call yourself an artist?

SCENE 24

EDNA. (*Song*) That's the beauty of it
The inexpressible beauty of it
Every stroke of a paintbrush
Is distinct from all others
And for all of your effort

It can not be repeated
One will always be denser
One will always be brighter
OR contain fewer ridges
Or have slightly more ochre
Every stroke of a paintbrush
Is distinct from all others
In a hundred ways
So unlike my days
That's the sadness of it
The inescapable sadness of it
A dream.

EDNA. Robert, what have you been seeing and doing and feeling
out there in Mexico?

ROBERT. I've been seeing the waves and the white beach of Grand
Isle. I've been working like a machine and feeling like a lost
soul. There was nothing interesting. (*Pause.*) And what have
you been seeing and doing and feeling in New Orleans?

EDNA. I've been seeing the waves and the white beach of Grand Isle.
I've been working like a machine and feeling like a lost soul.
There was nothing interesting.

SCENE 25

Edna and Robert meet on the streets.

EDNA. I guess I can only see you by accident. Why have you kept
away from me, Robert?

ROBERT. Why are you so personal, Mrs. Pontellier?

EDNA. You are the embodiment of selfishness. You save yourself
something, and in sparing yourself you never consider me for
a moment.

ROBERT. You are cruel.

They walk home. Robert lies down on the sofa. Long pause.

EDNA. Robert, are you asleep?

ROBERT. No.

Edna kisses him.

ROBERT. I've been fighting against it since last summer in Grand Isle.

EDNA. Why have you been fighting against it?

ROBERT. Because you're not free.

EDNA. I'm not?

Pause.

ROBERT. In Mexico I was longing for you all the time. I had a wild dream of you becoming my wife. There have been men who set their wives free.

EDNA. I'm no longer anyone's possession to dispose of. I give myself where I choose.

ROBERT. What do you mean?

A knock at the door.

EDNA. Adèle's baby is coming. I must go to her.

ROBERT. Don't go.

EDNA. Will you wait for me? No matter how late. You will wait for me, Robert?

ROBERT. Don't. Don't go. Edna, stay with me!

KATE. I write down life in a mystical place called Grand Isle at the mystical hour of 1899. When you emerge out of nothing, you will remember nothing. My words gone, my body gone, my memory gone, there will be no clue. Follow the wind to the burial site at sea to find me forever, to find my book, the last book of my life.

SCENE 25A: Time Break Scene

EDNA. Robert, what have you been seeing and doing and feeling?

ROBERT. The white beach of Grand Isle.

EDNA. The waves.

ROBERT. Lost soul.

EDNA. Seeing and doing and feeling.

ROBERT. There was nothing interesting.

SCENE 26

At Adèle's house. Adèle is having a baby and is in extreme pain. Edna watches in a daze. The words Adèle utters in pain are transformed into Léonce's past reprimand of Edna in her mind.

ADÈLE. There is no use, there is no use. This is too much!
This soup is really impossible. It's appalling that that woman hasn't learned to make a decent soup.
The fish is scorched. I will not eat this.
The roast is dry. And those vegetables!
I spend money enough in this house for at least one meal a day which a man can eat to retain his self-respect.
You must look after your household staff better.

Birth. Adèle is back to her sweet-self.

ADÈLE. Think of the children, Edna. Oh, think of the children. Remember them!

Edna moves back into her house and finds Robert gone. She picks up a note and reads.

EDNA. Goodbye—because I love you.

(*Song*) We shall return to the sea
You and I
We shall return to the sea
Once again we'll find that place
Of warmth and faith, of light, of grace
We shall return to the sea
And not come home
We shall walk into the waves
You and I
We shall walk into the waves

We'll continue hand and hand
Until we can no longer stand
We shall walk into the waves
And not come home
We'll become part of the sea
You and I
We'll become part of the sea
Glance upon the fading shore
And know we'll be at peace once more
We'll become part of the sea
And not come home

SCENE 27

*Winter at Grand Isle. Edna makes the trip alone. Dialogues are direct-
ed at the audience.*

EDNA. Years have gone by in dreams. Illusions. I might have kept
sleeping for a hundred years. How painful it is to wake up to
this life. All that I desire will not come true. All that the others demand of me will not be met. There is no place to be
alone. There is no beginning, no ending. How strange life is.
How very sad and mad and bad it is. How unbearably beautiful it is. Freedom is knowing that none of this stays. It will
all pass. As I will.

KATE. But I will come back and live again . . . The book will open,
and someone from the next century will dream about this
story. The day will come . . .

EDNA. The day will come when Robert, too, will melt out of existence. All things are inevitable. My children will grow up
without needing to take from me the key to the deepest chamber of my soul. I will not give up myself.

KATE. February 7, 1900, nine months after *The Awakening* was published, my publisher Herbert Stone wrote to me, canceling
the contract for my next story collection. The next day was my

IMAGE 4.5 **With her book in hand, Kate looks back on her own life.**
Dale Soules (left), Margi Sharp (right).
Photograph by Sonoko Kawahara.

fiftieth birthday. It was the coldest winter I had known in my
years in St. Louis.

EDNA. I am a melange of things lost
  things that cannot be obtained—
  but with this act, I will return to the present,
  to who I am now,
  and release the memory of everything
  all that I suffered
  all that I am yet to suffer.
  I walk into the ocean.
  I am awake.

  Edna freezes. Kate reads from the papers.

KATE. "*The Awakening* is too strong a drink for moral babes, and should be labeled 'poison.'"

"*The Awakening* is a decidedly unpleasant study of a temperament . . . the story was not really worth telling, and its disagreeable glimpses of sensuality are repellent."

I was born on February 8, 1850. My father died in a carriage accident when I was five. My mother, a wonderful, strong woman, raised me alone. I married Oscar, a mediocre businessman with a gentle, gentle soul. I had six children. Oscar died when our youngest was three years old. My children all grew up and were left to live and die their own lives. I died on

---

IMAGE 4.5 **Edna moves toward her death in the ocean, witnessed by the novelist Kate, her creator, and people who inhabited her life.**

Margi Sharp (left), Dale Soules (right).

Photograph by Sonoko Kawahara.

August 22, 1904. Five years after *The Awakening*. My last address was 4232 McPherson. I was one of the first in St. Louis to get a telephone in 1902. Lindell 1594M. (*With melancholy but deep love and pride*) The book is bound in light-green linen. There are green and dark red vines printed around the sides. The spine is in the same red. I like red.

She drops the papers, walks over to Edna and takes her hand with pride.

Blackout.

CHARACTERS

ALICE	Woman, late 20s to early 30s
MATT	Man, late 20s to early 30s
GHOST	Woman, 30s or 40s
BRUCE/MAN IN THE STATION	Man, late 20s to early 30s
WILLIAM/DOCTOR	Alice's father
PETER	Alice's brother
FEMALE CUSTOMERS	
MALE CUSTOMERS	

SETTING

Present,
New York City

FIREDANCE

IMAGE 5.1 **Alice confronts her lover Matt about his irregular behavior. Peter, her brother, is in another space—he is homeless (Scene 27).**

Michi Barall, Jonny Garcia, Timothy Altmeyer (from left to right). *FireDance*, directed by Marya Mazor, Voice & Vision Theater at the Connelly Theater, New York City, 1997.

Photograph by Ward Yoshimoto.

The characters of Alice (called Asia in an earlier version), Matt (earlier known as Rain), Ghost, Bruce, William, and Peter can be cast with a conscious and complete disregard to the superficial visual logic. An unpredictable and risky multicultural casting is encouraged. Ideally, the Male and Female Customers should be played by audience members.

Time and space can mostly be defined by lights and sound. No realistic props are necessary. The transition between scenes should be seamless.

Perhaps you could think of *Hamlet* as you read the play.

FIREDANCE

SCENE 1

A dim light comes up on a woman standing and staring straight ahead. She prepares slowly; then, with great calm, hangs herself. The same actor later plays Ghost.

Black.

Lights up on a street corner. Peter, slightly messy, is sitting on the street and singing at the top of his voice. Lights down on him.

SCENE 2

Lights up on a restaurant.

MALE CUSTOMER. Excuse me. Excuse me. Miss? What's your name?

ALICE. Alice.

MALE CUSTOMER. Yes, now, Alice. There is chicken in my soup.

ALICE. It's vegetable chicken soup.

MALE CUSTOMER. But I don't eat chicken, Alice.

ALICE. You ordered vegetable chicken soup.

MALE CUSTOMER. I didn't think there would be any chicken in it.

ALICE. . . . I see.

As she takes the soup away, she passes Ghost, who looks intently at her. They stare into one another's eyes.

Lights dim.

SCENE 3

Alice walks onto a subway platform. She is exhausted. Late night. A fuzzy announcement comes on.

VOICE. Attention downtown passengers. There is a delay in downtown service due to a fire in the 14th Street Station. We are sorry for the inconvenience.

Matt enters, notices Alice, and goes straight up to her.

MATT. Where have you been, April? I thought we were meeting at the usual place after work.

ALICE. Excuse me?

MATT. What happened? Why didn't you call me?

ALICE. You are mistaken . . .

MATT. Are you okay, April? Did you just forget?

ALICE. I'm not—

MATT. OK. OK. It's OK.

He kisses her cheek. She steps back.

MATT. I missed you.

Alice walks away from him. He follows.

MATT. Hey, you look great. I've always liked that dress on you.

Alice tries to walk away again.

MATT. I have to tell you something. I quit my job today.

Alice stops.

Pause.

ALICE. . . . I'm not who you think I am.

MATT *(laughs)*. Of course not. No one really is.

ALICE. That's not what I mean.

MATT. How was your day, anyway?

Pause.

ALICE. Why did you quit your job?

MATT. Well . . . I went to the park today. Sheep Meadow was crowded with beautiful people in bathing suits. Covered with goose pimples, fake happiness, and comfort. And I thought . . . *(abruptly)* Anyway, I should go now. See you later, OK?

ALICE *(surprised)*. Wait . . .

MATT. What is it?

ALICE. Uh . . . Finish your story before you go . . . Adam.

Pause.

MATT. OK . . . So I was watching these beautiful people in beautiful bathing suits. Suddenly I realized I was a black-and-white cutout image glued on a color postcard. Just for fifteen seconds, maybe. The air felt heavy and the sounds were muffled.

Pause.

ALICE. Then?

MATT. Then a frisbee came my way, and everything was back to—

ALICE. Back to?

MATT. Normal.

ALICE. Normal.

They look into each other's eyes. A fuzzy announcement comes on.

VOICE. Attention downtown passengers. There is a delay in service due to a sick passenger at the 42nd Street Station. We are sorry for the inconvenience. (*Echoes.*) We are sorry for the inconvenience. We are sorry . . . We are sorry . . .

ALICE. Is that why you quit your job?

MATT. I don't know for sure.

ALICE. What was the point of the story?

MATT. You know me, April.

ALICE. Right.

MATT. I couldn't decide what to do with my future, so I thought I might as well quit.

Pause.

ALICE. What will you do now?

MATT. I don't know . . . Any ideas?

Pause.

ALICE. Well.

MATT. I'm sure we can come up with something, between the two of us.

ALICE. Adam?

MATT. Yeah?

ALICE. Let's do the cross-country drive of our dreams.

MATT. That's a great idea! We've waited long enough to have our dreams come true, right? Maybe we'll get stuck in some god-forsaken part of Montana and live happily ever after.

ALICE. When do we start?

MATT. Soon. Very soon. I just have to take care of a couple of things.

ALICE. Okay.

MATT. Good, good. The future is becoming clear. (*Pause.*) Do you want to get married, April?

Pause.

ALICE. I don't think we are ready, Adam.

MATT. I guess not.

Pause.

Sound of an uptown train approaching from afar.

MATT. That's my train. I have to go. Shall we have dinner tomorrow?

ALICE. . . . Okay.

MATT. Eight? If something comes up, leave a message, OK?

The train comes in. Matt steps on and holds the door open. They kiss firmly on the mouth.

MATT. Meet me at our usual restaurant.

Sound of the doors closing. Lights down on Matt. Sound of the train moving away. Alice takes a few steps as if to run after the train. Lights down.

SCENE 4

Lights up on Peter sitting on the same street corner, still singing under the streetlights.
Lights down on him.

IMAGE 5.2 **Peter, Alice's brother, is homeless and sings on the street.**
Sheppard Pepper. *FireDance*, directed by Daniella Topol, Bard College, 2010.
Photograph by Rick Martin.

SCENE 5

Lights up on a pottery studio. Alice is making a vase. Morning.

BRUCE. It's hard to believe that he mistook you for someone else.

ALICE. He seemed honest.

BRUCE. He probably was, in his own world.

ALICE. Bruce, have you ever seen someone on the streets or in the subway and known that person belonged in your life? Hello. It's me. We are supposed to know each other. But you are paralyzed because you are afraid they won't recognize you.

One minute. Maybe. Then it's too late. She has passed by you or got on the train going the other way. You'll never get another chance. Gone. Forever.

BRUCE. Why are you so lonely?

ALICE. I don't know.

BRUCE. You may get another chance to pass the same person at the exact same spot. In twenty years. You'll meet again.

ALICE. You don't really believe that.

BRUCE. I really believe it.

Pause.

BRUCE. What are you making?

IMAGE 5.3 **Matt wants to engage in conversation with Peter.**
James Raid (left), Sheppard Pepper (right). *FireDance*, directed by Daniella Topol, Bard College, 2010.
Photograph by Rick Martin.

ALICE. Maybe an alternate universe. Lost moments. I don't know.

BRUCE. Looks like a vase.

ALICE. Yes. A vase.

BRUCE. I like the shape.

Lights down.

SCENE 6

Lights up on Peter singing on the same street corner. Matt walks up to him and gives him a dollar. Peter keeps singing.

MATT. What's your story?

PETER. Do you know fifteen thousand people die every day from starvation?

MATT. I didn't know that.

PETER. What's your story?

MATT. I'm looking for a job.

PETER. I'm not hiring.

MATT. OK.

PETER (*sympathetically*). I don't have any heartbreaking life story to share with you. I have a reasonably dysfunctional middle-class family. Except, oh yes, my mother is missing. This may be the cause of my troubles. I went to college for two years and dropped out. Perhaps this sense of failure is the cause of my troubles.

MATT. I'm not looking for any answers.

PETER. Of course you are. You want to understand me. You want to make sense of me.

MATT. Maybe I want to help you.

PETER. Help me do what?

MATT. What do you want from life?

PETER. If I tell you, you'll get it for me?

MATT. Possibly.

PETER. Why? Why not the homeless man with the big black dog on 14th Street? Why do I deserve you?

MATT. You sing.

PETER. There are better singers out there in the world. You can go to Carnegie Hall. After you get a job. I bet the tickets are like rockets. Sky rockets. High and almighty.

MATT. What?

PETER. Better stop paying too-close attention.

MATT. We can talk. I'd like that. Maybe you would, too.

PETER. I'm busy. I have to secure this street corner every day. I have to sing.

MATT. Is that enough?

PETER. What do you want me to want?

MATT. I want to know how you do it. Don't you doubt yourself on rainy nights? Don't you sometimes want a hamburger deluxe? Onions, lettuce, tomatoes? Pickles? French fries? How do you rest your head at night on concrete and believe that you will wake up tomorrow without fail?

PETER. You are wrong if you think I don't want. You are wrong if you think I don't cry.

He pulls Matt down and kisses him on the mouth.

PETER. Why are you so lonely?

MATT. Why aren't you?

PETER. I don't know.

Lights dim on Peter and Matt and up on another part of the street to reveal Alice.

SCENE 7

The subway platform. Alice is on her way to work.

GHOST. Hello. Hello. Alice.

ALICE. How do you know my name?

IMAGE 5.4 **Alice encounters Ghost and wonders about her missing mother.**
McCambridge Dowd-Whipple (left), Leonie Bell (right). *FireDance*, directed by Daniella Topol, Bard College, 2010.
Photograph by Rick Martin.

GHOST. Are you looking for Anna?

ALICE. You know Anna? Where is she?

GHOST. Are you looking for her?

ALICE. Yes, yes.

GHOST. How many hours a week would you say you spend looking for her? On average?

ALICE. What're you talking about?

GHOST. Just curious. Pretty traumatic to lose one's mother so early in life.

ALICE. I didn't lose her.

GHOST. But you don't know where she is.

ALICE. If you know, please tell me. She has been missing for fifteen years.

GHOST. I think you're looking for someone else.

ALICE. I've never stopped looking for Anna.

GHOST. In what way?

ALICE. What?

GHOST. Just curious.

ALICE. . . . I call random libraries and ask for her. She was a librarian.

GHOST. And?

ALICE. And I look . . . I look in obituaries in papers from all over the country. But I don't think she's dead. How do you know her?

GHOST. It was just a wild guess.

ALICE. What?

GHOST. Anna is a common name. Everyone knows one or two Annas.

ALICE. Are you crazy?

GHOST. I thought I could help you with the other person you're looking for.

Pause.

ALICE. I'm also looking for Adam. I call him Adam. I don't know his real name.

GHOST. Have you been to the restaurant called Tulips? I like the food there.

ALICE. That's where I work.

GHOST. I like the food there, my dear.

Lights change.

The restaurant. Matt comes in and runs into Alice. They are both surprised.

MATT. I was just—

ALICE. Looking for me?

MATT. Sure.

ALICE. How did you know I'd be here?

MATT. I didn't. I just got lucky.

ALICE. I see.

MATT. I'm looking for a job.

ALICE. I don't think they're hiring. But you can get an application from the Maître d'.

MATT. I was also looking for you.

ALICE. Would you like to sit down?

MATT. I don't have any money.

ALICE. Pasta with smoked salmon and watercress is good.

MATT. Good.

ALICE. Would you like a beer?

MATT. I don't have any money.

ALICE. Becks?

MATT. Good.

Alice walks away from the table. She comes back with beer, places it on the table, and walks away. Pause. Matt drinks. Alice comes back with pasta and sits across from Matt. He eats. She watches. Pause.

ALICE (*challenging him*). I'm ready now.

MATT. What?

ALICE. I'm ready to marry you.

MATT (*changing the subject casually*). How have you been?

ALICE. . . . Fine.

Ghost enters the restaurant. She sits at Matt's table. Alice stares at Ghost but she doesn't respond. Ghost is focused on Matt.

MATT. Can I help you?

GHOST. It depends.

MATT. It was a rhetorical question.

GHOST. You can free me. Forego what I owe for the voyage. Not hold me prisoner.

MATT. Excuse me?

GHOST. I came from Ireland to this new land when I was fourteen. I've been cooking, spinning yarn, making butter, cheese, and bread for my mistress for four years now. When I serve the meals, the master touches me when his wife is not looking. Touches me where it makes me shudder.

MATT. Have we met?

GHOST. Have you heard of indentured servants?

MATT. Is this a trick question?

GHOST. I was once in love with you.

MATT. Who are you?

GHOST. Who am I?

MATT. Do you have a name?

GHOST. Sometimes. But other times you make me nameless and invisible. I iron your handkerchief, make you hard-boiled eggs, walk the dog, and type your letters. I wear black satin.

MATT. I don't know you.

GHOST. I'm not talking about this life.

MATT. If you are here to haunt your lover, you've got the wrong man.

ALICE (*to Ghost*). Can I get you something? (*To Matt*) Would you like something else?

MATT. No, but . . .

ALICE. Dinner is on me.

MATT. Thank you.

ALICE. Goodbye.

MATT. Wait . . . I'm sorry I haven't—

ALICE. Do you have a story?

MATT. I've been busy being unemployed.

ALICE. You disappoint me. That's not nearly as good as your first story.

MATT. Can we meet after your work? (*Pause.*) We'll . . . We'll go to our usual bench. You know, on Broadway and 110th.

Pause.

ALICE. Midnight. What's your name?

MATT. Matt.

ALICE. I'm Alice.

She turns to go, stops, turns around, and looks at Ghost. They stare into each other's eyes.

GHOST. Going out on a date?

Lights dim.

SCENE 9

Lights up immediately on the bench.

ALICE. Why?

MATT. It's only a game. A harmless game.

ALICE. So there is no April.

MATT. You're my April.

ALICE. Are there other Aprils?

MATT. I don't remember.

ALICE. Do you have any real friends? People with real names?

MATT. I recognized you the first time.

ALICE. What do you mean?

MATT. Another black-and-white cutout in this colorful world.

Pause.

IMAGE 5.5 **Matt and Alice encounter a homeless woman with magical insight.**
Kati Kuroda, Timothy Altmeyer, Michi Barall (from left to right). *FireDance*, directed by Marya Mazor, Voice & Vision Theater at the Connelly Theater, New York City, 1997.
Photograph by Ward Yoshimoto.

ALICE. Is this bench our usual place? Or is this a universal usual place for you?

MATT. Does it matter?

ALICE. Of course it matters. I prefer routine to surprises. I don't want to have a mother one day and no mother the next day.

MATT. Has that happened to you?

ALICE. Yes.

Pause.

MATT. Do you like it here?

ALICE. Yes.

MATT. It's our place then. A routine place.

IMAGE 5.6 **Alice and Matt share stories of their families.**
McCambridge Dowd-Whipple (left), James Raid (right). *FireDance*, directed by Daniella Topol, Bard College, 2010.
Photograph by Rick Martin.

    He holds Alice's hand.

MATT. Did you see her?

ALICE. That mysterious woman? Yes.

MATT. Do you think she's crazy?

ALICE. No. She seems to have stories to tell.

MATT. But who am I to her?

ALICE. So many questions. Who am I to you?

MATT. That's easy. I've decided on you.

ALICE. Decided?

MATT. Here we are. Together, aren't we?

    Pause.

ALICE. Maybe you knew her once. In another time.

MATT. I don't feel it in my heart.

ALICE. What do you feel in your heart?

MATT. I only know what I don't feel.

ALICE. That can't be true.

MATT. I don't feel love for my mother.

ALICE. Why?

MATT. I don't think she ever loved my father. She didn't even cry for his death. She just became beautiful. She smiles. She sings. She wears a red dress.

ALICE. Would you love her if she wore black for your father?

MATT. Not at all. I want to forget her. I want to forget each day.

ALICE. Start your life over every day?

MATT. Wouldn't that be great? When you wake up in the morning, you have no regrets. You've made no mistakes.

ALICE. Why are you so lonely?

MATT. I don't know . . . I have a car.

ALICE. Yes?

MATT. Would you like to spend the night in the car at the bottom of the Brooklyn Bridge? The bridge will be beautiful in the night, like a monument made of light. And we can wake up to the sunrise.

ALICE. Yes.

Matt takes his silver chain off and puts it on Alice.

Lights down.

SCENE 10

Alice is in her father William's house.

WILLIAM. A wasted life. Your brother is a one-man freak show. And you? What is your profession?

ALICE. You know I'm a waitress.

WILLIAM. When do you feel most rewarded for your work? Is it when you are serving a big table and are able to carry all the plates of pork chops with one arm?

ALICE. You know what my answer is. We've gone through this before.

WILLIAM. No, no, please tell me. This is very interesting. I would like to know what's important to my daughter. Is it when a customer says, "Thank you, Miss, it was delicious"?

ALICE. It's when a middle-aged man comes in alone to eat because he has no other place to go, because he has no friends, and his wife has left him for some unknown reason, and his children hate him.

WILLIAM. I see. And where do his children sleep?

ALICE. What?

WILLIAM. What's that cheap thing you're wearing around your neck?

ALICE. It's a gift.

WILLIAM. From your sugar daddy?

ALICE. You don't know anything about my life.

WILLIAM. My son is a goddamn lunatic and my daughter is a fucking whore. You'll both die on the streets. Who cares? Your waitressing life isn't worth living anyway.

ALICE. Bastard.

WILLIAM. You deserve me.

ALICE. No, I don't. I don't I don't I don't. I'm leaving. I'm leaving your life.

WILLIAM. You'll never leave. Since your faggot brother is worthless, you will stay with me in my old age. This is the contract. I give you life. You eat my food until you are old enough to fuck. When I'm weak and ugly, you take care of me.

ALICE. I never signed that contract.

WILLIAM. You don't have a choice. It was invented at the beginning of human history. Why else should we reproduce?

ALICE. I don't think my presence in your old age is any comfort to you.

WILLIAM. Probably not. It'd be a constant reminder of failure.

ALICE. Whose failure? Yours or mine?

WILLIAM. Only one of us is a pathetic waitress. Tell me, why do you think you and your brother turned out to be such losers? Why don't you have what other people have, like ambitions and life goals?

ALICE. Why haven't you ever had what other fathers have? Love, for instance. Let's make a deal. You let me out of the contract with you, and I won't reproduce.

WILLIAM. Who do you think you are to make deals with your father?

ALICE. I'm a grown woman. I can make deals.

WILLIAM. Go to a whorehouse, then.

ALICE. Have a nice day.

WILLIAM. Become a prostitute, Alice. Become a nun. Go to a nunnery. Save yourself!

As Alice walks out, she makes the gesture of ripping a piece of paper. She exits. Lights down on William.

SCENE 11

Alice walks over to the street corner where Peter is still singing with his eyes closed.

ALICE. Peter, it's me. Your sister. Can you hear me? (*Peter keeps singing.*) Are you hungry? Do you need money?

PETER (*stops singing abruptly*). Do you know fifteen thousand people die every day from starvation? For God's sake, do they really have to die? Do you know fifteen thousand people die every day from starvation? For god's sake. Do you shari fifteen thousand igru bag every day from kokowaski? For jag yum. Do you know?

ALICE. Yes, but what can I do?

PETER. You can stop serving overpriced food to over-privileged people on the Upper West Side.

ALICE. Then what? Sit here and sing with you?

PETER. Why not?

Peter goes back to singing.

ALICE. I'm making a vase for you. It's blue. For your birthday.

Peter keeps singing.

ALICE. I thought you could put roses in it. Or maybe some broccoli.

Peter sings on.

ALICE. Or you can collect money in it.

Alice is in tears.

ALICE. I thought blue would go well with the pants you are always wearing.

She takes an apple out of her bag and places it in front of Peter.

Lights down.

SCENE 12

Lights up on Alice's apartment. Alice and Matt are in bed.

ALICE. If you were stranded on an uninhabited island, and you could only have one thing to eat for the rest of your life, what would you choose?

MATT. I'm going to have choices on a deserted island?

ALICE. For now. Once you make the decision, that's it. You can't change your mind.

MATT. What kind of an island is this?

ALICE. Are you going to choose or not? If you don't, no food for you ever.

MATT. Pizza.

ALICE. Pizza? You could eat pizza for every meal every day?

MATT. What would you choose?

ALICE. Rice pudding.

MATT. That's gross.

ALICE. It's not! It's comfort food.

MATT. If you have pizza, you can have different meals. You peel off the cheese, find some berries, and have cheese and fruit. You scrape off the sauce and put it on some leaves and have a salad. Then you have bread.

ALICE. That's more gross. Next topic.

MATT. Something less silly, please.

ALICE. Do you think death is a dream or suffering?

MATT. It's an undiscovered country.

ALICE. What do you think is waiting there?

MATT. I don't think about it. Next topic.

ALICE. Are you afraid?

MATT. No. I just thought about the strange woman at the restaurant. What did she want from me?

ALICE. Matt, just let her be. We can't explain her.

MATT. You like her, don't you?

ALICE (*uncertain*). I don't know. She reminds me of someone.

MATT. Your mother?

ALICE. No, not at all.

MATT. Tell me about your mother.

ALICE. I can't explain her either. She just disappeared when I was thirteen. I started menstruating on the day she left.

Pause.

MATT (*urgently*). You know I love you. I love you best. Never doubt my love. Believe it.

ALICE. What are you afraid of?

MATT. Believe it.

They kiss.

Time passes. The phone rings in the middle of the night. Lights up on William watching TV, holding the phone to his ear.

WILLIAM. Alice, are you watching the reruns of the daytime talk shows? There are men who con money out of multiple women. Very entertaining. Yesterday I saw a show on mothers and daughters who hate each other and sleep with the same man. Some of them even said it was better than not having anybody at all. Yep. Better than nothing. Stupid, aren't they? Anyway, you can forget your own troubles for a while. I recommend it highly. You know, I was the first in the family to get cable TV for your mother. Before your uncle the lawyer. Or was he a dentist? You know who I'm talking about, right? Alice?

Alice listens in silence and hangs up. Matt is asleep.

ALICE. Matt, wake up. I have to tell you something.

MATT. What?

ALICE. I don't think my mother loved my father either. I used to dream about this, her saying to me that she loved William. I wanted to call her a liar, but I always woke up before I found my voice.

MATT. When did it stop?

ALICE. Years ago. She doesn't come to me in dreams anymore. If I ever dream about Anna again, I won't interrupt her.

MATT. What do you think she can tell you in your dreams?

ALICE. The ending of the story. Unless I know how it ends, how am I ever supposed to tell it?

MATT. It hasn't been written yet. You can make it up.

ALICE. I might get it wrong and never find her.

MATT. Listen. My mother grieves terribly for my father's death. She wears a black housedress. Did you know they made house dresses in black? She doesn't ever go out.

ALICE. Anna has lived somewhere nearby and watched us grow up. She is healthy and has a job out of town somewhere. In a quiet library.

MATT. Is she coming back?

ALICE. I haven't written that part yet.

MATT. April and Adam do the cross-country drive of their dreams.

ALICE. When?

MATT. Soon. Very soon.

Lights down on Alice and Matt, and up on Peter singing under the streetlights.

Lights down.

SCENE 13

The restaurant.

ALICE. What would you like?

FEMALE CUSTOMER. I would like the grilled shrimp salad. What kind of greens are in the salad?

ALICE. Red leaf, arugula, and watercress.

FEMALE CUSTOMER. I don't like watercress. Can I have spinach instead?

ALICE. I'll check that for you.

FEMALE CUSTOMER. I don't care for watercress. And please grill the shrimp with no oil. I can't tolerate oil. What kind of dressing do you have?

ALICE. We have . . .

FEMALE CUSTOMER. I can't tolerate oil at all. Let me just have some lemon and mustard. On the side.

ALICE. Fine. Anything else?

FEMALE CUSTOMER. But if I can't have spinach, I don't want the salad. Let me see. This pasta, sautéed with broccoli, garlic, in olive oil. How is it prepared?

ALICE. It's pasta sautéed with broccoli, garlic, and olive oil.

FEMALE CUSTOMER. Can you make that without oil?

ALICE. Can you make the next train out of town?

FEMALE CUSTOMER. Yes, that's good. I'll have the pasta. Without oil.

Matt comes in followed by Ghost.

Matt sits. Ghost sits at his table.

Alice notices them, but walks out to the kitchen.

GHOST. Nice to see you again.

MATT. Are you following me?

GHOST. This place is a little expensive, isn't it? Where I come from, you can get a decent meal, meatloaf, mashed potatoes, and green beans for $1.25.

MATT. Where do you come from?

GHOST. In the middle of the desert in California. My baby is still-born in the camp on the day the bomb is dropped on Hiroshima. What happened to my parents? I never find out. Years later, I see a photograph of a solitary blind man against the vast wasteland. His eyes are blindfolded with a black rag. He looks like my father. Maybe he lived. Shortly after the bombing of Hiroshima, I am let out of the camp. Where should I go now? It's not safe anywhere.

MATT. OK, that's a new story.

GHOST. How would you feel if everything was taken from you? The house, the farm, the love of your country, most of your clothes and books and pots and pans, the backyard furniture you paid off just before the war, and your dog?

MATT. I never had so much.

GHOST. And be homeless, because white people still don't want you back in their neighborhood?

MATT. Do you . . . do you want to stay in my apartment?

GHOST. Sounds good. Do you have cable? I like old movies.

MATT. No. Sorry.

GHOST. Forget it, then.

SCENE 14

Lights up on the street. Peter is singing.

ALICE. Peter, it's me.

PETER. Do you know fifteen thousand people die every day from starvation? For god's sake, do they really have to die? Do you gugu shari fifteen thousand igru bag yoom kokowaski? For jag yum.

ALICE. Come home with me.

PETER. I am home, Alice. Don't be stupid. Nothing is for ever. Don't trust your Romeo. Go home and look at the violets he gave you. The scent has faded. Jag yum.

He goes back to singing.

Lights dim.

SCENE 15

At the bench.

MATT. I got you some violets.

ALICE. How pretty.

She inhales the scent.

ALICE. I love violets.

MATT. Good.

ALICE. Let's get some seeds and grow them in a pot. The flowers last much longer that way.

MATT. . . . How long?

ALICE. I don't know. I've never done it. It'd be an experiment.

MATT. It's too late for this year, isn't it?

ALICE. Probably. I think you're supposed to plant them right after the last frost.

MATT. That was months ago.

ALICE. I know. We can try next year.

MATT. There is no way to be sure that any given frost is the last one.

ALICE. We can guess.

MATT. We may get it wrong and never have violets again.

ALICE. Matt, it's not that serious.

MATT. No, of course not. By next year, there may be no frost. There may be an apocalyptic flood instead.

ALICE. . . . You mean like Noah's?

MATT. Don't be silly. Like global warming.

Pause.

ALICE. Thank you for the violets.

MATT. Sure. Anytime. They're cheap.

SCENE 16

The streets. Bruce is waiting for a bus. Matt approaches him.

MATT. Hey, remember me?

BRUCE. No.

MATT. We went to college together.

BRUCE. I don't think so.

MATT. Sure. We got drunk together once. You, me, and Donald. Don't you remember him? The number one football player.

Bruce examines Matt.

BRUCE. I was on the football team. 1998. University of Chicago. I don't know any Donald.

MATT. You know, it's good to see an old buddy. Especially when times are tough. How have you been? Joey, right?

BRUCE (*looks at his watch*). Fine. Yourself?

MATT. Good.

BRUCE. You said times are tough.

MATT. Well, I'm unemployed at the moment.

BRUCE. Sorry to hear that.

MATT. It's temporary. How are you doing?

BRUCE. Good.

MATT. Great.

Pause.

MATT. Do you know whatever became of Donald?

BRUCE (*pointedly*). I don't know . . . Todd. Maybe he is a famous professional football player. Maybe he is an astronaut on the *Enterprise*.

MATT (*defeated*). Maybe. It's good seeing you, Joey.

BRUCE (*sarcastic*). You, too, Todd. Here comes my bus. You still got my number, right? Call me if you get lonely.

He gets on the bus. Lights fade on him.

BRUCE. You just carry on, buddy.

Matt is left alone.

SCENE 17

Alice and Matt are coming out of a museum.

MATT. Every time I go to a museum, I get yelled at by the security guard.

ALICE. He didn't yell.

MATT. They should allow us to touch the sculptures.

ALICE. I guess the human touch is damaging.

MATT. The power of sculptures is in their roughness and smoothness. It's unbearably mediocre to stand there and look at them. Stand there and look at people looking at them.

ALICE. They won't be rough or smooth after a while if too many people touch them.

MATT. Don't you want people to touch your pottery?

ALICE. Yes, but pottery is for today. Sculptures are for the future.

MATT. What's for the past?

ALICE. Everything. In the end. I pressed the violets you gave me in my favorite book to dry.

MATT. At what stage of the decay did you do that?

ALICE. They weren't decaying. The flowers were still colorful.

MATT. You could have let them live longer then.

ALICE. They were cut flowers. Eventually the scent was going to fade.

MATT. Which book?

ALICE. Which do you think?

MATT. I know you told me what your favorite book was. I just forgot.

ALICE. I'll show you the book with the violets inside.

MATT. I was thinking, the vegetable curry you made the other day was just great. Can we make that again?

ALICE. OK. Tonight?

MATT. No, not tonight.

ALICE. How about Thursday?

MATT. No. Another time.

ALICE. Next week?

MATT. I'm not sure.

ALICE. In the past or the future?

MATT. It was really tasty. I can still remember it.

ALICE. . . .When?

MATT. When we think of it. Soon.

Long pause.

Lights down.

SCENE 18

Lights up on a hospital bed. Alice's dream. Alice is shivering, waking up from anesthesia. Ghost, dressed as a nurse stands by her bed.

ALICE. Are you my nurse?

GHOST. If that's what you want me to be.

ALICE. I was in deep sleep.

GHOST. No, you were unconscious. Under.

ALICE. I'm cold.

GHOST. Yes. That happens when you're waking up.

ALICE. I'm queasy.

GHOST. You are . . . ?

ALICE. Queasy. Crazy.

GHOST. Dreaming, my dear.

Alice pulls her body up on her elbows and spreads her legs with her knees bent—the position for a gynecological examination. Doctor enters and stands in between her legs. During the following scene, Alice looks straight at Doctor, but he does not look up from his clipboard once. Matt enters and stands directly behind Doctor. Ghost is invisible to everyone now. She dances around the three during the scene.

DOCTOR. We don't know the cause. There is no cure. One theory is that a portion of the menstrual fluid flows backward into the fallopian tubes rather than into the vagina. These cells in the fluid then attach themselves outside of the uterus, and develop into painful growths. These growths then bleed without leaving the body. This disease is most common in childless women between ages twenty-five and forty. I recommend an EWA, DEC, hysteroscopy and laparoscopy, a gonadotropin-releasing hormone followed by pasta sautéed with watercress.

ALICE. I don't understand.

DOCTOR. In the future you may need a oophorectomy or a bilateral olive oil salpingo-oophorectomy or a hysterectomy.

MATT. Don't depend on me. I have to go.

ALICE. I don't understand. Where are you going?

DOCTOR. After everything, it may not reoccur, but you may never eat grilled shrimp again and will be left in a permanent state of menopause. It's up to you. Don't depend on me.

ALICE. I love you.

MATT. To the supermarket. They're having a sale on potatoes. You know, for the vegetable curry.

DOCTOR. That will be all for today.

Lights out abruptly. The phone rings. A spotlight on Alice gasping for air. She is waking up from the dream. The phone keeps ringing. Lights out.

SCENE 19

Lights up on the pottery studio.

BRUCE. Here.

He wraps his arms around her tightly and lets go.

BRUCE. Wear this shield. Let everything bounce off it. You are safe.

ALICE. That's corny, Bruce.

BRUCE. Life is an amusement park.

ALICE. Do you know everything?

BRUCE. I don't have to know everything. I have a job. I pay my bills. I eat. I sleep. People I love are not hungry or cold. That's all I need to know.

ALICE. Do you need anyone?

Pause.

BRUCE. All I need is air, water, food, and shelter. Everything else in life is extra.

ALICE. Clothes? Don't you need clothes?

BRUCE. Yeah, that, too.

ALICE. Sunshine? What about music? Thunderstorm. Toothbrush. Pet turtle.

BRUCE. That's too much, Alice. Dangerous.

ALICE. Do you need me?

BRUCE. I don't think about it.

ALICE. How long have we known each other?

BRUCE. I don't know. A while.

ALICE. Ten years.

BRUCE. That's nice.

ALICE. Is it?

BRUCE. Of course it is.

ALICE. Bruce, what's not nice? What do you find abhorring?

BRUCE. What's this about?

ALICE. Tell me one thing that you don't like. One thing that disturbs you.

BRUCE. You shouldn't need so much. Want so much.

ALICE. Is that it? Do you find that annoying?

BRUCE. No. It's a waste of time, all this agitation. Dreams and drama.

ALICE. Why do you care about me?

BRUCE. Because I've known you for ten years.

ALICE. Why make pottery?

BRUCE. Because I like it.

ALICE. If I said I've never liked anything you've made, would you be angry?

BRUCE. No.

ALICE. Liar.

Alice walks out.

Lights down.

SCENE 20

Alice makes a call. The sound of a phone ringing. Lights up on Matt. He looks at his phone but does not answer. It goes on ringing. Lights down.

The corner. Peter is still singing. Matt enters.

MATT. I brought a hamburger deluxe.

PETER. Cheese?

MATT. Hey.

Matt sits next to Peter.

MATT. . . . So, are you gonna eat it?

PETER. What do you think? Do you think I'm gonna say no thank you plus some wise words?

MATT. No, I was just . . .

PETER. Testing me?

MATT. For what?

PETER. To see if I'm insane or saintly.

MATT. Maybe. Eat. It's the best hamburger deluxe you've ever had.

Peter eats. They sit in silence.

Lights down.

SCENE 22

The restaurant. Alice walks up to the table where Matt is.

ALICE. How are you?

MATT. Good. Good.

ALICE. Has something happened between us?

MATT. What do you mean?

ALICE. I thought I'd hear from you last week. Or the week before.

MATT. I'll call you tomorrow, OK? I'm meeting my ghost now, I'm sure.

Alice walks away. She approaches another table with two plates of hamburger deluxe.

MALE CUSTOMER. This is the best hamburger deluxe I've ever had.

FEMALE CUSTOMER. This is the best hamburger deluxe I've ever had. What makes this the best hamburger deluxe we've ever had?

MALE CUSTOMER. See these little onions? See these little French fries?

FEMALE CUSTOMER. I've been eating a lot of meat lately.

MALE CUSTOMER. I've always eaten meat. Meat and potatoes. People, like, eat fish. Do you eat fish?

FEMALE CUSTOMER. Yeah, I make, like, a fish sandwich. It's good.

MALE CUSTOMER. I used to eat fish.

FEMALE CUSTOMER. Fish sticks?

ALICE. How is everything? Can I get you another gallon of grease? Can I get you a book called *An Unexamined Life is Not Worth Living*?

CUSTOMERS. No, thank you. We're fine.

Ghost walks in, sits across from Matt. Alice looks over to their table, then exits.

GHOST. Do you want to buy silver and turquoise bracelets? Handmade by a genuine Sioux. Six hundred dollars each.

MATT. I can't afford them.

GHOST. Maybe we'll trade. How about the piece of land your chair is sitting on right now?

MATT. It doesn't belong to me.

GHOST. It never did.

MATT. All right. What have I done now?

GHOST. Dead bodies around me become gradually cold. It is dark and quiet now. I cuddle against my mother's butchered body. Days pass. Then they find me. People who shot every old man, pregnant woman, and child in my tribe. I'm nine months old. I live because they missed me. The only survivor of the massacre. But the blood stain on my face never fades. I live with my mother's blood on my face.

MATT. Let me guess. The Battle of Wounded Knee. 1890. This is just an educated guess. I only know this because I read the famous book. I'm not one of the soldiers.

GHOST. Who are you then?

MATT. I'm Matt. Born in 1980. In Brooklyn.

GHOST. How does that not make not one of them? You're not free from blood or history.

MATT. Why are you here? Why me?

GHOST. Because you're blind to your responsibility.

MATT. My responsibility? What responsibility? I didn't imprison you, rape you, rob you, humiliate you, beat you, burn you or sell you. I went to college in Kansas. I'm unemployed.

GHOST. But your ancestors did.

MATT. Fuck you. I don't have time for this. I don't have time to contemplate history. I have to come up with this month's rent.

GHOST. How is Alice?

MATT. What?

GHOST. Alice.

MATT. I don't know. I'm not responsible for her. I know what you are getting at, but you're wrong. Alice and me, we are not history. I don't injure humanity because I don't call her. It's nothing, and it's not my fault anyway. I just don't have the time.

GHOST. So little time.

Lights down on the restaurant.

SCENE 23

Matt sits on the bench alone and looks at his phone. He doesn't make a call.

Long pause.

Lights down.

SCENE 24

Lights up on Alice and Bruce on the street.

BRUCE. Where are we going?

ALICE. We're looking for the ghost.

BRUCE. OK.

ALICE. What do you mean, OK? You don't believe in ghosts.

BRUCE. No, but I know you do. You believe that the lines between all things are fragile—life and death, life and dreams.

ALICE. Life and amusement parks?

BRUCE. Now, *you* don't believe that.

ALICE. We are looking for the woman who comes to the restaurant.

BRUCE. Won't she show up there if you sit tight?

ALICE. Not every day. Never on Wednesdays, and I need the answer right now.

BRUCE. Answer to what?

Suddenly, Ghost is standing in front of her.

GHOST. Looking for me?

ALICE. I want to know.

GHOST. What?

ALICE. Do you . . . do you think the sautéed spinach at Tulips is too salty?

GHOST. Just right.

ALICE. I think so, too . . . . Do you like rose or mint?

GHOST. Rose.

ALICE. Me, too. I'm buying a new dress. Rose.

GHOST. Your friend?

BRUCE. I'm Bruce.

GHOST. Are you Indian? Irish? Indonesian? Italian? Iranian?

BRUCE. American. And you?

GHOST. You know, Bruce. Some men are unaware of the contract.

When you are born a white man, you have options. You can sign your name on the document called history in blood, or not. But you, you don't have options. It's automatic for you.

ALICE. I don't understand.

BRUCE. My friend has a question she wants to ask you.

GHOST. You're not a conversationalist, are you, Bruce? You only talk to a handful of people, people you are sure don't hold any grudges against you. That limits your range of activities. Because when you're born a man, that means you're not a woman, and that means—

ALICE. I think you should leave. Right now.

GHOST (*transforming into Anna*). You want me to leave, my dear?

ALICE. Yes. Instead of saying things we don't understand. Instead of pretending to be a happy mother.

GHOST. I am a happy mother. I love my children, Alice and Peter. But I'm not sure if I have the right.

ALICE. What right?

GHOST. To sign the contract to love and care for you.

ALICE. Why not?

GHOST. The rest of my life is a long time.

ALICE. You mean you got tired of us?

GHOST. No, of course not. But this may not be the right story.

ALICE. You created the story. *You* did.

GHOST. Not entirely. I was very young when I met William. I knew nothing.

ALICE. What did you need to know?

GHOST. The ending of the story.

ALICE. It hasn't been written yet.

GHOST. It makes me anxious. Not knowing. I have to—I have to—

ALICE. You have to leave.

GHOST. Do you understand, then?

ALICE. No.

GHOST. You're a lovely girl. You have braces and occasional pimples.

ALICE. I don't have them anymore.

GHOST. I love you for your braces and pimples.

ALICE. I don't have them anymore.

Pause.

GHOST (*back to herself*). So what do you think about the new chicken wings appetizer?

ALICE. It's good.

GHOST. Hmmm . . . I'll try it next time. You better get to work, shouldn't you?

Ghost exits.

BRUCE. Alice?

ALICE. I wanted to know why Anna left. Why she didn't take Peter and me with her.

BRUCE. And?

ALICE. It was a long time ago. It doesn't matter anymore.

BRUCE. What are you going to do now?

ALICE. Make a vase. Rose. What are you going to do?

BRUCE. Walk you to Tulips.

ALICE. You've never done that before.

BRUCE. Life is a constant surprise. Why do you like him?

ALICE. Who? Matt?

BRUCE. Never mind.

ALICE. Because I thought he belonged in my life—at the beginning, when we first met. I guess it became a habit. (*Pause.*) Bruce?

BRUCE. Yeah?

ALICE. Did you see her?

BRUCE. Of course I did.

ALICE. I mean Anna. My mother.

BRUCE. . . . Of course.

ALICE. I've always loved your pottery.

Lights up on Peter on the street corner. Matt sits with him.

PETER. Even though people are starving all over the world, I don't
   have to. The church behind the park gives out hot dogs on
   Tuesdays. They taste terrible, which helps me contemplate all
   the unfortunate souls who don't have hot dogs. Hunger is a
   metaphor anyway in the United States of America. Even for
   those who are actually hungry. Anyway, I don't believe in any
   of this.

MATT. Do you have family somewhere?

PETER. Is that necessary?

MATT. Most people have family of some kind.

PETER. Maybe that's the cause of my troubles.

MATT. Family? Or no family?

PETER. I used to believe in something. What was it? Maybe it will
   come back to me someday in the middle of a song.

MATT. Would you tell me someday?

PETER. What?

MATT. Anything. Just.

PETER. Take care of yourself. Holding your breath will kill you.
   Jug yum.

He sings.

Lights down.

SCENE 26

*The restaurant. Ghost is sitting alone at a table. Alice is working. Matt
walks in, and goes straight to Ghost.*

MATT. Life is hard for you, isn't it?

GHOST. I'm watching that little girl with yellow hair and a pink dress
   holding a doll with yellow hair and a pink dress. I know
   things. I know slavery.

MATT. Slavery? Aren't you getting a scholarship to college or a job at an Equal Opportunity Employer?

GHOST. I know my great grandparents were chained and whipped, and they worked barefoot in the field, and said, yes, sir, and ate nothing but rice. And their babies were sold like cows.

MATT. Don't you get into Harvard or Manhattan law firms before someone like me?

GHOST. That girl doesn't even know anything. I know that we've suffered. She hasn't. Her mama wore a pink dress and her grandma wore a pink dress. Now I should wear it. I should be the one now.

MATT. Don't you get food stamps? Aren't you on welfare?

GHOST. Does this look like a perfect world to you?

MATT. No. I lost my job.

GHOST. You also lost your memory. Did I always sit next to you at restaurants?

MATT. As far back as I can remember. Why do you always show up when I'm eating here anyway?

GHOST. I like the food.

MATT. You like the food?

GHOST. What. You think I should be eating fried chicken and watermelon?

MATT. No, that's not . . . I don't care what you eat. Eat whatever you like. Just leave me alone to eat my little white-man dinner in peace from now on.

GHOST. Cooked by Mexicans.

MATT. What?

GHOST. Cooked by Mexicans.

MATT. What do you want me to do? Avenge all the injustice in the world?

GHOST. No.

MATT. What, then?

GHOST. I want you to remember.

Alice walks up to Matt's table.

ALICE. I have to talk to you.

MATT. Hi. Come home with me tonight.

ALICE. No. But I'll meet you at our usual bench.

MATT. Sure. Whatever.

Ghost and Alice look at each other. There is an understanding between them.

Lights down on the restaurant.

SCENE 27

The bench.

ALICE. You have been avoiding me.

MATT. You and me, this may not be the right story.

ALICE. You created this story. You did.

MATT. I can't make a mistake.

ALICE. Without making mistakes, you'll never be able to change the ending of your story. You may not even notice that there is a story.

MATT. I'm not going to repeat my father's life.

ALICE. What is your father's life?

MATT. It was ordinary, like any other ordinary life. A picture of middle-class happiness and then suicide.

ALICE. I'm sorry.

MATT. He didn't succeed the first time, because he only slashed his wrist.

He takes Alice's arm

MATT (*menacingly*). If you really want to succeed, this is what you do. You cut open the blood vein vertically on your arm. All the way.

Pause.

MATT. After the first attempt, he was committed to the hospital where they made him do pottery. Rehabilitation, you know. Actually, he made a nice teapot before his next attempt.

ALICE *(tense)*. What do you want from me?

MATT *(sarcastic)*. You do pottery, don't you? Maybe you can make cups to go with my father's teapot. He kinda ran out of time.

ALICE *(challenging)*. What color is it?

MATT *(equally challenging)*. It's blue.

SCENE 28

The pottery studio.

BRUCE. What are you making?

ALICE. Blue teacups. Bruce, what is the saddest memory you have?

BRUCE. Why the saddest? Why not the happiest?

ALICE. Because I'm interested in the saddest just now.

BRUCE. Well, when I was five, my cousin told me that midnight is the next day. I couldn't believe it. So one night, I forced myself to stay up to see if the sun would rise at midnight. Of course it didn't. I found out that there was darkness in the morning. Waking up has never been the same since that day.

ALICE. Is that absolutely the saddest memory you have?

BRUCE. Yes.

ALICE. Are you insane? No one has broken your heart? No one you love has died? Haven't you lost anything in your life?

BRUCE. You expect too much. Every moment in life has to have some unknown but deep meaning for you.

ALICE. That's not true! Most of my hours are spent on meaningless activities—washing my hair, doing dishes, picking lint off the carpet, waiting on tables. It is a great day if I have one hour that means something. If I added all the lost hours over my lifetime, the number would be enough to make me want to stop living.

Pause.

ALICE. I probably didn't think of you once yesterday.

BRUCE. But you see me every Wednesday and remember I exist. It's a small surprise. A nice surprise. Here. (*Hands her a small pot.*) Years from now, during one of your spring cleanings you will come across this pot. You may recognize the color. You may remember me. Wouldn't that be nice?

ALICE. No no no no. There is a Wednesday in every week. For the rest of our lives. Wednesdays. Promise me.

BRUCE. You know that's not possible.

ALICE. Don't you ever need promises in your life?

BRUCE. I have you now. On Wednesdays.

ALICE. You can't admit that you have doubts, that you fear death, that you stay awake at nights wondering if the sun will ever rise at midnight in your lifetime. You can't admit you are lonely. Because you are a coward.

Long pause. Bruce gets ready to leave.

BRUCE. I will see you next Wednesday. Right? Alice?

Bruce walks out.

Lights down.

SCENE 29

William on the street. Ghost catches up to him.

GHOST. Hello. William.

WILLIAM. I don't know you.

GHOST. Story of my life. Always an anonymous woman.

WILLIAM. I can't help you.

GHOST. Did I ask for help?

WILLIAM. Is there something you want from me? Otherwise, go
away.

GHOST. You're not a friendly type, are you, William?

WILLIAM. Dammit.

GHOST. That's right. You can't ignore me the second time I call you
by your Christian name.

WILLIAM. How do you know my name?

GHOST. From the phonebook.

WILLIAM. I knew it. A lunatic beggar.

GHOST. I haven't seen Anna in some time.

WILLIAM. You know my wife? Where is she?

IMAGE 5.7 **William encounters Ghost, who reminds him of his missing wife.**
Christian Scheider (left), Leonie Bell (right). *FireDance*, directed by Daniella
Topol, Bard College, 2010.
Photograph by Rick Martin.

GHOST. Now you're interested.

WILLIAM. Tell me where Anna is!

GHOST. You haven't said hello yet.

WILLIAM. Please. I haven't seen my wife in fifteen years. Here is a dollar. Tell me where she is.

GHOST. A dollar? Where do you think I'm from? The nineteenth century?

WILLIAM. That was a mistake. Here's twenty.

GHOST. I'm not selling anything.

WILLIAM. Then what do you want?

GHOST. Why do you think I want something?

WILLIAM. In exchange for information. Everyone wants something.

Ghost transforms into Anna.

GHOST. You were always unhappy that I didn't have a list of things I wanted.

WILLIAM. Anna? Anna.

GHOST. But I had no idea what I should want. Over time, I got tired of not knowing.

WILLIAM: I worked hard. Gave you everything. All I wanted in return was a normal life. Homemade meatloaf on Wednesdays.

GHOST. But I didn't want everything. And I was too sad on Wednesdays to make meatloaf.

WILLIAM. Why should you be sad?

GHOST. I don't know. I just was.

WILLIAM. You never told me anything.

GHOST. I did. I told you everything. After that, you bought me a TV.

WILLIAM. You are spoiled. Ungrateful. How dare you abandon me and the children. It's your fault they amounted to nothing.

GHOST. You haven't asked.

WILLIAM. What?

GHOST. How I felt leaving the children.

WILLIAM. Is that my responsibility? To worry about how you felt leaving, while being left alone with two kids?

GHOST. Peter was a good boy. He used to sing to me.

WILLIAM. He's nothing!

GHOST. You never appreciated his singing. William, you haven't asked why I left.

WILLIAM. This isn't what life should be! This isn't right! I don't approve!

Ghost transforms back to herself

GHOST. Stop yelling.

WILLIAM. What? . . . Oh.

GHOST. I'll take that twenty. It's only fair since women are paid less than men for the same work.

William hands Ghost the bill.

GHOST. Well, see you around.

WILLIAM. Wait.

GHOST. What?

WILLIAM. Who are you? Do you know my wife?

GHOST. Who is your wife?

WILLIAM. Anna.

GHOST. Never heard of her.

WILLIAM. Because if you knew her—I forgot to ask her something . . .

Ghost exits, leaving William behind.
Lights dim.

SCENE 30

The bench. Alice is waiting. Matt enters.

ALICE. Where have you been? Cross-country driving?

MATT. I was looking for a job.

ALICE. Any luck?

MATT. No. I'm tired.

Alice takes her chain off and tries to give it back to Matt.

ALICE. Take this back, Adam. It's poisoned.

MATT. It's not mine. It was never mine.

ALICE. You gave it to me.

MATT. No.

ALICE. It was a gift. From you.

MATT. I've never seen it.

Alice throws the chain on the ground.

ALICE. You're a liar.

MATT. Who isn't? Did you think I loved you? April?

ALICE. You led me to believe that you needed me.

MATT. It's not my fault. I never held you prisoner.

ALICE. No. You are the prisoner.

MATT. Needing someone can fuck you up. You are out having a beer at a bar, and you start talking to the guy sitting next to you about the Middle East, before you know it, it's 2 am, and you told that person you "need" you would call her before midnight. Well, midnight was two hours ago. You can't go back. For two lost hours, you are just a little bit fucked for the rest of your life.

ALICE. You'll never be free. You'll be haunted for everything that you are and you're not; everything you can't do, haven't done, won't do. You'll never even figure out the differences.

MATT. When you need someone, you somehow think that person can save you from death. Then one day you notice pain in your right elbow that doesn't go away and realize that person has nothing to do with your death. You are going to die anyway.

ALICE. Did you ever love me?

MATT. You are fucked and dead.

ALICE. You poor, poor man.

Matt walks away. Ghost approaches Alice.

GHOST. Are you looking for Anna?

ALICE. No.

GHOST. Who are you looking for now?

ALICE. William. And Peter.

SCENE 31

Night. Alice's apartment. She is asleep. Peter enters and begins looking for something. She awakes. Alice's dream.

ALICE. Peter? Are you OK?

PETER. Yes, yes.

ALICE. Are you looking for something?

PETER. Anna's story.

ALICE. What're you talking about?

PETER. Don't worry. I just need to find the ending. I think an unfortunate death is coming.

ALICE. Who's going to die?

PETER. I am.

ALICE. Peter. Please. Look at me.

PETER. Don't you see, Alice? Anna left to change the ending of her story.

ALICE. Anna left because of William.

PETER. She left for a new story. You should, too. Take no luggage.

ALICE. Peter. Shall I make a bed for you?

PETER. I found it. The original ending. There is a suicide. She drowns. Poor thing.

ALICE. But it's not your death. And it didn't happen anyway.

PETER. It's my death. Baloon yak the ee ee ta dome.

ALICE. What?

PETER. Pa dundun yanp wa ee . . .

ALICE. Peter, I don't understand. I don't understand!

The phone rings. Alice wakes up. Peter disappears.

SCENE 32

Lights up on the street corner. Peter is singing in a whisper. William enters.

Late night.

WILLIAM. It's your fault that my wife and daughter are gone.

Peter keeps singing throughout.

Alice is mine. She is all I have. She should love me, not you. I did everything I was supposed to do. The breadwinner. What makes you different? Why shouldn't you be a breadwinner? I've fulfilled my commitment to forty years of meaningless rituals and boredom. When do I get to sing?

Peter keeps singing as if he doesn't see William. William is worked up to a violent rage. He grabs Peter and lifts him off the ground. He beats Peter but Peter keeps singing. Matt approaches with a blanket.

MATT. What're you doing?

Matt tries to get William off Peter.

MATT. Leave him alone!

WILLIAM. You're killing me with your filth, your unforgiveness, your blood gone bad.

Matt and William struggle.

WILLIAM. I don't approve! I don't approve! I don't approve!

William is choking Peter. Matt throws William on the street. He hits his head.

Silence.

Peter resumes his singing in a whisper. William doesn't move.

MATT. I have to, I have to . . .

PETER. Dead. No more fear of death. Poor thing.

MATT. I have to, I have to . . . call the police.

PETER. Forget it. People die every day.

MATT. Do you know him? Has he harassed you before?

PETER. He looks familiar. (*In rage*) For god's sake, did he have to die?

MATT. I didn't mean to . . . What should I do?

PETER. I have no answers for you. Do you know fifteen thousand people die every day from a knock on the head? Jug yum.

Matt runs out.

Goodbye.

Peter picks up the blanket Matt dropped, wraps himself in it, and resumes singing.

Lights down.

SCENE 33

Outside Alice's apartment. Matt runs up and almost bumps into Alice who is leaving.

MATT. Hi.

ALICE. I have to go.

MATT. Wait, please. I need to talk to you.

ALICE. My brother needs me.

MATT. . . . You never told me you had a brother.

ALICE. Because we could never get to any truth over the mountain of bullshit you shoveled in between us.

MATT. One can't be true all the time.

ALICE. Right. I need to go to my brother.

MATT. Wait, Alice. Stay with me. I need you more than any brother can ever love you.

ALICE. You make no sense.

MATT. No brother can match what I feel for you.

ALICE. Let me go. My father is dead.

MATT. . . . What?

IMAGE 5.8 **On the Brooklyn Bridge, Alice mourns her father's death. Matt cannot console her. Ghost is present.**

Timothy Altmeyer, Mary Magdalena Hernandez (left to right). *FireDance*, directed by Marya Mazor, Voice & Vision Theater at the Connelly Theater, New York City, 1997.

Photograph by Ward Yoshimoto.

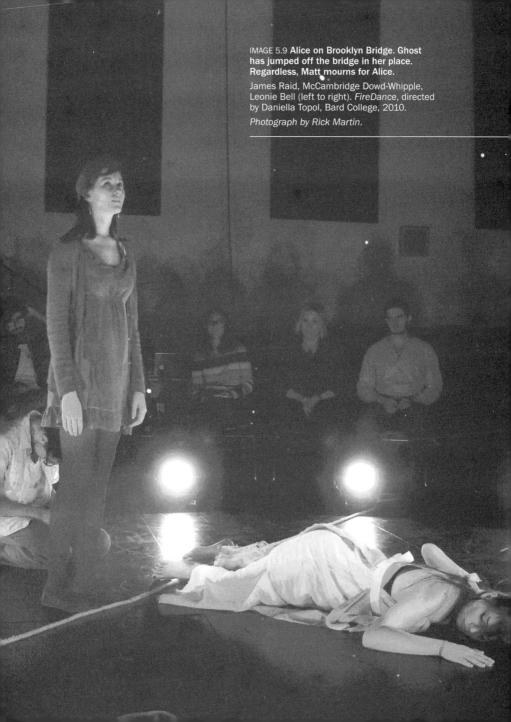

IMAGE 5.9 **Alice on Brooklyn Bridge. Ghost has jumped off the bridge in her place. Regardless, Matt mourns for Alice.**

James Raid, McCambridge Dowd-Whipple, Leonie Bell (left to right). *FireDance*, directed by Daniella Topol, Bard College, 2010.

Photograph by Rick Martin.

ALICE. My brother killed him.

MATT. . . . When? Where?

ALICE. On the street where he lived. He was homeless. Now he's in jail. I have to go.

MATT. . . . Wait.

Matt gasps for air.

MATT. What am I supposed to do?

ALICE. About what?

MATT. About this interview I have coming up. It's a job at a bookstore. Should I get a haircut?

ALICE. I can't help you.

Alice walks away. Matt follows her.

Lights dim.

SCENE 34

Brooklyn Bridge at night. Alice is walking fast. Matt follows.

MATT. Wait. Wait. What are we doing on Brooklyn Bridge? Wait.

Alice stops and looks at him.

ALICE. Isn't this our usual bridge? Huh? Adam?

MATT. Alice, let me take you—

ALICE. Did I ask you to be here with me tonight? Did I ask you to see the sun rise over the bridge tomorrow morning?

MATT. No. I was worried about you.

ALICE. Did you follow me from the police station? Why am I suddenly so interesting to you? Because I have a brother who is a murderer? Because my father's dead?

MATT. I'm sorry about your father. And your brother. (*Silence.*) What do you want me to say?

ALICE (*violently*). I want you say that you loved me. I want to hear you say it. I didn't imagine it. You loved me. Say it.

MATT. What is that going to accomplish?

ALICE. Absolutely nothing! Did you ever love me? I want to know before it's all over. Did you or was I just insane?

MATT. What is insanity?

ALICE. Insanity is remembering your brother's face when he was seven, when he had his first big fight with his father, saving a postcard from Mexico that your mother got before you were born, believing it when some unemployed loser tells you that he loves you.

MATT. What did your brother and father fight about?

ALICE. I don't know! He wouldn't talk to me. He wouldn't talk to his appointed lawyer. He confessed, and then stopped talking. Stopped singing.

MATT. I mean when he was seven.

ALICE. What?

MATT. His first fight.

ALICE. Why don't you make it up?

Alice climbs over the wall of the bridge.

ALICE. Do you want to come with me?

MATT. You're not going to kill yourself.

ALICE. No, I'm going to be free.

She turns and looks at Matt. Tense silence.

Ghost appears. Matt doesn't see her this time.

The two women look at each other. As Alice makes the move to jump, Ghost jumps instead. Alice sees Ghost jump. What Matt sees is Alice jumping.

ALICE and **MATT.** No-o-o-o-o-o!

Matt sinks down to the ground.

MATT. Alice. I'll drink vinegar and eat crocodile for you, but I can't go with you. I can't . . .

Alice looks at Matt in a daze. Matt does not see Alice anymore.

ALICE. I freeze time on this winter night. The city lights, weary amber. Random memories of the lost tribe of my family. We dance for the first time, for the last time, to take us back to the beginning of everything, to forget our names, to kill the fire in my eyes. Hold my hand, Adam. I'll read your future. There is a curse on your life. On the nights you are afraid of death, you will miss me.

Alice exits.

Lights down.

SCENE 35

A sad little train station. There is a sad little snack stand with a sign, "Part-Time Help Wanted." The man behind the counter is played by the same actor who plays Bruce. Alice enters with a small suitcase and sits at the counter.

MAN. Hi.

ALICE (*surprised*). Hi.

MAN. Is something wrong?

ALICE. No. You remind me of someone.

MAN. I hope that's a good thing.

ALICE. May I have mint tea, please.

MAN. Huh?

ALICE. Tea. What kind of tea do you have?

MAN. Regular tea.

ALICE. OK. Regular tea, then.

MAN. Are you visiting someone in Poughkeepsie?

ALICE. No. Just passing through. (*Pause.*) Well, if I were staying for a few days, what would I see in Poughkeepsie?

MAN. Diners. Gas stations. A nice university campus. A movie theater. Trees. People.

ALICE. Can I get sushi in town?

MAN. You mean raw fish? Forget it. But you can get baked clams.

ALICE. I guess that's close enough. Who comes through this station?

MAN. Oh, I don't know. Some students. People visiting families. Ghosts.

Pause.

ALICE. Are you looking for part-time help?

MAN. Yeah. $7.50 an hour. Thirty hours a week.

ALICE. OK.

MAN. What?

ALICE. I'm applying for the job.

MAN. I thought you were just passing through.

ALICE. I was. But there is no place I can go where I don't need luggage.

MAN. Are you traveling without luggage?

ALICE. Yes. No. Some.

MAN. Which is it?

ALICE. I have what I need to start over.

MAN. Do you have any experience?

ALICE. I'm a professional waitress.

MAN. Good. It's easy-going here. Life is an amusement park.

ALICE. What?

MAN. What's your name?

ALICE. Alice. April. Anna. And you?

MAN. Which is it?

ALICE. Sorry. I've had many nicknames. I should decide. You can call me May.

MAN. OK, May. I'm Peter. Your hours are Tuesday through Saturday, 7 a.m. to 1 p.m. A guy called Steve will take over at 1 p.m. I'm here at nights and all day Monday. We are closed on Sundays. You'll see me every Wednesday when I do the stock.

ALICE. Wednesdays . . .

MAN. Welcome to Poughkeepsie. (*Walks away, humming a familiar tune that Peter used to sing.*)

ALICE (*turning to look at Man as he walks away*). Peter?

A train has arrived. A few people with small suitcases pass by. One of them is Ghost.

Lights down.

BROKEN MORNING

Stories from the Death Row Factory

IMAGE 6.1 **The sewing factory on death row.**
Sophia Skiles, Margi Sharp, Kaipo Schwab, George Hanna, Brian Nishii (from left to right). These five actors performed twenty-five roles in the play. *Broken Morning*, directed by Sonoko Kawahara, co-produced by Crossing Jamaica Avenue and HERE Arts Center, New York City, 2003. (All subsequent photographs of this play are of this production.)

Photograph by Adrian Buckmaster.

CHARACTERS

SHEILA	Young African American woman. Her daughter Terry was kidnapped from home, raped, and murdered. She has three other children. She lives with strength and hope.
ANNE	Caucasian woman in her 50s. Her only son Alex was killed on his sixteenth birthday. She is devastated by the enormous loss.
EDWARD	Latino man in his late 40s. On death row for rape and murder of a young Latina. Cold and edgy.
MARK	African American man in his early 30s. Charming. A con artist.
PAMELA	Young Caucasian woman. Mark's ex-wife.
WALTER	Caucasian man in his late 50s. On death row. He thinks he is trying to be a better human being but is hateful and confused.
CAPTAIN GREEN	Caucasian man in his late 50s. Death-row captain. Enjoys his business. Proud.
LAURA	Young Caucasian woman. Captain's daughter. Lost. Looking for a different life.
A. L.	Asian Pacific Islander. On death row. Uneducated, remorseful.
TIM	Caucasian man in his 20s. A college student. Awkward and shy.
PAUL	African American man in his 40s. On death row for robbery and murder of a Caucasian man. He had a difficult childhood and a criminal adulthood.

DIANE	African American woman in her 30s. Paul's wife. Uneducated. Lost without Paul.
JANE	Caucasian woman in her 40s. On death row for robbery and murder of two men. She had a troubled past but is now a changed woman.
CHRIS	Caucasian man. Jane's son. Sixteen. Smart. Always supportive of his mother.
CHUCK	Young biracial man. On death row for rape and murder of an old woman. Troubled and dangerous.
OFFICER KELLY	Asian Pacific Islander. New on the job. Conservative but sensitive.
CHAPLAIN	African American man in his 40s. Blindly devoted to the men on death row.

Others:
YOUNG MAN
YOUNG WOMAN (victim)
CARLOS LOPEZ
OLD WOMAN (victim)
TEACHER
LIBRARIAN
DAD (Tim's father)

Broken Morning is a fictional play inspired by people the play-wright met in Huntsville, Texas. The project was supported by Theater Communication Group's Extended Collaboration Grant and Dallas Theater Center.

Though most of the characters are based on the interviews, some are composites of several people, including some people the playwright read about in various books.

Because there are numerous overlappings of spaces, and the time shifts often throughout the play, a bare stage would serve the play well. The time and space should be defined by lights. Some costume pieces will be needed, as actors transform into many different characters. For the New York City production directed by Sonoko Kawahara, twenty-five roles were played by a diverse company of five actors, resulting in gender, age, and race crossings. One male actor played the Writer.

BROKEN MORNING

With Lyrics by Mark Campbell

Lights up on Writer.

WRITER. The beginning. We hear a sound of glass shattering in the dark. Lights come up on Sheila, a young woman with a beautiful, strong face.

Sound of shattering glass.

SHEILA (*song*, *"An Empty Bed"*).
I didn't hear it
Didn't hear it
The window breaking
Slept right through it

I only found out
In the morning
When I went down to
Wake the kids up

I stepped on pieces
Little pieces
Of glass all scattered
In the kids' room.

Their room was cold.

That's when I saw him
Saw my youngest
He wasn't sleeping
He was sitting

And staring straight ahead

I held my stomach
And looked over
To where my daughter
Would be sleeping

And saw an empty bed

Gone.
My Terry,
My angel girl,
Just five years old.

WRITER. Lights change. We see Anne, a heavyset Caucasian woman in her fifties. White face. A young man of about sixteen enters.

Young Man walks across stage. Anne notices him. She is shocked. Hurriedly she takes off after Young Man and chases him. Finally she catches up with him and grabs his arm. Young Man turns around. Anne drops his arm.

ANNE. I'm sorry. I thought you were someone else.

Young Man exits, leaving Anne standing alone, lost.

Sound of sewing machines and general factory noise.

Anne, Young Man, and Sheila fade away.

Prison-bar lights.

WRITER. Huntsville, Texas. Ellis One Unit. Death row. Edward is a Latino man in his late forties. Stocky with a harsh face.

EDWARD. The first time I killed, I was just a kid. Bar fight. Mostly I was trying to make a path to get outta there. This dude was in my way, so he got shot. Next morning I heard on the radio he was dead and they had no suspects. I thought about it for about ten minutes, and said to myself, well, there ain't nothing I can do now. So I went out partying again. I didn't think I'd get caught.

He walks out and takes Young Woman's hand. They dance under romantic lights.

EDWARD. I got out in '82. For about two years, things were all right. Then I started doing coke and speed. I should've just stayed with marijuana and beer.

Loud sound of shattering glass. Lights change to a harsh color. Young Woman freezes.

WRITER (*reads from the fact sheet*). Edward Cruz was convicted of capital murder of a nineteen-year-old woman on June 13, 1986. Police said the woman was raped and beaten to death with a motorcycle chain under an overpass in East Austin. An autopsy showed that the Hispanic female was hit sixteen times on the head and eight times on the face with the chrome-plated chain.

Young Woman remains frozen. Edward walks back to the prison area.

EDWARD. Eight years later, I got an execution date, August 4 or 5, I think. Back in '94. They gave me the date on Good Friday, so my mom had to give up Easter. Can you believe that? They couldn't wait until the holiday was over? It bothered Mom a lot that she had to miss Easter, but she brought my daughter and my son to see me. Mallie started crying. She was seven then. I've never even touched her once. She was born when I was going to court for this case, and I've been here since. I got a stay four months later. Mallie was real happy. She says she's gonna become rich so she can get me outta here. She is my angel girl.

As Edward and Young Woman fade, lights come up on Sheila again.

SHEILA. Why didn't I hear it? The window breaking in my angel girl's room during the night.

Sheila fades. Lights come up on Mark.

WRITER. Mark is an African American man in his early thirties. He is very charming.

MARK. I went to New Mexico Junior College on a rodeo scholarship. I started out roping calves and, later, got into bull riding. It's a real exciting lifestyle. People think you are a hick if you ride the rodeo circuit, but it's a major sport. There are a hundred and twenty thousand blacks in the Professional Rodeo Cowboy Association. I didn't quite make it in rodeo. I mean, I was good enough. The money was good. I guess I didn't want it bad enough, I don't know. Now I miss it.

Lights change to prison-bar lights. Walter walks in.

WRITER. Walter. A tall and muscular Caucasian man in his fifties. There is something physically uncomfortable about him.

WALTER. You don't suck your fingers or scratch your dick and then touch the basketball, nigger. Do you hear me? I can barely stand your dirty hands, I'm not gonna put up with the rest of your filthy self, got it, nigger?

Mark ignores Walter. Walter exits.

MARK. I have plenty of friends here. I'm the type, you know. Good personality. Character. I'm very sociable. There is no problem with race here as far as I can tell. Actually I've never experienced it in my life. I've read about it in papers and watched some on TV but I've never been around it personally. I know nothing about racism.

WRITER. Edward appears in the next cell.

EDWARD. Hey Mark, I have a gut feeling. I got a chance. I may have to do some more time. Ten years maybe. I can do it. I've done ten already. Doing time never bothers me. What's up with your appeal?

MARK. You've been here a long time. A lot of people here need to go home if you ask me. Edward, you should go home, before me I mean. I'm an innocent man, but I'm not selfish. If I had a choice, I'd let you go first.

EDWARD. You're full of shit.

MARK. I'm innocent. I hardly know the people they accused me of killing. I met Barbara once. I guess I was friendly. But I never even met her cousin. I didn't go to their house. I didn't steal money from them. I didn't stab them. It's a case of mistaken identity.

EDWARD. Were they white?

MARK. Huh?

EDWARD. What were you doing hanging out with white women in the first place?

MARK. I'm good with people. I have lots of friends. Lots of women.

WRITER. Mark's wife is Pamela, a petite, young Caucasian woman.

Lights up on Pamela.

PAMELA. He writes me from death row. How he misses me and his son. How he wants to take Brendan to the boys' club for baseball. Just like his daddy did. Well, Mark has seen Brendan twice since we got divorced when he was nine months old. He turns seven on August 4. When Mark was free, he avoided paying child support. I had the attorney-general's office find him to get his wages, but as soon as we knew where he was, he'd move on to some other job before I could get a penny. We had to start looking for him all over again. He was spending all his money on drinking, cocaine, and women, I heard.

WRITER (*reads Pamela's letter*). Dear Mark, thanks for your letter. I'm in a relationship with a good man. He has a steady job, and he is kind to Brendan. It's nice for Brendan to have a father figure. I'm moving on with my life. You shouldn't write me anymore. Take care of yourself.

Lights down on Pamela.

Mark reads the letter silently in his cell.

MARK. I was raised in New Mexico, in a pretty nice lower-class family. Never really wanted for nothin'. My mom's been in restaurants all her life, working real hard for her kids.

WRITER (*reads Mark's letter*). Dear Pamela, after quitting rodeo, I lived life in the fast lane. I wasn't a very good father then. But it was fun. When we were married we had fun, too, didn't we? I have no regrets. If I could do it all over again I'd want the same exact life. I'd want everything to be just as it was.

Lights up on Captain Green.

WRITER. Mr. Green is the death-row captain. A Caucasian man in his fifties. A short, round man. Very proud.

CAPTAIN GREEN. Mark Williams, it's been six months since you caused trouble. I'm going to return you to the factory. You are basically work capable. Just don't get into any more fights. Report to work Thursday morning.

MARK. No problem.

WRITER. Texas has the largest terminally condemned population in the United States. Over four hundred. This is the sewing factory operated by the death-row inmates. Several men are cutting fabric with scissors or working at the machines. The factory has two shifts that accommodate up to one hundred and twenty inmates, and there is a long waiting list for a sewing job.

A. L. is a very large Asian Pacific Islander.

Sound of the sewing machines.

A. L. You want some coffee?

EDWARD. Coffee? In this weather?

A. L. I don't mind. I'm used to being hot.

EDWARD. Maybe later. I have to soak in the air conditioning for a coupla hours before I can drink coffee.

A. L. It's nice the factory is air conditioned.

EDWARD. In exchange for slave labor.

A. L. I don't mind.

EDWARD. Hey, is there anything you do mind?

MARK. You have to admit, Edward, it's not a bad deal. We get to talk to each other, you know, as friends.

EDWARD. Speak for yourself.

MARK. And it's hot in the cells. We get to sit in air conditioning. The work isn't hard.

EDWARD. What're we making, man? Prison guards' pants!

MARK. I have a pretty good life. I don't care to be negative.

EDWARD. Alright, Mark. Your life on death row is pretty good. How 'bout you, A. L. You have a pretty good life?

A. L. Well . . . I can drink coffee anytime I want. I think about the Bible all the time. Maybe God will forgive me and I'll leave here someday. I don't even know what it's like out there anymore. I don't want to get into a dangerous place. I just want a little air, a little peace.

WRITER. The factory fades away. Lights up on Captain Green.

CAPTAIN GREEN. When I first came to the Texas Department of Corrections, TDC, I worked in the food service for a while. I was Assistant Food Service Manager. Then I was promoted to Food Service Captain. Twenty years in the correctional business. Now I'm the Death-Row Captain. I'm in charge of all the death-row operations. I supervise a lieutenant, six sergeants, one hundred and forty-five guards. We have three full-time psychologists, two full-time dentists, and three full-time doctors just for death row. My wife works for TDC, too. She drives the bus, transports inmates back and forth. Our kids are TDC brats. My daughter works as a guard. It's a family business.

Lights up on Laura.

WRITER. His daughter Laura is twenty-nine, though she looks older. She has two children.

LAURA. I wanted to go to college. I don't know, it just didn't happen. All my family worked for the system and there is nothing else to do in this town. It's a decent job, good benefits.

She is on the phone with her father.

CAPTAIN GREEN. Laura, are you coming over this weekend? I'll take Jack fishing.

LAURA. What about Beth?

CAPTAIN GREEN. Sure, if she wants to come. I was just thinking Jack and I'll have a little man-to-man talk. You know, he has been asking about what I do lately. I think he's beginning to think about his future.

LAURA. He's going to college.

CAPTAIN GREEN. He can study criminology at Sam Houston. If he works as a guard, he can go part-time and get his education paid for.

IMAGE 6.2 **Laura, Captain Green's daughter, once had a different dream from becoming a death-row prison guard.**

Margi Sharp.

Photograph by Brian Nishii.

LAURA. Dad, he's only seven.

CAPTAIN GREEN. It's never too early to start planning. He's got things going for him. I can direct him to the right people.

LAURA. Do you have plans for Beth?

CAPTAIN GREEN. She's a smart girl. I'm sure she will follow your mom's and your footsteps.

LAURA. She is not going to be a prison guard.

CAPTAIN GREEN. What's wrong with being a prison guard? She should be so lucky.

They hang up the phone. Captain Green fades away.

LAURA. It gives me the creeps when Dad smiles and says, "We're a TDC family." It sounds like we are victims of some awful medication that resulted in deformed babies or something.

She puts on a uniform jacket and moves into the prison area.

WALTER. Can I be next for the shower?

LAURA. No, you can't. I'll call you when I'm good and ready to let you take a shower.

WALTER. It's almost time for work.

LAURA. Did you hear me? In here, you do what I tell you to do. That's the rule . . . for a change.

Walter mumbles.

LAURA. What? Did you say something?

WALTER. Bitch.

LAURA. I think we're out of time for showers today. Tomorrow, think about holding your tongue and showing some respect, big man.

Walter and the prison lights disappear.

WRITER. Laura's past. Seven years back. She is in a local bar. She meets Tim, a Caucasian college student. Laura is a pretty young woman. Tim is short and nerdy.

Tim enters and sees Laura, hesitates for a while, then goes up to her.

TIM. Um, hi. Can I buy you a drink?

LAURA. OK. Gin and tonic.

TIM. Can I sit here?

LAURA. Sure. You live around here?

TIM. Nearby. I go to Texas A&M. Oh, I'm Tim.

LAURA. Laura. I'm thinking about applying to Texas A&M. Is it nice?

TIM. It's alright, I guess.

LAURA. What're you studying?

TIM. Biomedical science.

LAURA. What do you do with it?

TIM. Um, I may go to pharmacy school. Possibly. I don't know.

LAURA. Is your father a pharmacist?

TIM. No, he is—what do you call it?—a shift operator. For an oil company. Would you . . . um . . . would like to go out to dinner?

LAURA. Right now? I haven't finished my drink yet.

IMAGE 6.3 **Laura once dated a college student, Tim, a Caucasian man, who later ended up on death row where she would become a guard.**

Margi Sharp (left), George Hannah (right).

Photograph by Brian Nishii.

TIM. I'll buy you another one at the restaurant. Do you like lobsters?

LAURA. I don't know.

TIM. Steak, then? A T-bone steak and a baked potato. Sounds good?

LAURA. You got money for that?

TIM. You can order anything you want.

LAURA. OK. I'll go.

Tim and Laura fade; Sheila appears.

SHEILA. Why didn't I hear it? The glass breaking in the night.

Young Man walks across the stage. Anne notices him, and follows him. Finally she catches up with him and grabs his arm. He turns around. She drops his arm.

ANNE. I'm sorry. I thought you were someone else.

Young Man exits, leaving Anne standing alone. Sheila and Anne fade away.

WRITER. Prison lights up on Paul, an African American man in his forties.

PAUL. "In God We Trust." That means money, right? And it's not about African Americans either. If I had some money, I wouldn't be sitting here on death row right now. I'd be partying with my wife. It's been a nightmare and a half for her. After she spent all that time in prison needlessly for supposedly being my accomplice, I didn't want her to work no more. Fortunately, I'm something of a good planner when it comes to economics, right? So from here I figured out a situation for her that successfully allowed her not to work, get a car, and rent a house. She is a strong woman. She'll make it now without me. Yeah.

Lights change.

WRITER. Paul's memory. Carlos enters.

CARLOS. How you doing, Paul?

PAUL. Alright.

CARLOS. It's Christmas, man. You going to commissary?

PAUL. No.

CARLOS. You got money?

PAUL. No.

CARLOS. Here, take this money.

PAUL. I'm independent, man. I don't ask nobody nothing.

CARLOS. You don't owe me. Take it. Get some cigarettes. Merry Christmas.

Carlos disappears.

PAUL. The thing that messed me up was that he wasn't black. Carlos Lopez. He was from Colombia. It was my first Christmas in here; my wife was still in prison, so I had no one. After that, from time to time, Carlos gave me cigarettes and ice cream. But he wasn't black, you see. That really messed me up. I guess you'd say he was a friend. He got executed last year. Sometimes I wonder what it's like in Colombia.

Lights shift to A. L. in the visiting room. Chaplain enters. They are separated by glass and steel.

WRITER. The death-row chaplain is a thin white man with glasses, in his sixties.

CHAPLAIN. Hello, friend. You sent for me?

A. L. I hear a voice in my head. It's my uncle's voice.

CHAPLAIN. Where is your uncle?

A. L. He's back home. In Samoa.

CHAPLAIN. You're just missing him. No need to worry.

A. L. He's gonna beat me, he says. He won't leave me alone.

CHAPLAIN. Do you have family here?

A. L. No, they had nothing to do with it.

CHAPLAIN. I meant, do you have people who come to visit you here?

A. L. Oh, no. My mom is in Hawaii. I send her cards sometimes.

CHAPLAIN. How many visitors did you have this year?

A. L. I don't really . . . Like I said, Mom's in Hawaii, I got two kids I don't know where . . . My brothers and sisters call me sometimes.

CHAPLAIN. Would you like me to visit you every week? We can talk about the Bible.

A. L. I don't mind. Sure.

CHAPLAIN. Good. Think of me as family.

A. L. and Chaplain exit in opposite directions.

WRITER. Jane is a Caucasian woman in her forties. Short and round. Her son Chris, a skinny boy with a determined face, is sixteen. They are in the visiting room at the Gatesville Prison in Texas, where seven women are on death row.

Lights on Chris.

CHRIS. (*song, "About That Sweater"*)

About that sweater.
It totally doesn't fit.
It pretty much looks like shit.
The one thing you can say.
It does look hand-knit.

Sometimes I swear I don't know who she is.
Sometimes I think that might be for good.
She isn't what you'd call a sitcom mom.
Whatever, she did the best she could.

My mom, a former junkie on death row.
You'd think a normal life might be a reach.
And then she goes and makes some sweater thing,
Or gives you the "you're-a-man-now" speech.

Sometimes I don't know who the fuck she is.
And other times I feel like I'm her kid.
No, she doesn't act like she's a sitcom mom,
I'd probably hate her if she did.

About that sweater
So it's not a work of art.
But made with her hands and heart,
I'll wear the ugly thing
'Til it falls apart.

JANE. Happy Birthday, Chris.

CHRIS. Thanks, Mom. I love the sweater you made for me.

JANE. Did it fit? It's hard for me to guess the right size.

CHRIS. Perfect.

JANE. So what do you got planned for your birthday?

CHRIS. I think Bud and Nancy are taking me out to dinner.

JANE. That's nice. They couldn't come with you today, huh?

CHRIS. I think they wanted me to have private time with you. They think it's special to be sixteen.

JANE. It should be . . . Chris, I wanna tell you something today.

Pause.

JANE. When I was sixteen I got pregnant. I was so excited, I even quit doing drugs. I was getting my act together. I had a girl. Stephanie.

CHRIS. What?

JANE. Stephanie was all mine. I loved her, and there was nothing wrong. It was all good love. But she only lived for four months. I'd never heard of crib death before then. My baby died in her sleep for no good reason. Just like that. I was sent to a mental institution afterwards.

CHRIS. What happened to her father?

JANE. I heard he died in prison. He didn't know anything about Stephanie anyway.

CHRIS. Why are you telling me this now?

JANE. Because you are sixteen today. I want you to see how different your life is. You're going to college in two years. Isn't that something? I want you to know I did the best I could.

CHRIS. I know.

JANE. I'll never leave you as long as I can help it, Chris.

Chris exits.

JANE. Well, I guess I'm not going anywhere for a while anyway. But I tell him that every time I see him. When I was six, my mom just got up and left everybody—a husband, three boys, and two girls. Didn't even take her clothes. Two days later she called to say she found someone else who could love her better. Dad destroyed all her pictures in the house. A year later she died in a car crash. The man died, too. I can't remember what she looked like. If I have to leave, I want Chris to remember my face.

Jane fades away.

Paul and his wife Diane enter the visiting room.

WRITER. Diane, Paul's wife, comes to visit him often. She is an African American woman in her thirties with a noticeable amount of make-up.

PAUL. Honey, do you remember I told you about this guy, Carlos?

DIANE. Mmm hmm.

PAUL. He was from Colombia. I wanna see pictures from there.

DIANE. Where's that?

PAUL. It's a country in South America.

DIANE. How am I gonna get that?

PAUL. . . . Never mind. Were you able to open up a money market account?

DIANE. Yeah, honey. I can read and write, you know.

PAUL. I know. I'm the one who taught you how, remember?

DIANE. Paul, do you think I should try to get my kids back?

PAUL. How you gonna feed five kids?

DIANE. I got six. Anyway, three are grown already.

PAUL. Baby, you gotta take care of yourself. I'll worry if you get yourself in an impossible situation.

DIANE. I'm lonely, that's all. Maybe I should try to find your family.

PAUL. Are you nuts, Diane? All they'll do is try to swindle money outta you. They're illiterate drunks. Every one of them. You know that.

DIANE. I need somebody.

PAUL. No, you don't. Don't be foolish now. You gotta be careful out there. They are watching you. One wrong move and you lose everything. Do not trust anybody.

DIANE. I can't take it anymore.

PAUL. What's wrong with you? You wanna end up waiting tables or something? How am I gonna rest in peace?

DIANE. Paul, don't even say that.

PAUL. Don't let me down, Diane.

DIANE. It's only a few months away.

PAUL. I'll get another stay. Don't worry.

DIANE. I've gone through this ten different times in the past three years. How many more times . . .

PAUL. Would you rather have me dead?

DIANE. No, no, no. That's not what I'm saying. I wish you could come out, Paul. That's what I'm saying.

PAUL. No, baby. I'm never coming out. Be strong. Keep the car. Keep the house. My only hope is you now.

Paul fades away.

DIANE (*song, "Paul"*).

I was thirty when I married Paul
He was my fourth husband.
Married my first when I was thirteen

Paul was different from the other men.
He was a good husband.
Never did beat me, never was mean
And he taught me things
Good things
Things I didn't know before
Like how to talk
And drive, and use the ATM

And he bought me things
Nice things
Things I never had before

A house, a car
Expensive shoes—six pairs of them.

And I knew he'd been locked up before
Did him a few break-ins
Held up a bank, but I didn't mind

I'd have done hell anything for Paul
Anything he'd tell me
He was that kind.

WRITER. Diane was convicted as his accomplice. Received two life
sentences but got out in six months on a technicality.

DIANE. The crime we were accused of—Paul taught me to say that,
"what we were accused of"—was a robbery and murder of a
white clerk at the Holiday Inn.

WRITER. He was tied up in the closet and shot, and $2,500 was
missing from the register.

DIANE. Paul was good to me. I would've done anything for him.

Diane fades. Tim and Laura enter.

WRITER. Back to Tim and Laura again. Their past story in progress.

LAURA. Where are we going?

TIM. Um, I'm taking you shopping.

LAURA. What for?

TIM. How about some shoes? Nice, classy shoes.

LAURA. I don't need shoes.

TIM. You don't have to need shoes. Remember Imelda Marcos?

LAURA. Uh . . . I don't like her designs. I usually just buy Nine West.
They're cheaper.

TIM. Imelda . . . Um, today, you are going to do better than cheap.
Much better.

LAURA. Look, I can't accept gifts from you. I hardly know you.

TIM. Well, let's get to know each other, then.

LAURA. How do you have so much money?

TIM. Um, I guess you can say I come from money.

LAURA. Not your father's side.

TIM. Huh? Oh, no. My mother is from Morocco. She's British. She is a nobility of some kind in Morocco, by her uncle's marriage.

LAURA. How did your parents meet?

TIM. Um, her family is in the oil business. They have dealings with the company my father works for. Tell me something about yourself. What do you do?

LAURA. I just got a job in the sanitation department as a secretary.

TIM. That's nice.

LAURA. No. But my parents are pretty happy about it. Good benefits, you know. I wanted to check out California after high school. But my parents weren't into that. Whatever. Are you really gonna buy me shoes?

TIM. Yeah, and some jewelry. Moroccan style, maybe.

Tim and Laura exit. Lights change.

WRITER. Chuck, a light-skinned black boy with a clever face, was fifteen at the time of his crime. Mrs. Paterson was his favorite teacher.

Lights up on Teacher and Chuck.

TEACHER. Chuck, where is your paper?

CHUCK. Oh, I forgot. I'll bring it tomorrow. I promise.

Teacher smiles and pats him on his head. She walks away. Chuck spits.

CHUCK. I never had no friends. At school white kids called me darkie and blacks kids called me whitey. I'm illegitimate and I'm a mulatto. A mulatto is an outcast. Another thing that get's me no respect is that I'm little. People always treated me like I was a domestic pet. Sometimes I wanted to scream, "So you think I'm cute, huh, motherfuckers? You know I break into rich people's houses and trash them? I shred the wallpaper. I piss on their nice white carpet. That's cute, huh?"

Lights change.

WRITER. Chuck is ransacking a house. He takes out his penis and pees all over the carpet. An old woman enters and surprises him.

IMAGE 6.4 **Chuck, a biracial boy, confesses his crime to his high school teacher, who is a Caucasian woman.**

Sophia Skiles (left), George Hannah (right).

Photograph by Brian Nishii.

In the following scene, neither Chuck nor Old Woman moves. They stand apart the entire time.

OLD WOMAN. What are you doing in my house, nigger?

CHUCK. I'd been making so much noise, I didn't hear her coming. She was a tiny woman. Didn't look scared at all. That made me mad. Her eyes moved down to my pants and saw my dick hanging out. I rushed her, knocked her down on the sofa and raped her.

Old Woman gasps and cries out. Chuck, after a while, tries to catch his breath.

OLD WOMAN. I wish I was dead. I wish I was dead.

CHUCK. "OK then," I said. And I put my hands around her bony neck and strangled her. It didn't take no time at all.

Old Woman gasps for air. Lights go down on her.

CHUCK. She shouldn't have said that.

Lights change.

Chuck walks back to school. Teacher approaches him.

TEACHER. Chuck, where were you this afternoon? You missed Mrs. Johnson's class.

CHUCK. I hitched a ride to North Dallas and killed an old woman in one of the houses.

TEACHER. . . . OK, Chuck. Come and sit in my office. When the police come, don't tell them anything unless someone else is with you in the room. Do you understand?

Teacher disappears, and prison lights come up on Chuck.

CHUCK. I turned sixteen by the time I was tried, and that was old enough to be put to death. During the trial, a psychologist said to me that I was a classic case. I fucked my mother. I didn't know where he came up with that. The woman looked nothing like my mother. I loved my mother but I never wanted to fuck her. So what was he talking about? Anyway, I'll never have to file a tax return, or worry about where to spend my vacation, or any shit like that. For now, I can lead my life exactly like I want to. So that's OK by me.

Chuck fades out. Jane fades in.

JANE. When I was growing up in L. A. shooting heroin all the time, I used to say, I'm a hope-to-die dope fiend with a needle in my arm. Never did I think my dream would come true in a weird way. Last month, I actually dreamed I was executed. I even felt the stuff going into my arm. That was my third execution dream.

Chris enters.

JANE. They gave me a date.

CHRIS. You'll get another stay.

JANE. I don't know. I was twenty-four when I came here. I'm forty now. I've lived a lot on death row. I'm tired.

Pause.

JANE. I want you to keep all your plans. I want you to go away to college. There'll be a lot of publicity, but you have Bud and Nancy's last name, so people far from here won't figure it out.

CHRIS. I'm not going to hide. I'm going to give interviews on TV and newspapers.

JANE. You know I've been sober for seventeen years. I've gotten my GED. You can be proud of me at the end.

CHRIS. When?

JANE. March 2.

CHRIS. I'll make the funeral arrangements.

JANE. Bud and Nancy will do it.

CHRIS. I'll do it. I'll do it myself.

JANE. You know what's good about all this? The new warden is gonna give us a contact visit.

Jane fades away. Chris is alone.

CHRIS (*song, "Your Son"*).

I'll never be ashamed of you
I won't let that happen
I know all you've been to me
All the good you've done

I'll never be ashamed . . .
As much as they'd want that
I'll always be proud of you
Otherwise they've won

I'll never be ashamed of you
I won't let that happen
I'll always remember you
Always be your son

(*Chris continues*) A letter from one of her victims' mothers arrived. She wrote to Mom to say hurry up and die, give her some peace. When I was twelve, mom told me about her crime. She and her partner killed two men in a robbery. Her partner was executed three years ago. That was hard for her. I know during her trial, nothing was mentioned about her being a heroin addict since thirteen, or her father having sexual relations with her when she was nine, or her being tossed around juvenile halls and foster care for eight years. I think all this counts. I think it counts that a person suffers a hard life. It counts that a person is really sorry for the mistake she made. Waiting was always part of my growing up. Waiting to see Mom. Waiting for an appeal. Waiting for execution. Waiting for a stay. Now I wait some more. Mom and her partner were running from parole violation out of California. Just passing through Texas. That's how Texas became my home.

Lights change. Chris fades away. Sheila fades in.

SHEILA (*song, "Before You Know It"*).

That was a dark
That was a dark
A dark and very hateful place

I had to fight
Hard as I could
to get myself away from there

What do you do
How do you keep
From thinking of it all the time

Then there's the guilt
Like all the rest
Just isn't terrible enough

It's all your fault
You are to blame
And all that other awful stuff

When will it be over?
Will you last?

Then this one needs a band-aid
Or this one's fish has died
Or this one has a birthday

And before you know it
Time has passed.

WRITER. Lights up on Anne. She is in a library, going through microfilm.

ANNE. I had remembered a story of a woman in Texas whose daughter was murdered. She committed suicide some months after

IMAGE 6.5 **Anne, a Caucasian woman, has never recovered from the murder of her sixteen-year-old son. Writer listens.**
Kaipo Schwab (left), Sophia Skiles (right).
Photograph by Brian Nishii.

that. In October, my life became unbearable. I went to the library to look up this woman's case in the papers. I wanted to figure out how long it would take for a mother to take her own life after her child's murder. There were three months between her daughter's death and her own. My Alex was murdered in July. It had been three months.

WRITER. Anne throws up. A young African American woman, the librarian, approaches her.

LIBRARIAN. Are you alright?

ANNE. No.

LIBRARIAN. Can I get you something?

ANNE. No.

LIBRARIAN. Would you like to sit down?

ANNE. No.

LIBRARIAN. If you need any help . . .

ANNE. Please go away. My son is dead.

Pause.

LIBRARIAN. I'm sorry.

WRITER. Anne's only son was killed on his sixteenth birthday.

ANNE. Alex was sleeping in his father's house on his birthday. This creature was hiding in the backyard for some reason, and heard them celebrating earlier in the evening. He was mad because when he turned sixteen, his parents didn't pay attention to him. Alex was turning sixteen, and he had love. So this creature broke into the house late at night and stabbed Alex twenty-five times. My son was killed because he was happy.

Anne is sobbing. Librarian holds her hand.

LIBRARIAN. Was he . . . black?

ANNE. No, no, dear. He wasn't.

Lights change. Librarian fades away.

ANNE. I couldn't figure out what to do with my son's dog, so I decided to live. The average time on death row was twelve years and nine months when I first started waiting. Now it's supposed to be eight years. The creature has been there nine years. I'm still waiting.

Sound of sewing machines. Anne fades away as the factory fades in.

WRITER. The sewing factory. Walter and Edward.

WALTER. Edward, I feel like we got things in common. So you're half Mexican, or whatever. But that's still cool. You know what I'm saying?

EDWARD. What do you want, Walter?

WALTER. I wanna talk to you. You see, I think the nuclear warheads are evil. Can't believe I had anything to do with them, but I didn't know any better back then.

EDWARD. What are you talking about?

WALTER. In the Navy, my thing was nuclear warheads. I was involved in transporting them. It was wrong, I admit that. It's harmful to you and me, you know. Devoid of humanity. That's it, devoid of humanity.

EDWARD. Right. Whatever.

WALTER. I think the government should abolish nuclear warheads, or anything nuclear. It pollutes the environment, and that's not good for the kids.

EDWARD. You don't got kids.

WALTER. But you do, right? How many?

EDWARD. Three.

WALTER. So you know what I mean. You just can't be pro-nuclear and be a decent human being at the same time, right? What're their names?

EDWARD. Ricky.

WALTER. Yeah?

EDWARD. Mallie.

WALTER. Yeah?

EDWARD. What?

WALTER. You said three.

EDWARD. Two.

WALTER. You said three.

EDWARD. I got two.

WALTER. So why did you say three?

EDWARD. I didn't, 'coz I got two.

WALTER. Alright. So Ricky and Mallie. Good.

EDWARD. There's another girl. But I ain't sure if she's mine.

WALTER. All right, so maybe another girl. They need a safe place to grow up, I'm sure you agree. I'm doing something about that.

EDWARD. What?

WALTER. Well, I think sewing helps. It raises people's consciousness.

EDWARD. Whose?

WALTER. People's.

EDWARD. Which people?

WALTER. You, for example. I talked to you about the dangers of this world, and now you can protect your kids better.

EDWARD. From here?

WALTER. Whatever, still, it's a good thing. It's my mission. I realize I once did damage by handling those nuclear warheads, so I'm willing to take responsibility for it.

WRITER. Paul has been listening to their conversation.

PAUL. Do those kids you're so concerned about include black children?

WALTER. I wasn't talking to you.

PAUL. And what other wrongs have you done?

WALTER. What?

PAUL. Why you here? Not because you transported nuclear warheads for the Navy.

WALTER. Shut the hell up. I got brains to think, all right. Not like you.

PAUL. Oh, I'm thinking. About what it's gonna feel like to die. About what I'm gonna ask for my last meal. Should I have cheeseburgers or chicken wings? You know most cheeseburgers are decent, but you can really fuck up chicken wings. Do you think I wanna have a lousy last meal?

WALTER. Shut up.

PAUL. Mission, my ass.

Tense silence.

The factory fades out. Lights change.

WRITER. A gardening shop. Anne has been browsing. She goes up to Diane, Paul's wife.

ANNE. Excuse me, do you work here?

DIANE. No.

ANNE. I'm sorry.

DIANE. Are you looking for something?

ANNE. No, not really.

DIANE. I'm Diane.

ANNE. I see.

Pause.

DIANE. And you?

ANNE. . . . Anne.

DIANE. You garden?

ANNE. Well, yes, this is a gardening shop.

DIANE. I know. I don't garden myself. I'm just looking.

ANNE. I see.

Anne moves away from Diane.

DIANE. Do you want me to get somebody?

ANNE. No.

DIANE. You had a question, didn't you?

ANNE. You don't have to help me.

DIANE. I was just trying to be friendly.

ANNE. I don't feel very friendly.

DIANE. Excuse me.

Diane gives up. Anne thinks for a moment, then reluctantly approaches Diane.

ANNE. I was just wondering if I should buy more bird feed. There is one hummingbird left in my yard, and I'm hoping she'll fly south soon. She is supposed to be in Brownsville already, on her way to South America. I guess I'm supposed to take the feeder inside, so the bird won't linger.

DIANE. You're kidding. Are you really worried about a silly bird?

Disgusted, Anne moves away from Diane.

IMAGE 6.6 **Anne encounters Diane, an African American woman. She realizes that her husband, Paul, is on death row for a murder.**

Sophia Skiles (left), George Hannah (right).

Photograph by Brian Nishii.

ANNE. Well, I tried. I have no patience for people anymore. I can't say I'm a good person these days. I just keep my head low and pay my taxes. I don't owe the society anything. I love no one. I talk to no one. Since I don't invite anyone to my house, I don't clean much. I just garden. For a while, every time I closed my eyes, I saw the creature stabbing Alex. So I'd go out and pull Johnson grass, the kind with terrible roots, until my hands would bleed. Then when I closed my eyes, I just saw the grass. This suits me fine. Alone with my garden. I don't want any friends or another husband to disturb my memories of Alex.

DIANE. You're not upset, are you?

ANNE. No.

DIANE. I meant to say that you are lucky the only thing you have to worry about is a hummingbird.

ANNE. I guess so.

DIANE. My husband, he's in jail. He's on death row. I have to worry about him.

Anne is horrified. She stumbles, trying to get away from Diane.

DIANE. Hey, are you OK?

As Diane reaches for her, Anne opens her mouth to scream but nothing comes out. Silent scream.

Lights down on both.

WRITER. Tim and Laura's past. Again.

LAURA. I wish I could travel. What my father wants me to do is to marry some correctional officer in town and settle down.

TIM. He works for TDC, right?

LAURA. "We are a TDC family." He wants me to get a job there, too.

TIM. Good benefits, right?

LAURA. My father is the Death-Row Captain.

TIM. Fun job.

LAURA. Yeah. Do you wanna meet my family?

TIM. Um, not yet. Hey, do you like camping?

IMAGE 6.7 **Death-row captain Green, a Caucasian man, talks about how to handle the prisoners to a newcomer, Officer Kelly, a young Asian American man.**
Brian Nishii (left), George Hannah (right).
Photograph by Sonoko Kawahara, from Brian Nishii's video.

LAURA. It's ok.

TIM. I love the outdoors. I was a Boy Scout until I was eighteen.

LAURA. You're kidding.

TIM. No, even now, I help them out sometimes.

LAURA. I get it.

TIM. What?

LAURA. Why you're not interested in sex. The oldest Boy Scout in the country.

TIM. I'm interested in . . . I'm just not interested in committing a sin. I'll meet your family when the time is right, OK?

LAURA. OK.

Tim and Laura fade away.

WRITER. Captain Green and Officer Kelly. Officer Kelly is an Asian man in his late twenties. He is new on the job.

CAPTAIN GREEN. There are two levels on death row: work capable and segregation. If you are work capable, you can get a job in the sewing factory. You work, and receive some privileges. Education if you want. Mail from anybody. Exercise anytime you want. Watch cable TV. We open the cell door on the hour, and you can go to the dayroom. No handcuffs. But if you are a seg, you stay in your cell twenty-one or twenty-three hours a day.

OFFICER KELLY. The segregation must be rough.

CAPTAIN GREEN. You must recognize these men for who they are. They're murderers.

OFFICER KELLY. I think some men deserve a life sentence instead.

CAPTAIN GREEN. They give you sad stories?

OFFICER KELLY. Everyone is poor.

CAPTAIN GREEN. Right. No one on death row has any money. They are all public defender cases. Burdens to the society.

OFFICER KELLY. Some of them may even be innocent.

CAPTAIN GREEN. I don't care if they are innocent or guilty. We didn't try 'em. That's between them, their lawyers and the courts. It's your job to watch them. They're dangerous individuals, and you have to treat them as such.

Chaplain walks in.

CHAPLAIN. Captain Green, Ronald in segregation would like to attend the service this Friday.

CAPTAIN GREEN. Ronald. Ronald Howard? No way.

CHAPLAIN. He is a good Christian. Very solemn.

CAPTAIN GREEN. He's dangerous.

CHAPLAIN. Trust me, Captain Green. He has found Jesus Christ.

CAPTAIN GREEN. I don't care if he found Queen Elizabeth. He's much too dangerous to the rest of the inmates, and I promise you he'll at least spit at you if you give him the opportunity.

CHAPLAIN. Don't you think people can change?

CAPTAIN GREEN. The answer is no. Excuse me, Chaplain, I have some business to tend to.

CHAPLAIN. Yes, of course. God bless you.

Captain Green exits. Officer Kelly follows.

CHAPLAIN. I love these men on death row. I devote my life to teaching them the word. I laugh with them, hug them, have coffee with them. Sometimes I cry with them. God forgives. Every person is new once he finds Jesus Christ. I don't care to know what they have done. Yesterday, I read about a new arrival's case in the Houston paper. Something about the next-door neighbor. But I didn't pay attention to the details. I wouldn't remember them anyway. My mission is to bring glory to God by helping these men on their Christian walk.

Anne fades in; Chaplain remains visible.

ANNE. People say Alex is in a better place. I tell them if they ever lose their children, they can comfort themselves with that. The best place for him was here. He was getting my Chevy for his birthday. He was really excited. He wanted to be here. Not in a better place. Here. With his friends, his dog, his family, his mother. I don't go into stores round Mother's Day anymore. I don't want to be wished Happy Mother's Day. Same with Christmas. I buy enough of all my necessities like toothpaste and soap way before Thanksgiving, so no one wishes me Happy Holidays. I don't celebrate Christmas. But they celebrate it on death row.

CHAPLAIN. One inmate asked me if he would meet his victim in Heaven. I had never thought about that. The Bible says you recognize your loved ones. I told him to put his mind at rest. Don't dwell on the victim. Just think about the Lord Jesus Christ.

IMAGE 6.8 **Paul, an African American man, does not think his trial was fair.**

Margi Sharp.

Photograph by Brian Nishii.

Chaplain and Anne fade away.

Prison lights up on A. L.

A. L. I miss little bananas from Samoa. Sometimes for Christmas they have bananas here, but it's not the same. When I was a kid, Mom left me and went to work in Hawaii. Left me in charge of my little brothers and sisters. My uncle, he beat me, he took care of me. I still hear his voice in my head: "If you don't quit drugs, one day you gonna regret it." But I started with vodka and whisky. He got me drunk one night and I was hooked. I wish it was all a dream. Dying is bad, you know, if you don't go to . . . I wish it was a dream.

The factory fades in around A. L.

A. L. Wish it was a dream.

MARK. It was a case of mistaken identity.

EDWARD. I didn't think I'd get caught.

PAUL. "In God We Trust," that means money.

MARK. I'm good with people. Lots of women.

WALTER. Devoid of humanity.

EDWARD. I lived the way I wanted to live.

PAUL. I didn't recognize the things they were saying at the trial.

WALTER. Self-education.

PAUL. All white jury.

MARK. Race didn't play a role. Just a poor investigation.

EDWARD. Guess I should've stayed with just marijuana and beer.

WALTER. Capital punishment is political. We're used as tools.

A. L. Wish it was a dream.

WALTER. I believe in the second chance. I educate myself in here for that day. You never know. I read science magazines. I always loved science. That's why I went into the Navy. You see, people, they are hard to guess. They change their minds all the time. One minute they are OK and the next minute, all fucked up. I don't have time for that. You can depend on science. To move forward. That's what I need. To move forward.

JANE. Chris was one year old when I came here. So it'll be fifteen years since I last touched him. In here, the benefit of death is being allowed to hug your son just once . . . We've always been very close. He comes to see me every other week. When my lawyer and his wife offered to take Chris when he was six, I thought, finally I can give him a normal home. When I was a child, I used to look at other families and think why, why, why can't my family be normal like them? They'd sit down and eat dinner together. Why can't we be like that? But now Chris has that. Nothing but private schools. I've done it. He's got a real chance now. I've broken the cycle. I'm ready.

Jane fades away.

WRITER. Tim and Laura. The past moving toward the inevitable present.

LAURA. Let's do something. All we ever do is spend your money. Why don't we do something exciting tonight?

TIM. Such as?

LAURA. I don't know. There's nothing to do in this town.

TIM. I don't need excitement. I'm happy with things as they are.

LAURA. I'm bored.

TIM. I've always been quiet. I see people at college being loud and going off to parties all the time. I've never been part of that.

LAURA. What? Instead you go to church?

TIM. Um . . . Sometimes. Maybe you should, too.

LAURA. No, thank you.

TIM. What're you upset about?

LAURA. Because nothing ever changes.

TIM. Why do things have to change?

LAURA. Have you been to Morocco?

TIM. Huh?

LAURA. Didn't you say your mother is from Morocco?

TIM. Um, yes. I have. When I was a child.

LAURA. I'd like to go far away. But instead, I'm gonna be a prison guard, to make my father happy.

TIM. I'm sure he'd understand if you pursue a different career.

LAURA. Probably. But I have no idea what else to pursue.

Tim disappears.

WRITER. This is the end of their past together.

LAURA. I don't know why I thought he could change something in my life, in me. It didn't happen. I became a security guard at the prison. Good benefits, you know. Two years later, I woke up one morning to find his face all over the front page.

WRITER (*reading from the paper*). Tim Warner broke into an ex-classmate's home to steal money and shot Cathy Brown in the head when she woke up. Afterward, he probed her head wound with a knife in an effort to retrieve the bullet. Unsuccessful, he then poured gasoline on her body and set it on fire. He then left her house, called his minister at home, and later walked into the police station. He had been burglarizing homes for a few years, spending the money on luxury items.

LAURA. Lobster dinners and designer shoes . . .

WRITER. Tim is on death row.

Laura fades away as Tim fades in. Prison lights on Tim. Captain Green goes by.

TIM. Are you Captain Green?

CAPTAIN GREEN. Yes. What do you want?

TIM. Nothing. Nice to meet you.

Captain Green walks away. Officer Kelly passes him.

CAPTAIN GREEN. Kelly, are you going to lunch?

OFFICER KELLY. No, Captain. I brought a sandwich with me.

CAPTAIN GREEN. C'mon. Today, they are serving double beef cheese-burgers. It's the inmates' favorite last meal. You should have a taste.

OFFICER KELLY. I'll pass on that today.

Captain Green exits.

OFFICER KELLY. In the dozen years before I got here, one hundred and eighty-six people were executed. I expected the death row to be a dangerous place. But it's strangely peaceful here. I'm surprised to see teenagers on death row. For them, sewing in the factory is their first job ever. I look at the older men who have been here for years. This is their home. I hear stories of men who rape and kill just to get on death row. For a place to sleep and three square meals. For a peace and quiet they cannot get out there on the streets.

Officer Kelly fades away.

Prison lights up on Tim. Chaplain enters.

CHAPLAIN. Are you the new inmate?

TIM. Yes, Sir.

CHAPLAIN. Do you have anything to confess?

TIM. I confess with my mouth and believe with my mind.

CHAPLAIN. I thought so. You know the Lord Jesus then?

TIM. He is the only way to salvation.

CHAPLAIN. Be at peace, son. You'll go to Heaven.

TIM. Yes, I know.

Tim disappears. Laura enters wearing a uniform jacket.

LAURA. There are almost four hundred men on death row here. I haven't run into Tim more than a few times during the last two years. I married another guard soon after I broke up with Tim. We have a boy and a girl. We are a TDC family.

(A flashback.)

LAURA. Let's go to Morocco and visit your relatives.

TIM. Um, that's an expensive trip.

LAURA. But you come from money.

TIM. I have a busy year at Texas A&M. I'm a senior this year.

LAURA. What are you gonna do after college?

TIM. I don't know. I could get a job in the same company where my father works.

LAURA. So we won't travel.

TIM. We should wait.

LAURA. And we won't make love.

TIM. Um, we should wait.

Lights down on Tim and Laura, and up on Captain Green. Present.

CAPTAIN GREEN. I have some travel opportunities in this job. I went to a seminar in '93 in Colorado, called Management on Death-Row Principles. It was really interesting. Twenty-seven states were represented. Louisiana, they got lethal injection. Georgia has the electric, Utah's got the firing squad, Washington's got hanging. We all got together and compared notes. I actually did a lot of teaching and advising, because we're the largest, and everyone was looking up to us. Some of them only got six or seven inmates on death row. So they were learning from us.

Laura fades in.

LAURA. Life is what it is. It's fine. I want my kids to make it, though. I want them to be something big. Away from this town.

WRITER. Lights up on Chuck and Officer Kelly. Chuck is now eighteen, but still small.

CHUCK. Hey, Kelly have you tried the prison chow yet?

OFFICER KELLY. No, Chuck, I usually bring lunch.

CHUCK. What's the matter? The buffet doesn't look good to you?

OFFICER KELLY. I'm sure it's alright.

CHUCK. Well, I'm not so sure. I'm not sure at all if it's fit for human consumption.

OFFICER KELLY. . . . . I'll try it next week.

CHUCK. Whatever. I don't give a shit. It's all free.

OFFICER KELLY. Chuck, how do you like working in the factory?

CHUCK. What's there to like?

OFFICER KELLY. Do you like having a job?

CHUCK. Hey, what's this? What're you getting at?

OFFICER KELLY. Nothing. I was just having a conversation.

CHUCK. A conversation, huh? Let me ask you something.

OFFICER KELLY. What?

CHUCK. Do you think I can have a guitar?

OFFICER KELLY. I don't think so. Why? Do you play?

CHUCK. I usedta play for this teacher I had. She liked it. She thought I was talented. Oh, well. Whatever.

OFFICER KELLY. I'll find out for you.

CHUCK. Forget it. Who cares.

They fade out. Sheila fades in.

SHEILA. Terry was raped before she was killed. For a while, I had a list of things I would do to the killer. Pound his head with a sledgehammer. Pull his nails out. Break a huge piece of glass on his head. Smash his feet until they were mush. They play basketball on death row. I got three kids, and I can't afford a basketball net. That's not right. But I try not to think about any of that. I'm making enough money waiting tables at IHOP to keep this house for me and my kids. A lot of my customers know about Terry, so we talk sometimes. But mostly I live for my kids. Christina is five now. The same age as Terry when she was killed. Christina was born afterward, but she knows about her sister. It was a blessing for me to get another girl. And my new baby makes two girls. Double blessing. No child will ever replace Terry, but I've learned to love my memories.

Sheila fades away as the visiting room fades in.

WRITER. Tim is visited by his father.

DAD. We're moving away in a few months.

TIM. Where?

DAD. I'm taking an early retirement. Your sister is finished with college. So.

TIM. Where?

DAD. Tim, you know it has been difficult for us since . . . Your mother says the neighbors are constantly watching us and

IMAGE 6.9 **The ending tableau.**

Margi Sharp, Sophia Skiles, George Hannah, Kaipo Schwab, Brian Nishii (from left to right).

Photograph by Adrian Buckmaster.

talking about us. I've had some unpleasant times at work. Your sister should be able to do things like date and go on trips with friends. We just want to be a normal family again. If we move far away, no one will know us. We can start over.

TIM. You mean you'll move away and pretend you don't have a son.

Pause.

Don't worry, Dad. If you don't tell, no one will suspect it. You can look like a normal family, I'm sure.

DAD. It was a hard decision to make.

TIM. I was once part of the normal family, too. Always a good boy, remember? Never in trouble. Never even smoked pot. Everyone else was having fun, but not me.

DAD. It was a long time ago.

TIM. I was working at McDonald's while other students were running around with brand new clothes every week and going on ski trips every weekend. I wanted be part of that just once. I wanted to have friends. Is that abnormal?

DAD. Nobody forced you to become . . .

TIM. What? What have I become? Don't you know I'm a tailor? My responsibility is the belt part of the pants, Dad. It requires the most skill.

DAD. Grandma is getting so old, we thought it might be nice to move to California to be near her. Your mother misses her, you know.

TIM. Not Morocco?

DAD. What?

TIM. Nothing. Hey, California, that's a neat state. Do you know that they spend more money on their prison system than the state universities?

DAD. What have we done wrong?

TIM. Absolutely nothing. We were a completely normal, dull family. There was nothing extraordinary about my life.

As Tim and his dad fade away, Young Man walks across in front.

Anne follows him, catches up with him, and grabs his arm. He turns around.

ANNE. I'm so sorry.

Anne bursts out crying.

YOUNG MAN. Are you OK?

ANNE. I thought you were Alex, my son. I don't know why. I know he is dead.

YOUNG MAN. I'm sorry. Is there anything I can do?

ANNE. No, no. Thank you. You remind me of Alex. He was kind. You see, Alex didn't like pickles. We had to special-order at McDonald's, because he didn't want pickle juice on his hamburger. The autopsy report said there were dill pickles in his stomach. I smiled because, see, his father's new wife didn't know Alex hated pickles. So she served them on his birthday, and he ate them to be polite. Alex had a generous spirit.

Anne smiles proudly through her tears.

YOUNG MAN. He sounds like a good person. I should go. Take care.

ANNE. You too, dear. Thank you. I just wanted to tell you . . .

YOUNG MAN. Yes?

ANNE. I was really proud of you for making honors math. I didn't have a chance to tell you that.

YOUNG MAN. You mean Alex.

ANNE. I also wanted you to know that this year, I had great tomatoes. Thanks to your help.

YOUNG MAN. I understand.

He turns to go.

ANNE. These days, you should keep your doors and windows locked when you sleep, don't you think?

YOUNG MAN. I guess.

ANNE. You can never be too careful. Try to remember that.

YOUNG MAN. I will. Goodbye.

ANNE. Goodbye.

Young Man leaves. Anne is alone.

ANNE. I'm glad I got to say goodbye.

Anne fades away.

Jane and Chris fade in. Sound of a gate unlocking and opening. The prison lights lift from Jane. She walks out and stands next to Chris. They hug tightly for a long time.

Jane steps away; lights down on her. Sheila fades in.

SHEILA (*song, "Frankie"*).

Going on eleven,
My Frankie
How did that ever happen?
Eleven.

Seems to have forgotten
That morning.
Though he still has to sleep with
The light on.

Moving was a good thing—
That helped some.
Though we still have our nightmares
Glass breaking . . .

He is such a great kid,
My Frankie.
Sure I love all my children,
But Frankie . . .

There's really something special about him
We're a team
Me and my son
And I don't know what
I would have done without him
He taught me
That you have to move on . . .

Chris has entered quietly, upstage.

CHRIS. The wait is over.
   March second has come,
   March second has almost gone.
   Amazing how quick the whole thing was,
   Now comes the hard part I guess . . .
   To move on

SHEILA. To move on

CHRIS. To move on

SHEILA. To move on

CHRIS (*overlapping with Sheila*). To move on

WRITER. A silhouette tableau of all the characters come up. The sound of sewing machines is heard.

   Blackout.

IMAGE 7.1 **Antigone and her fiancé Harold find themselves in the underworld after their deaths.**

Angel Desai (left), Joey Collins (right). Women's Project, as part of *Antigone Project*, New York City, 2004. (All subsequent photographs of this play are of this production.)

Photograph by T. Charles Erickson.

RED AGAIN

After Sophocles's Antigone

CHARACTERS

ANTIGONE	A woman
HAROLD	Antigone's lover
IRENE	Antigone's sister

TIME	All times converging into one instant
PLACE	The underworld and the world of the living

Red Again is the last scene of a play in five parts—*Antigone Project*—written by Karen Hartman, Tanya Barfield, Caridad Svich, Lynn Nottage, and Chiori Miyagawa. The project was conceived by Miyagawa and director Sabrina Peck and developed by Crossing Jamaica Avenue.

SOPHOCLES' *ANTIGONE*

Antigone was written in 442 BC. In the play, Eteocles and Polynices, sons of Oedipus, go to war over the city of Thebes and die at each other's hands. Antigone, their sister, defies the new king's edict to leave Polynices' body exposed for vultures to devour—because he attacked Thebes—and buries his body. She is punished and condemned to a slow death, sealed in a cave. Ismene, her sister, who refused to help Antigone bury their brother, comes to regret her decision. Haemon, Antigone's fiancé and the King's son, kills himself when he learns of Antigone's death. This is where my play begins.

RED AGAIN

Antigone and Harold find themselves in beautiful blue light. There are piles of books around and nothing else. A portion of downstage remains dark.

ANTIGONE (*disoriented*). Harold. Where are we?

HAROLD. The underworld, I assume.

ANTIGONE. The underworld. Then you followed me here.

HAROLD. It was my destiny.

ANTIGONE. We didn't say goodbye, did we?

HAROLD. I would not have expected anything so sentimental from you, Antigone.

IMAGE 7.2 **The opening video by Nick Schwarts-Hall.**
Photograph by T. Charles Erickson.

IMAGE 7.3 **Harold and Antigone reminisce about their lives together.**
Joey Collins (left), Angel Desai (right).
Photograph by T. Charles Erickson.

ANTIGONE. You could have lived.

HAROLD. I didn't.

ANTIGONE. I'm sorry.

HAROLD. For what?

ANTIGONE. For bringing tragedy into your life.

HAROLD. I don't mind tragedy.

ANTIGONE. I had to do what I did. Something colossal went wrong, and it was changing the composition of human decency.

HAROLD. I know.

ANTIGONE. The rich grew greedier and greedier with suspicion and destruction, and the poor stood mute. The earth was mutilated, animals tortured and discarded, rivers poisoned. People began to disappear. I had to bury my brother's body. I couldn't just let him disappear. He was my last brother.

HAROLD. Antigone. I don't mind tragedy. You did the right thing.

ANTIGONE. It was the right thing to do. I had to be courageous.

HAROLD. You were courageous.

ANTIGONE. The end was dark and cold. A long time passed, or no time at all. Time stopped. I was afraid of death.

HAROLD. Didn't you know that I would follow you?

ANTIGONE. I was afraid to die.

HAROLD. Now I'm here with you.

ANTIGONE. Yes. I'm no longer afraid.

Pause.

ANTIGONE. I did not expect the underworld to be so serene. I thought I would see my doomed family.

HAROLD. This may be Bardo. A transition place.

ANTIGONE. It's rather beautiful.

HAROLD. It reminds me of the ocean. The air smells salty, too.

Pause.

ANTIGONE. What would you have preferred to this?

HAROLD. Nothing. I prefer you to everything. But if you weren't so enraged all the time about the injustices of the world, I would've been happy just meditating.

ANTIGONE. You can't change the world by meditating.

HAROLD. You're wrong.

ANTIGONE. How?

HAROLD. It's too complex to explain right now.

ANTIGONE. I think we have a lot of time.

HAROLD. The point is, I knew the fire in you was irreconcilable. You were born with that fire. I didn't try to change you.

ANTIGONE. I tried to change you, didn't I? But I couldn't find a revolution that I could sign us both up for.

HAROLD. So you left me.

ANTIGONE. Because the society had gone intolerably wrong and you were still meditating. Not burying my brother, the un-patriot, would have meant that I consented to surrendering my rights to perform rituals and honor my ancestors. What would we have lost next?

Freedom of speech and thought? The right not to reproduce? The right to eat meat or not to eat meat? Freedom to go roller-skating?

HAROLD. Antigone, you did the right thing.

ANTIGONE. Yes, I did.

HAROLD. After you were executed,

ANTIGONE. I wasn't. I hanged myself.

HAROLD. After you hanged yourself . . . I tried to kill the King. I failed.

Pause.

ANTIGONE. Thank you for following me. I was desperately lonely.

HAROLD. We were engaged. I'm keeping my promise.

Pause.

ANTIGONE. What now?

HAROLD. We wait.

From the dark side of the stage, a bloodcurdling scream is heard. A stark light comes up on Irene, facing the audience.

Irene is in the world of the living. Harold and Antigone freeze.

IRENE. I'm reporting a double suicide. My sister, Antigone, hanged herself, and her boyfriend, Harold, found her body and then stabbed himself. My name is Irene. I live in Manhattan. Please hurry. We are being evacuated. All people of Japanese descent received notice to relocate in forty-eight hours. I'm packing my life into two suitcases that I can carry. I can't carry two dead bodies. I can't carry my sister. I can't carry her. I have to carry linen and silver and our family curse. Antigone is dead. Forever. I can't carry any more. I'm being sent far, far

IMAGE 7.4 **Irene is left alone in the world of the living where time is collapsed and human atrocities play like a film on a loop.**

Tracie Thoms.

Photograph by T. Charles Erickson.

away from home. Somewhere called Treblinka. Do you know where it is? I think it's in Bosnia. Or Cambodia. Please. I need help. I'm reporting a broken heart, broken bodies, broken humanity.

Irene freezes.

In the blue light, Antigone shivers.

HAROLD. Are you cold?

ANTIGONE. What are we waiting for?

HAROLD. An opportunity for reincarnation.

ANTIGONE. I don't want to go back. Leaving was an immense effort. Leaving my little sister was as excruciating as the thought of continuing to live without dignity. After Polynices' death, I could not reconcile the two planes of my existence—my critical stance of the kingdom and my love for you and Irene. I didn't think personal love was enough when I no longer trusted humanity.

HAROLD. It was enough for me. The world didn't have to be larger than the people I loved. Until you were taken away from me. Then the world became painfully enormous.

ANTIGONE. Why do you want to go back?

HAROLD. We didn't get to finish our story.

ANTIGONE. Will you touch my face? (*Harold does.*) I like it when you touch my face.

Antigone and Harold freeze. Lights up on Irene again.

IRENE. Yes, you might have called my brother dark-skinned; though not really dark, but definitely not creamy white. That did not make him a terrorist. He didn't have any weapons. All he had was a wallet which transformed into the shape of a gun in the presence of police officers. But I'm not calling about Polynices. Children are being murdered everywhere by fictitious weapons of mass destruction and economic sanctions and postwar deprivations. I'm calling on August 6, 8.15 a.m. The mushroom cloud from Hiroshima is choking Manhattan.

IMAGE 7.5 **Antigone finds books in the underworld that correspond to all human lives ever lived.**

Joey Collins (background), Angel Desai (front).

Photograph by T. Charles Erickson.

It's April 22 , and the mustard gas released at the eastern front in France is choking Manhattan. It's September 11, 8.46 a.m. I'm reporting a broken city. Antigone and Harold are both dead.

Irene freezes again. Antigone reads one of the books from the pile.

ANTIGONE. Harold, look at this book. I know the woman in the story. I went to school with her. She married a doctor and had a life of suburban luxury, but one day, she woke up screaming. She walked right out the door of her big white house screaming, through the garden full of roses and geraniums, and became an artist. It's all in here.

HAROLD. What was her name?

ANTIGONE. Kate.

HAROLD. You've never talked about her before.

ANTIGONE. I lost touch with her after school. I often wondered what became of her.

HAROLD. What does the book say?

Antigone flips the book to the end.

ANTIGONE. The book is not finished. There are blank pages at the end. Kate lives in Germany. She hears about my death in the news and remembers me. Remembers that I was not so wild with rage back then. She is sad for me.

HAROLD. Look, Antigone. Here is your book.

ANTIGONE. Mine?

HAROLD. Here are some things you said to the King that got you in trouble.

"I do not think your edict has such force that you, one man, can override the great, written, unshakable traditions."

"Your moralizing repels me; every word you say is a greedy lie. The public's lips are locked in fear of the ruthless power that can randomly accuse anyone of being a traitor for any reason."

ANTIGONE. I spoke the truth.

HAROLD. You sure did. I mean, I was proud of you. Here is the fight you and Irene had.

As Harold continues to read, we see the past re-enacted by Antigone and Irene, breaking the invisible wall between them.

ANTIGONE. How can you bear to leave our brother disgraced?

IRENE. They are watching us every minute. Our phone is tapped, our e-mails are scrutinized, our activities are photographed.

ANTIGONE. You didn't answer my question.

IRENE. Have we not had enough tragedy in our family? Have we not been persecuted enough? Please, let's hold on to what is left of us.

ANTIGONE. You will always know your own compromise. You will have to live with that knowledge for the rest of your life.

IRENE. Yes. I'll live to regret it. But you won't, because you'll be dead.

ANTIGONE. I won't submit to an unreasonable authority. There are certain things that are true about being human, no matter who rules us. We have the right to bury our own brother.

IRENE. We have the right to live. Some things are bigger than you. There is a time to wait and a time to act. You must be patient.

ANTIGONE. Waiting and keeping silent only degrades one's soul. You are a coward.

IRENE. Lack of survival instinct is insanity. You're a madwoman.

ANTIGONE. I will bury him myself.

IRENE. No, Antigone. Live. Live with me.

ANTIGONE. You are no longer my blood.

End of memory. Harold stops reading.

HAROLD. You are severe.

ANTIGONE. Poor Irene. She is left alone with everyone's grief. Let's not excavate tragedy any more.

Harold hands Antigone her book, picks up his own and opens it.

HAROLD. Here are things I said about you: softness, intelligence, poetry, stubbornness.

IMAGE 7.7 **In a flashback, Antigone and her sister Irene argue about burying their brother's corpse.**

Joey Collins, Angel Desai, Tracie Thoms (from left to right).

Photograph by T. Charles Erickson.

Antigone looks in her book.

ANTIGONE. Here are things I said about you: light, humor, beauty, talks too much.

HAROLD. I stopped talking so much since I met you because you talk constantly.

ANTIGONE. Here are some other things: tendency toward behavior commonly considered manly.

HAROLD. Chivalrous.

ANTIGONE. Tendency to claim that you know everything.

HAROLD. I know more than you do. Tendency toward occasional hysteria.

ANTIGONE. Tendency toward occasional political incorrectness. Like telling a woman she has hysteria.

HAROLD. Tendency to point out everything that is ever so slightly wrong.

ANTIGONE. Will you touch my face? (*Harold does.*) I like it when you touch my face.

Antigone and Harold freeze.

IRENE. Yes, I've called a few times before. My family was dysfunctional. Yes, Oedipus, who gouged his own eyes out for his crimes of unnatural sex and patricide, was my father. Jocasta, who hanged herself, was both his wife and his mother. And my mother. My two brothers, Eteocles and Polynices, born of incest, died at each other's hand. Yes, I called the ambulance service each time. I'm still entitled to police assistance. I'm an American citizen.

Antigone and Harold each left a note. What do you mean that you know the contents already? I have them here. The notes are addressed to me. These were the last private and intimate words of the last two people who cared about me. How did you get them? They weren't even mailed. They were left on my bedside table.

You're not sending any help, are you? I'm on my own with two corpses. You are busy because it's nearly dawn on April 30, and the last Marines in Saigon are lifting off. It's January 17, 2.38 a.m., and the air strike over Baghdad has begun . . . (*Breaks from addressing the audience. Distraught*) Antigone, Antigone, my sister—

Antigone hears Irene for the first time.

ANTIGONE. Irene?

Irene does not hear Antigone.

IRENE. You shouldn't have chosen death. There are things to live for. There is always something to live for. Even here in Rwanda during the civil war, no, I mean during ethnic cleansing. No,

IMAGE 7.8 **Irene regrets her disagreement with her sister Antigone.**

Tracie Thoms.

Photograph by T. Charles Erickson.

IMAGE 7.9 **Antigone regrets her disagreement with her sister Irene.**

Angel Desai (left), Joey Collins (right).

Photograph by T. Charles Erickson.

that's not right either. Afghanistan? No. Even here in occupied Manchuria. What? What do I have to live for? Oh, Antigone, I am so alone. So completely alone. So unnaturally alone.

ANTIGONE. Irene, Irene. Can you hear me? I want to tell you about the books I found in the underworld. Each person has a book; and as one lives life, her story gets recorded in the book. I looked in your book. You have many blank pages still. Your story continues.

IRENE. You were right. The damage done to human decency, democracy, and rational thinking is too great. There is no turning back. We live in lies, and racial profiling, and threats disguised as freedom speeches, and no one will help me bury your paleness and Harold's bloody red. The city is under high security alert, the color Red. Red City. Red in my house. Red human history.

ANTIGONE. No, Irene. These books. I found the books of human effort. There are more books here. Completely blank ones for new lives.

IRENE. They read Harold's and your notes. So now I have nothing. Nothing is mine. They own my memories.

During Antigone's next speech, lights fade on Irene.

ANTIGONE. I know right now it feels like all the violent acts and atrocities in human history are converging and happening in one instant. I know it feels like that instant is a loop, and it plays and plays and never stops. Red, again and again. But there is white in these books. Irene, please hear me.

HAROLD. Antigone, Irene will survive. You always thought you were the stronger one, but in the end, the strongest lives. She lives.

ANTIGONE. I wrote in my note to her that I had no choice but to leave her; I had to be brave.

HAROLD. I wrote to her that I was following you because otherwise you'd be afraid.

ANTIGONE. Tendency to divulge unnecessary information.

IMAGE 7.10 **Harold and Antigone are ready to go back to the chaotic world of the living.**
Angel Desai (left), Joey Collins (right).
Photograph by T. Charles Erickson.

HAROLD. Tendency toward bravado. Gets us killed every time. (*Pause.*) I found two blank books. One cover says "Former Harold" and the other says "Former Antigone." We are going back.

ANTIGONE. Going back to Red again.

HAROLD. We have work to do.

ANTIGONE. Will we find each other?

HAROLD. It's our destiny.

ANTIGONE. You should look for me fighting in a revolution.

HAROLD. Look for me meditating in a monastery.

ANTIGONE. Did you really try to kill the King?

HAROLD. It was a pathetic attempt. But I spat at him at least.

ANTIGONE. We won't remember each other, will we?

HAROLD. Not initially. But before the end of our story, we will love each other again.

ANTIGONE. Yes, and I'm no longer afraid.

HAROLD. I follow you.

> *They look into each other's eyes. And then look to the audience. Lights become intensely white.*
>
> *Black.*